CHRIST
ABOVE CULTURE:
The Answer To
Farrakhanism

By Robert McElroy

CHRIST
ABOVE CULTURE:
The Answer To Farrakhanism

Copyright 1997 by Robert McElroy
All Rights Reserved

Library of Congress Catalog Card Number 97-61846

ISBN 0-9660529-0-0

Manufactured in the United States of America
First Printing 1997

Published by
UNION GROVE PRESS
Mesquite TX

Produced by
PPC BOOKS
Westport CT

CONTENTS

INTRODUCTION AND AUTHOR'S ACKNOWLEDGMENTS

The problems which these writings address are primarily a response to the imposing presence and influence among African Americans of the fiery-tongued, black militant leader of the Nation of Islam, Louis Farrakhan. This man, who has most often been described as a preacher of hatred against whites and Jews, has at other times been referred to as a strong black leader, who advocates black pride and progress. Most would agree that he is currently capitalizing on the continually, volatile, black-and-white racial climate in America. Realizing the historically tense nature of these issues and tensions, Mr. Farrakhan has embarked on a surprisingly successful national campaign, using trendy, race-explicit, anti-white, anti-Jewish, and anti-Christian (whether black or white) teachings, aimed at winning sympathizers and converts to the Nation of Islam. To the shame and the shock of the black Christian churches, and, indeed, all of America, for either creating or maintaining fertile conditions which allowed this evil to thrive, this man is succeeding far beyond what any could have imagined. I say "shame," because for the first time in history, the leader of a counter-Christian movement has been highly successful in driving a wedge between a large segment of the black race and Christianity. The only thing similar in magnitude would be the efforts of Marcus Garvey, the militant, black nationalist leader, in the early 1920s. Through his great oratorical and organizational skills, Garvey was able to attract hundreds of thousands to his movement, before it finally failed. Although many of Mr. Farrakhan's ideas seem to be borrowed from Garvey's, which were more socio-economically based; however, being primarily a religious leader, Mr. Farrakhan's movement has developed along a more religious and political line, which also has many economic and social overtones.

Mr. Farrakhan, who is a fiery-tongue rhetorician, far beyond even what the legendary Garvey was, has proven himself adept at, not only moving a large segment of the black race toward his militancy, but of overcoming past Christian resistance to his movement. On the negative side, he has also proven to be a master craftsman at twisting historical facts (which we shall examine), then using these mangled facts, sometimes mixed with verifiable truths, in creating disharmony between the races, and now, between Christ and the black race. Having found some measure of success in accomplishing this, Farrakhan has moved forward with his "cold war," between the races. However, much of his fiery rhetoric, which, at times, grossly exploits and over exaggerates the race issue, seems to be nothing more than a fabricated smoke screen, contrived to disguise his move toward black nationalism and super-culturalism; and the creation of a separate nation within our nation, with him as the chief ruler.

The question becomes: How has Louis Farrakhan managed to be so enormously successful, in such a short period of time, among a culture which has traditionally been so loyal to Christ and Christianity? At first glance, his success seems to ride, primarily, on the current crest of a resurging wave of white racism in America. He is quick to point out that he believes white racism to be one of the major flaws in white Christianity; and along with that comes other societal ills, such as oppression, injustice, and discrimination. In order to overcome the strong religious resistance from Christians, he is quick to point out the often baffling positions black Christians find themselves in, as they try to explain the segregation and hostility they face from a large segment of white Christianity. Most of us are aware of the phrase which states that "The eleven o'clock hour on Sunday morning (the traditional worship hour among most Christian churches), is still the most segregated hour of the week!"

With these and other weapons in his well-armed quiver, Mr. Farrakhan has been shooting many fiery darts at, what he views as, the hypocrisy of Christianity; the oppressive conditions in America, brought on by white racists, Jews, and the national government; and other social ills being faced by its African American citizenry; and all who oppose his own racists views, whether black or white.

As I previously mentioned, Mr. Farrakhan is careful to always include selected tidbits of, undeniable truths documenting American racism, in his remarks. What seems to strengthen his arguments is that it appears that most of the social and economic ills of our nation always tend to fall, disproportionately, on the backs of African Americans. Such conditions often breed social unrest. This unrest is exacerbated by many things: the inability of the local, state, and national governments to deal effectively with the nation's crime and drug problems; the entrenched poverty among many blacks; a feeling, among African Americans, of being victims of a well-designed personal attack by Congress, with cut-backs in many social programs, Affirmative Action, and the like; and then, within the black community, there is the stagnated, and often out-of-touch ministries, of many black churches. Farrakhan has cleverly used these negative things, along with his distortions, in order to add credibility to his arguments and gain a hearing among those who have traditionally shunned him.

Some of his distortions and, what I believe to be, intentional omissions, we shall discuss in these writings. These include: The fact that more whites, Jews, women, and even little children, marched, protested, and even died for the freedom of African Americans during the Civil Right Struggle than all of the Nation of Islam combined, including Farrakhan, himself, who, now that it's safe to come out of hiding, wants to rise up an be our leader! We will also look at Farrakhan's false claims that Christianity is the religion of the white man; his failure to recognize the extent of black progress in America; his implied assertion that Islam is the historically correct religion of African peoples; his false claims that he is "the prophetic Jesus;" his failure to recognize that it was Arabic Muslims, and not Jews, who were first and foremost among slave traders, and that the Prophet Muhammad, himself, was a slave owner (easily verified in the Hadith, the second most sacred Islamic document). I shall discuss in some detail, these facts, which Mr. Farrakhan has been so adept at distorting, or ignoring.

In spite of my remarks, it would be foolish, counter-productive, and even untruthful of me, no matter how I personally feel about Mr. Farrakhan, or how much I might detest some of his teachings and racist actions, not to give him the credit he is due. No one can doubt his skills as an orator; nor his fiery zeal concerning the causes which he champions. When he speaks, he does so with such great passion and emotion, until the actual truth often becomes clouded by the emotional-moment. If one listens to him emotion-ally, concerning the conditions of black people in America, he can almost make people believe that we have not made any progress at all within the last twenty-years! Listening to him, with mind and reality disengaged, one could get that impression. However, when you really take a few moments to earnestly and honestly reflect on where we are, you suddenly discover that most of the cities where he has delivered his fiery speeches, either currently have black mayors, or formerly had black mayors; black police chiefs and county sheriffs, county commissioners, city councilpersons, superintendents of schools, and, in many instances, lower rates of unem-ployment among those seeking jobs. Now, of course, I am not blind. I am well aware that many problems with racism, poverty, unemployment, and the like, still exist. However, I do think that it is unwise to never give credit for the progress that we have made. Everybody needs to be "stroked" at one time or another.

Not only do these writings look at many of the unheralded facts concerning Islam and African people; and the false claims of Farrakhan concerning the Nation of Islam and black people; but they also look at Farrakhan's denigration of the historical Person of Jesus Christ; and the attempted elevation of himself in the place of Christ! Among the vain and ridiculous claims he makes, in an attempt to bolster his own credibility, is that he is the fulfillment of "the prophetic Jesus;" and that he is the "savior." It is in response to such outright misrepresentations of truth and bending of historical facts and prophecies, that further drives me toward my mission. I am, therefore, driven by both my desire to counter the deceptive claims and practices of Farrakhan, as well as my personal commitment to Jesus Christ, to witness to, and now contend with, the enemies of the Christian faith. If the readers would dare take up the challenge of reading and reflecting on the informative, and sometimes, shocking, revelations contained in these writings, along with their own research, I believe that they will share my concerns, and choose to reflect more deeply on matters of faith and race, before rushing to embrace this controversial personality, along with his controversial teachings. I do believe that the open-minded reader will discover that it is not the black race and Christianity which are incompatible, but rather, the doctrines of Islam and Christianity which seem to be mutually exclusive.

While these writings focus primarily on Louis Farrakhan, they also take an honest look at the conditions of our nation as a whole, both good and bad. And, although, there are many areas where I disagree with Mr. Farrakhan, and feel very strongly that he has intentionally and deceptively slanted the truth, I am also fully aware that our paths and experiences do cross, and often merge, in the area of the traditional American reaction to our mutual blackness. However, I believe that few, among those who read these writings, have suffered more the humiliating, dehumanizing, and violent effects of racism, than I have; including Louis Farrakhan, himself. This requires further explanation.

In Chapter One, I reveal the full details of a brutal and horrifying attack on my life, by two bloodthirsty, white racists, who tried their best to murder me. It is truly a miracle that I am alive today! I have attempted to offer a frank discussion on how my personal theology and philosophy of life evolved after having my own blood spilled to the ground by these racists, and the damage-control instituted by my mother in order to save me from a future of counter-violence and hatred toward whites. Consequently, I have been able to resist the temptation to become a white-race-hating follower of Louis Farrakhan, or any other racist, in spite of my ordeal. Given the fact that I could easily rationalize and legitimatize my decision to my personal satisfaction, based on this attack, I still choose to resist that temptation.

Wisdom informs me that it was because of the ignorance generated by white racism, that I nearly lost my life. Why, then, should I turn and add to, or become a continued victim of that ignorance? My decision not to go that route is based on early life wisdom teachings; and the knowledge and "common sense" acquired from life's many varied experiences, most of which were founded upon the Christian ideals of love, and forgiveness, and the other teachings of Jesus.

In addition to my personal commitment to this work, I have also been encouraged to pursue this effort by many close friends and relatives. I owe a special debt of gratitude to my good friend, Scott Johnson, who was the first to read the initial writings and to offer me great encouragement in this work. This is not to imply that Scott agrees with all of the ideas expressed here; his comments were strictly limited to the story in Chapter One, which describes my near death experience at the hands of white racists.

In some parts of these writings, as well as in our frank discussions, Scott says that at times I sound like a Republican (which he is). But, as I told him, when it comes to truth and the real issues of life, such as morality, responsibility, ethics, and right and wrong, we cannot afford to live strictly by political beliefs; for truth is not limited to one particular group. I believe that in the quest for truth, each person must choose for himself or herself, which road to travel. After all, this is what Christianity, and moral and social responsibilities are all about.

I must also mention the importance which family has played in my life and in these writings. Much of that which form the substructure for the theme, exalts the importance of family in developing lasting religious and social traditions. I am deeply indebted to my family for their prayers and support, throughout life and in this effort. First on the list is my dear mother, Lola M. Cason, who, from infancy, has been my primary source of encouragement, and the driving force behind my moral and spiritual development; as well as, all other worthwhile achievements in my life. She has never let me forget that I am a child of God, and that "I," therefore, must, and "can do all things through Christ, which strengthens me" (Philippians 4:13). Mother, along with my stepfather, and the only true dad I had, Leroy Cason, made many sacrifices in order to help me get a college education; for this I shall be eternally grateful. Then, I am most grateful to my wife, Carolyn, who has been a constant source of support, encouragement, and joy during this project. And to my profoundly intelligent son, Robert, the philosopher and educator, who, like Dr. Martin Luther King, Jr., holds a degree in Philosophy from Morehouse College, I am deeply indebted for the critical thoughts offered on this, and other subjects; which we have often discussed until the wee hours of the morning, and sometimes, all night long. He has been a continued source of love, inspiration, support, encouragement, over the last 25 years.

Last, but not least, I express my gratitude to two of my high school teachers. The first is the late Mrs. Gertrude Cotton, my preeminently profound high school English teacher, who challenged us to master the English language; and to her associate teacher, Mrs. Jean Bryant, sponsor and adviser to our senior class. It was Mrs. Bryant, who, painstakingly, and patiently, pondered with me over a career choice for my life. It was this wonderful lady, who helped convince me to choose the profession of Pharmacy as a career goal. Without these individuals, my life would be decidedly different.

Finally, I believe that God advanced the idea of cosmic relatedness, that is, living in the world as caring neighbors. I, therefore, believe that there should be universal "rejection" of all ideas which pit "us against them," whether from Louis Farrakhan, David Duke, or any other racist. The Apostle Paul seemed to advance the idea of universal brotherhood while speaking to the men of Athens, on Mars Hill,

God . . . hath made of one blood all nations of men
for to dwell on all the face of the earth . . .For in him
we live, and move, and have our being . . .
For we are also his offspring (Acts 17:24, 26).

This idea was stated very simply, but quite eloquently, by the words of Rodney King, the victim of the world-renowned, infamous, video-taped beating by Los Angeles policemen. King pleaded for peace among the races following the rioting which broke out after the policemen were exonerated by an all-white jury. King pleaded:

"Can't we all just get along?"

If there is ever to be peace in America, we must all learn how to put race and prejudices behind us all; and learn how to get along together. Our belief systems, therefore, must not be race-based, but through faith in a higher power. I, therefore, firmly take my stand in my decision to choose Christ over Race and Culture; and to speak out boldly on issues to the contrary.

SPECIAL NOTE: At times, the name of the Prophet Muhammad is spelled Mohammed, but refers to the same person. In like manner, Elijah Muhammad's name is sometimes spelled Mohammed. The different spellings seem common when translating Arabic names into English.

CHAPTER ONE

LOOKING DEATH IN THE FACE

The following story from my personal life is told in order to inform the reader of the fact that I know from firsthand experience, the depths of this sickness called "white racism." Yet, in spite of this enigma, I take my stand with Christ, above my race and above my culture; along with my wounds and scarred-till-death body; until His eternal kingdom shall finally be ushered in.

I was born in the deep South, and there grew up. As a youngster, during the `50s and `60s, I was fortunate, on the one hand, to experience the full flavor of Southern hospitality, with its accent on living in community with one another. Neighbors and friends in the community shared in each other's needs, hurts, and blessings. There was a certain friendly atmosphere, unsurpassed anywhere else in the world. Most people were just naturally kind and neighborly to each other. They shared what they had, with those who might be going through some tough times. Very few went lacking, if they were part of the community. Even black and white people got along quite well, that is, as long as we, black people, "stayed in our places," and in our own community. The introduction of this negative attribute of our seemingly harmonious community, also introduces us to the other side of the world of Southern living: black and white relations and white racism.

I have experienced, first-hand, the gamut of racism's monstrous effects and consequences in my personal life. I am no stranger to this pervasive evil. While I knew of, or got to know some fine white folk, for the most part, these were two separate worlds. A black person was wise to "stay in his place," if he or she was to get along well in the community.

We knew that the best and the first was always reserved for White folk. If you were in line at the local department store and a white person came up after you to be checked out, especially if it was a white woman, you knew that it would be wise to step aside till the white person was waited on. You also knew that you had to get off the sidewalk if you met two white folks walking toward you. You knew that you must never, I mean NEVER, be caught drinking from the "white only" water fountain. And Lord knows that you didn't make the mistake of sitting on the white side of the waiting room and cafeteria at the bus station. If you had good sense you sat in the little rectangular space next to the bathrooms, which you couldn't go in, because they were reserved for white folks. When you wanted to go to the restroom, you had to hold it until you could make it to the county courthouse, and then go down into the basement. It was like going down into the sewers under New York City. It was usually wet, dirty, and filled with horrible odors. After you left, you could forget about going to the back door of the bus station diner for a sandwich, which was the only place where blacks could be served. You usually did not have any appetite left for any kind of food, after going in that place!

Another bitter Southern experience in my young life was the near lynching of the late Mr. Buddy Gammons, a mentally retarded man, who lived in my hometown. He was accused by a cowboy truck driver, which we called "Weasel," (name changed by author), of peeping through the window of their trailer home, in order to take a look at his wife. If you had seen this lady, you would wonder why even a sane person would want to go through the trouble! There just wasn't that much to look at; nevertheless, old "Weasel" stirred up enough of the vain white folks, mostly those living in the trailer community, to attack old Buddy. Before poor Buddy could be rescued by Mr. Frank Ward, the black store owner, they had beaten him severely, cut off some of his fingers, and, as I recall, had already tied and put the hanging rope around his neck, and were getting ready to string him up. I am told that Mr. Ward defiantly confronted the mob, along with some other good white folks, and rescued Mr. Buddy. Later years, "Weasel" would suffer and die in a horrible manner: he was burned alive in the house where they had later moved to. When the fire was extinguished, they found his heart in the ashes; and those who were there said that old "Weasel's" heart was still beating! The black people in the area attributed it to Divine retribution, or pay back for the evil that he had instigated against Mr. Gammons. Many felt that it was a sign that God doesn't like ugly. This saying was more aptly put by a dear friend, and one of the best pharmacist in America, Mrs. Frankie Roland, of Dallas, Texas, whom I met many years later, after coming to Texas. Frankie said, "God doesn't like ugly, and He's not too crazy about pretty, either. God's main interest is in us doing right!" Unfortunately, many of us have to learn this valuable lesson, the hard way.

These experiences, among other things which I have shared with you, constitute a sampling of the wide variety of the unfortunate situations of growing up in the deep south, amid Southern hospitality.

One among the "other things" in my Southern experience was learning to know your new name when around white folk: "boy," or "gal," if female. Another was seeing old men being treated worse than dogs. Having seen men kicked in the butt, slapped, and talked to like dogs, make up some of the sad experiences of the Southern culture of times past. I was determined that when I became a man I would never end up like that. I knew, by the constant teaching of my mother, that a good college education was the only way out; therefore, I began early preparing myself.

The majority of work in farming communities was slaving in the hot fields, from dawn to dusk. I remember wages of $3 per day (the day consisted of just after sunrise till just before sunset). The elders told us it was good because it used to be worse. The miracle of it all was that they were able to keep their families fed and clothed on their meager earnings. This was not exclusive to black families; for most poor families, including poor white folks, who feared God and loved their families, always seemed to find a way to feed their families. It reminds me of the song title from the hit TV show, "The Beverly Hillbillies." The song says something like this, "Let me tell you a story about a man named Jed, a poor mountaineer; but he kept his family fed." This has been the wonderful and miraculous story of the God-fearing, poor all over the world; that through trust in God, hard work, and ingenuity, they have been able to make it, some way and some how. Where I came from, they often quoted Psalm 37:25 and 26,

I have been young, and now am old;
Yet I have not seen the righteous forsaken,
Nor his descendants begging bread.
He is ever merciful, and lends;
And his descendants are blessed.

I suppose it will always be a mystery how so many of the very poor and the oppressed were able to make it through all of the obstacles they faced. Only God knows how the few pennies, nickels, dimes, and other small change was able to build homes, churches, and provide food and clothing; but there are still many living witnesses that our foreparents did it; and they did it with dignity and style.

In spite of the many faith stories of the patience of our forefathers and mothers, who learned to be content and endure their hardships and effectively use what they had, most young people are not willing to wait, no less suffer hardships. We were much like this during the 1960's, when the Civil Rights Movement was in full force. I suppose that in every generation, it has usually been young people who press and push for change, in search of a piece of the real action. In our day, the youth energized the Movement with our vigorous zeal and energy; while our elders supplied the guidance and wisdom. With the coming of television, we could see in many cases just how far behind we were, as we watched ordinary people all over the nation enjoying the good life, while most Southern black citizens still lived in poverty and impoverished conditions.

Many African Americans were still living in "shotgun houses," which were antiquated remnants from the near-plantation days (a "shotgun house" was one in which there were many small holes in the roof, enough, sometimes, that one could count the stars.) In many cases, there were also holes in the old wooden floors, which looked like someone had shot up the place with a shotgun filled with buckshot, both roof and floor. The rain came through during the rainy season; and in some places, you could look through the holes in the floor and see the chickens walking under many of those old house, which had stilt-like, stacked-up, foundation stones. Summers down South, were usually very, very hot and very muggy. For the most part, we knew nothing of air conditioning; and many did not even have electric fans. I suppose that this is why many of our women didn't mind so much being a maid, because they could at least enjoy the fine air conditioned environments that many white people lived in. The young people, however, were tired of these impoverished living conditions; they simply wanted a better way of life; therefore, they turned to those who had escaped, hoping for their own escape; even if it was only for the Summer.

Changes in the South, at that time, were very slow, or none at all. Many young men, and sometimes young ladies, who had relatives who had escaped the drudgery of hard Southern living, went North, or to larger and more progressive Southern cities, in order to find work during the Summer months, while staying with relatives and friends. They found work in hotels, restaurants, and factories in places like Atlantic City, New York, Baltimore, Jacksonville, and Miami. I could only listen to their adventuresome stories about the bright lights of the city, and the liberated northern

4

girls. I would not experience this sense of "escape," until after my second year of college.

During my youth, I had terrible headaches, what I now understand to be migraines. Only a migraine sufferer truly understands the almost unbearable suffering the victims of this disease endures. I could only work in the fields, in the unbearable hot Summer sun, for short periods of time before I had one of those nauseating, gut wrenching, eyeball popping, excruciating headache attacks. I remember working in a field, shaking and pulling peanuts; then, during one of these attacks, literally crawling to the end of a row of peanuts in order to drag myself to a shade tree. I lay there for what seemed like several hours before the field hands broke for lunch and somebody could take me home. Some probably thought that I was just lazy, but inside of me, I felt as though I was about to die (and sometimes actually wished that I could, because of the pain and agony). At other times, I felt that God didn't like me, but still wouldn't let me die, until my suffering on earth was done. Because of the disease, I had to stay indoors a lot. It was at this time that I developed a great love for books: reading about science, music, and the great cities and cultures of the world. I was determined to be somebody. I didn't want to end up like others that I had seen who had ended up being nothing but worn out farm hands; smelling the obnoxious fumes from the farm animals or from the smokestacks on the old two-cylinder farm tractors. These weird looking, green and yellow monsters looked like a fire-breathing dragon, on wheels. The loud, smoky machines could be heard for over a half mile away, with its "putt-putt-putt," sound. I had to get away.

I studied hard during high school and involved myself in many extracurricular activities. I was short and small, but with great determination and effort, I made the starting varsity basketball team in high school. Coach Abraham Johnson, who is now deceased, said that I had something called "heart." I was also a starter on our town's baseball team. And because I tried my best to follow my mother's teachings, and treat everybody right, people tended to like me. I was voted "Most Likely to Succeed," by my Senior class members. I was voted president of our Senior class, president of the Student Government Association, and president of the "4-H Club." If there was something good going on, I wanted to be a leading part of it. Most recently (April 1997), I was voted President of the Dallas-Ft. Worth Chapter of the FAMU Alumni Association. I guess I'm still trying to do what my mother told me to do. The Bible clearly says,

"Train up a child in the way he should go: and when he is old

THE GAIN AND LOSS OF A MUCH-NEEDED SCHOLARSHIP

Back in 1961, while competing in a "4-H Club" sponsored, oratorical contest in Jacksonville, Florida, I had the distinct honor of meeting the late Dr. Richard V. Moore, then President of Bethune-Cookman College in Daytona Beach, Florida. Dr. Moore had been at the contest listening to all the young speakers. When I had finished my presentation, not making it to the finals, I was told by my sponsor that Dr. Moore wanted to meet with me. Although I didn't win any awards at the oratorical contest (as a matter of fact, I felt that I had been "blown out of the water" by the flamboyant antics of the big city contestants), Dr. Moore said that he was truly impressed with the message and sincerity of my oratorical presentation. He felt that my speech was from the "heart." I believe that if there is any two things which will help us overcome our shortcomings, one thing would be sincerity of heart, and the next would be determined effort. I lost the oratorical contest, however, through my efforts, I had gained an even greater thing, a desperately needed key to unlock the door to a good college education.

After we talked, he said that I was the kind of student he was looking for, and then guaranteed me an academic scholarship from his College, if my grades were as good as I had told him. If it was one thing that I wasn't worrying about, it was my grades; because, with my mother's encourage-ment and help, I had always maintained nearly an "A" average in most subjects. In addition to that, I was a bona fide member of the National Honor Society. I held the number 2 scholastic ranking in our senior class until just a few days before graduation. This occurred when a disgruntled classmate demanded and helped carry out a re-calculation of our scholastic averages. They said that she came out something like 0.003 points ahead of me! Well, they snatched my little salutatory speech and gave the honor to her. I was devastated at first, until my mother came to the rescue, once again. Fathers are great, but I think the world would collapse without those good mothers who are always there to help us through the tough times and to teach us "the finer points of life." When "Dr. Mom" got through, I could care less about the incident and it made me stronger in the long run. Unfortunately, the person who displaced me did absolutely nothing with her life, when measured against what she had the potential of becoming. It was sad because she really was a rather talented person. Anyway, as a result of this, I became one of the few students in our school's history, who has ever been a "temporary Salutatorian." I think that I still, and forever shall, hold that distinction because they closed the school a few years after integration came.

Dr. Moore gave me a full scholarship, and I took a major in Chemistry. What a wonderful experience that was, going to school in this beautiful city by the sea. The city was also famous because it was the home of the world-famous "Daytona 500 International Race Track." In addition to these wonders, we could watch the launching of rockets at Cape Canaveral (now called "Cape Kennedy"). Being a young, college teenager, I realized that there were also other things to "watch" in Daytona Beach, especially during Spring Break. What a wonderful time it was when all of the beach beauties invaded the beaches from the northern and Ivy League colleges. It was especially nice, being able to enjoy the camaraderie of fellow college students, who happened to be white, since had been mostly forbidden in the South, until Civil Rights Legislation had been enacted. For me, these experiences were simply sharing stories and drinking beer with the guys; and playing co-ed volleyball; Frisbee tossing; and playing football. It was just, basic, good, clean, college-type fun.

As a matter of fact, I began having too much fun; on the beach and on campus. My math grade plummeted. I had been on the Dean's List for the first semester; but, being heavily recruited, I decided to pledge 2 fraternities the second semester: one social fraternity and one service fraternity (Alpha Phi Omega); along with all the other fun. I didn't complete the social fraternity because it required 2 semesters, which I was to complete in the Fall. Well, my foolishness cost me my scholarship, and I could not afford the tuition at this private school. My mother saw where I was headed, and I had to transfer to the only state-supported college for blacks, Florida A&M University (FAMU), which had a Pharmacy School, which prepared me for my chosen profession.

I had no scholarship at FAMU, so I had to work during the Summer, in order to help out. At the end of my first year there, I headed North to "the Promised Land," to spend the Summer with my older cousin, William, and his family, in Newark, New Jersey. He had indicated that there were great possibilities of summer jobs in Newark, where I could earn much more money than down South. I had been in the North only once in my life; and that was when I won a trip to Washington, DC, while working with the "4-H

Club." That was one very neat experience: for the first time in my life I could see black people in important jobs; being treated with dignity and respect. Now, I was being offered the great opportunity to go "up North." "Hallelujah," I was going to what many black folks felt, at that time, was the "Promised Land!" However, I would soon learn some valuable lessons about the seemingly "cursed" condition of being born black, anywhere, on Planet Earth; for the only thing which we seemed to be "promised," was a-hard-way-to-go. Many things happened which reminded me of the old saying, "If you're white, you're right! If you're yellow, that's mellow; if you're brown, stick around; but if you're black, get back!"

THE NORTHERN EXPERIENCE: RACISM AND A CALL FROM BLACK MILITANTS

My first job after landing in Newark, New Jersey, was with Klines Department Stores. This firm readily hired me as a stock clerk, and asides from this unchallenging work and the very low pay, they treated me kindly. I was so glad to have an inside job, with the luxury of air conditioning and nice people to work with, and for that I never realized that with 2 years of college, I was a victim of the "glass ceiling," even at that level. There were certain jobs and positions that were not available to most blacks. I soon accepted that; because I felt that it would be useless, and even counter-productive for me to demand more. It just goes to prove that when you don't know any better, you'll accept just about anything. The late, Dr. Carter G. Woodson, noted African American historian and educator, once wrote that:

> The Problem of holding the Negro down, therefore, is easily solved. When you control a man's thinking you do not have to tell him not to stand here or go yonder. He will find his "proper place" and will stay in it. He will go without being told. In fact, if there is no back door, he will cut one for his special benefit. His education makes it necessary. [1]

I was happy with my position because I had been taught that certain positions had been reserved for white folks. I was glad to be in the big city; not working outside in the blazing sun. And to top this off, I got my first chance to experience the northern culture: eating pizza from sidewalk vendors; gazing at skyscrapers (I tried to be discreet, for I had heard of country folk getting run over by cars, after walking out into the street while looking up at big buildings). One of the great experiences was riding subway trains between Newark and New York City; and browsing in great department stores. I even walked through Central Park, all alone, at night, and was not mugged or accosted.

After a few pay checks, I got to be a real big shot. I would often take my hard earned money and go to the local bar near my house, grab a barstool, light up a cigarette, rear back and tell the bartender to give me a scotch and soda, just like in the movies. How foolish and immature I was. I was darn near broke before too long. Because of low wages, I kept looking for a better paying job. Finally, I landed one with Federal Pacific Electric Company. Having 2 years of college; I felt qualified me to land one of the advertised positions, working in the main office as an office assistant. However, I soon found out that whether North or South, it didn't work that way for young, African-American men, no matter how intelligent or educated. The young white boy who came into the office with me, who had just finished high school, got the office the job and I was sent out to the warehouse to carry buckets of steel, as an "Electroplater's Helper."

My job was to dip buckets of metal parts into acids and other dangerous chemicals, in order to strip off corrosion, prior to the electroplating process. Maybe, they felt that since I had two years of Chemistry and other Sciences, that I wouldn't mind risking my eyes and life, seeing how these chemicals stripped metal, and your clothes right off your body, too, if you weren't careful! What was really happening was that I was "just another black nigger," destined only for back-breaking, hard labor. I soon found that racism was the same whether North or South. It was during this experience that I first learned of the "Black Muslims," or as they are now more widely known, "the Nation of Islam."

THE FIRST CONFLICT BETWEEN CHRIST AND CULTURE:

One of the black fellows who worked there continually pointed out the injustices I was suffering, along with the other brothers. He told me that he was attending Black Muslim meetings and learning to follow the teachings of "Brother Malcolm X and the Honorable Elijah Muhammad." He pressed me weekly, almost daily, to come to the meetings. I told him about my faith in Jesus Christ and that I was a Christian, to which he replied that it was foolish for black people to follow the White man's religion. He was well indoctrinated; which is what I find to be true of most sects and cults. They often know and recite the teachings of their leaders, (and the Bible, also!), far better than most Christians who have had the Bible lying around their homes all their lives, collecting dust. Perhaps, this is why we have so much trouble within Christianity, is that we don't really know the Bible; nor the demands of the Christian faith. This one factor is most probably the reason Louis Farrakhan has been able to influence and win so many "Christians:" Farrakhan knows the Bible better than many Christians do!!!

Consequently, my co-worker tried to use his learned indoctrination techniques in order to confuse me and weaken my resistance to his proselytizing efforts. He was good, but my faith was better! He said that Christianity had never done black people any good. To him and the Muslims, it was a religion designed to control the minds, hearts, and souls of black people in order to keep them locked into mental slavery, so that white folks could keep using and abusing them, like they were doing me. He would also say things like, "Look at you. You're an intelligent, young black man, a college student, you have a good education, and where does the white man put you? Out here lugging buckets of steel, like any other common laborer!"

How could I deny his argument? Most of what he said concerning me, was true, and I knew it. I had followed most of the rules and instructions given me by my parents, relatives, teachers, and elders. They would tell us, "You've got to know twice as much and be twice as good as the white man, to be given any kind of chance; and even with all that, he's still gonna be given a place ahead of you." My great-uncle, Uncle Richard, a very short but powerful man in will and constitution, who resembled one of the cowboy character in the old westerns, recognized the value of a good education. He told me that they (the white man and the demands of farming) wouldn't let him go to school but a few weeks out of the year, but he wanted me to go as far as I could. He would say, "Pie" (my childhood nickname), "stay in college, till you get your first degree, then your second degree, then your third degree . . . " I would say to myself, "My God, how many degrees does he want me to get?" Well, I have done just like he said. This was great advise given me way back in the 1960s, by a Christian man, who experienced far more racial abuse and oppression than I will face in a lifetime. Uncle Richard, died before I could get all the degrees he wanted me to, but, I went on and did just what he said. I thank God for him, and his seemingly "impossible" challenge.

But while I was in that dangerous, chemical "sweat shop," in New Jersey, I was being challenged to abandon all of the religious foundation that Uncle Richard, mother, and all others, who helped form my religious pathway, had told me to hold onto. If I had not been thoroughly convinced in my heart that there was something to this "Christ" thing, I would have changed my name long ago to one of those "X" names. But I did believe, with all my heart, that Jesus was the way. My mother had told me He was; my great grandmother, Hettie McElroy, (an angel in disguise), had told me about Jesus; and my Bible had confirmed all that I had been told. In spite of my hurt and my suffering, I just knew that Christ was above culture; that Christ was bigger than race; and that true Christianity was that which was found in the Word of God, and not necessarily the hypocrisy found in much of white Christianity, which I had a bitter taste of in my experiences through the years. I was to the point that I felt that Billy Graham was the only white Christian, whom I could trust as a true Believer.

I was helped in my struggle with the relationship between race, culture, and racism by several things: the fact that I had experienced as many, and probably a whole lot more acts of unkindness from so-called 'brothers," than from the so-called "white devils," which was my Muslim friend's erroneous and prejudicial description of all white people. The first, and only, switchblade knife held at my throat was in the hand of a black "brother," who showed up as an uninvited guest at my high school sweet-hearts house. One of the earliest, and greatest betrayals in my young life was from a black high school teacher, whose name was Albert.

Albert was one of our youngest teachers and was very popular. We got along very well; and eventually became very good friends. He would tell me about his college days and interesting things about his young, successful life. Albert had majored in Industrial Arts, or something like that, and knew a lot about electricity and electrical gadgets. The latter have been my great weakness, for many years, up until this very moment. I just had to have some creative contraption, or know how everything worked. I spent much of my extra time in his classroom learning about this fascinating subject, and the gadgets he had around. In spite of the negative events which follow, I still appreciate the interest which Albert showed in me; and the extra time he took to teach me this interesting subject, far beyond what his position required.

When Albert saw my intense interest in the subject of electronics, he began teaching me about radio parts and circuitry, and even had me building my own radio from scratch. What I didn't know was that in addition to the parts we worked on, he also had his eye on some other "parts," which belonged to my 16-year old girlfriend, Rhodia.

Rhodia was truly a sight to behold. This young girl had many others panting after her. She had a perfect hour-glass figure and full, luscious lips. She was very active around our school. She was always on the honor roll; she was a cheerleader; on the basketball team; and played a mean game of volleyball. All of these activities required her to wear those tiny little shorts, which exposed more of her than I desired. One could recognize that she was a "knockout," even while wearing a below-the-knee skirt, but those shorts started blood to boil in hormone-stuffed teenage boys (and men). But even the full length dresses she would wear could not hide the beautiful figure they contained. She would wear those wide belts, and long, flaring dresses, like the one's Marilyn Monroe used to wear, and what a sight she was! Most of the time I tried to keep a sharp eye on her, but you can't keep watch all the time; nor be there all the time. I was just glad that she was mine. Unbeknownst to me, my good friend, Albert, the teacher, wanted to share my prize with me. Apparently, he was just a snake-in-the-grass, waiting to lunge on her.

AN ATTEMPTED RAPE:

One night we were having a class play at the school and Rhodia was late and didn't have a way to get there. Albert gladly, and enthusiastically, volunteered to go and pick her up (I would later find out why he was so eager). It seemed as if it would take forever for them to get back to school. Rhodia broke the news to me later as to why it took them so long to get back: my good friend, Albert, the high school teacher, had pulled off the road in a secluded spot, and became very aggressive toward her sexually, attempting to force her to have sex with him! She said that he had done his best in an unsuccessful attempt to seduce her, by both force and coercion, before finally giving up and bringing her on to the school.

I knew that something was dreadfully wrong when they first arrived. I took her aside and began drilling her about what happened to them. It was during this time that she broke the shocking news to me. At first, when I heard what Albert had done, I was almost in a murderous rage. I immediately confronted him about what she claimed he had done, or attempted to do. He immediately went into a state of denial concerning most of it; but as I kept pressing him, he finally broke down, stating that he acted improperly toward her. He began begging me not to take to it to the principal or other teachers or parents. I wanted to tell the whole world; but, for the life of me, I couldn't do it. In spite of this evil thing he had done, I couldn't forget that, for a very long time, we had been very good friends (at least, that was my impression). When my friends saw my hesitancy, they wanted to take matters into their own hands. The main leader was one we called "Ralph," after Ralph on "The Honeymooners" TV Show. He got many of the fellows together, mostly from the varsity basketball team, on which I was a starter, and proposed that they all get together and beat the hell out of him. Before I knew it, another friend came and told me that several of my friends had him cornered outside the school building, with no place to run, and no one to call out to. These, young brothers, knowing that whatever they did to him, Albert couldn't tell it, in that he would have to tell the whole story, and risk being fired by the school principal; and/or killed by her irate father, or one of her brothers. My friends would have beaten him to a pulp, but I felt sorry for him and stopped them just in time. After all, Rhodia insured me that nothing happened between them.

As much as I hated what he did, and even hated him at that moment, for the life of me, I just couldn't let him go out like that. Although, what he had done was a low-down, and a dirty shame, I chose not to make a public display of him for his inexcusable action, neither would I bring him up on charges, because I knew that he would get fired. And though he had proven himself a poor friend to me, I still considered myself his friend. It was a hard decision, but I had to make it. I called the boys off, just when they had him where they wanted him.

I figured too, that it was hard enough for a young black man to finish college; but then to get fired and possibly barred from teaching, would probably ruin his life forever. I reasoned that since he was not successful in his efforts and since he had been discovered and confronted, he had learned his lesson. He would have to live with his conscience; and be reminded of his betrayal every time he saw me, Rhodia, or any of my friends. It was really tough for him, trying to teach at our school, and command respect from the students. Fortunate, for us all, he got a transfer the next semester. I still talked to him and would sometimes visit with him and his girlfriend, one of the most attractive young teachers at out school, but our relationship never was the same again. This betrayal would have a very detrimental effect on me, for the rest of my life, for I never would have many friends that I felt I could trust.

But, you know, it's always hard on a relationship, when you have a super fine lady as your companion. There always seems to be another young buck, trying to invade your territory. Years later I heard a kind of crazy song, which makes a lot of sense, now, once I got to thinking about it. The song goes something like this:

> *"If you want to Be happy for the rest of your life,*
> *Never make a pretty woman your wife,*
> *So, from my personal point of view;*
> *Get an ugly girl, to marry you."*

Perhaps, if I would have followed the songsters advise, life would have been less complicated. What do you think?

Truly, the challenge for her attention didn't stop there, for there were several other so-called friends, who moved in on her. After high school, I went off to college and she stayed at home, attending the local Junior College. I began hearing all kinds of things, and I knew that it was time for each of us to move on. After I broke off with her, I moved into other relationships, only to find that other young men, and not-so-young men, are always waiting in line, for just the right opportunity to step in. These were all my "black brothers" stepping in, on me. Honesty demands that I also say that I did my stepping also.

UNFAVORABLE TRAITS WITHIN THE FAMILY:

Now to top off my argument that evil is not confined to the color of one's skin, let me bring my argument as close to me as possible. My own biological father, who helped to conceive me, both denied and abandoned me when I came into the world: he was black. While I have faced my share of prejudice and racism, I have received more blessings, honors, promotions, and other rewards from people of opportunity, many of whom happened to be white, than negative experiences described by black racists.

It is sad, but I must honestly admit, that in most of the earlier years of my supervisory and managerial experience, the most surprising opposition, as well as the most severe challenges to my leadership, have not come primarily from other racial groups, as one might be led to believe. I am not stating that I have not faced opposition from other racial groups, only that I have often been blind-sided by those whom I had naively thought would give me the greatest support. Perhaps the source of this way-ward thinking stems from the fact that when all are oppressed, we speak the same basic message concerning the need for liberation. However, when one among us actually experiences some small degree of liberation, some in our past coalition suddenly become our opposition. We become an "Uncle Tom," or "Just a token black," by those we thought of as our allies.

14

Fortunately, there have been other black workers, who were some of the best workers, and supporters, on the face of the earth. In this group were both men and women who were happy to have a decent job and who gladly did their jobs, performing their jobs far above the average crowd. In addition to this positive group, within the last few years I have had the great opportunity of supervising an all-black staff of superior performers. This group could be classed as "super stars!" The entire group is self-motivated; mission oriented; well informed about what we need to be doing; and they do their jobs with a very high degree of efficiency. This just proves that it is ignorant, irresponsible, and damaging to individual, as well as group pride and esteem to ever group all people under a pre-conceived set of stereo-types, whether black, white, or otherwise.

Life informs those who are teachable, that neither wisdom nor evil comes wrapped up for one race or culture. We must come to that noble and wise position that Dr. Martin Luther King, Jr., proposed to us many years ago. He said that a person should "be judged on the content of his character rather than the color of his skin." [2] This same principle must apply to all men and women, regardless of what color they might be.

THE RAINBOW COALITION OF FRIENDS

There had been many kind White people in my life, as well as, a number of evil ones. In our Civil Rights meetings we experienced the kindness of a White college professor and his wife, who met with us secretly to tell us of the strategies planned by racists in the community. Through this brave couple, and many courageous blacks in our community, who risked harm to their properties and families by sharing their homes with us much progress was made. One such brave black couple was Mr. and Mrs. Scott Marks. Another was Mr. and Mrs. Guy Long; and there were many more.

Perhaps, one of the greatest couples, which I ever encounter, was Ken and Peggy Flaming (last name changed to protect their privacy), of Georgia. They happened to be white. We met during the turbulent years of the 1970s, while we were both stationed at Ft. Sam Houston, Texas. Ken was a Registered Pharmacist, as I was; however, unlike me, he was a US Army Officer, and I was an enlisted man. Ken had completed ROTC at the University of Georgia, and had received a commission as an Army officer.

As I got to know them, I soon discovered that there were no pretenses about Ken and Peggy. They were just down to earth, living and breathing, regular, good hearted, human beings. Although Ken was the Officer in

Charge of our section, and therefore, my boss; he chose to work together with me, side by side, each day. We were both hard workers, so we got along well. Even though I was equal in education, however, being an Army officer, Ken was still my boss. And in response to him as my boss, I never failed to carry out an assignment to the best of my ability. My work habits made a lasting impression on him. His willingness to work with me as a fellow pharmacist and not "lord over" me, as a superior, which as a military officer, he had the authority to do so, really made an impression upon me.

In our off-duty time, Ken and I, along with our wives, usually took advantage of almost every opportunity we could in finding time to socialize and get to know each other. As you can imagine, the Army had very strict rules prohibiting officers from fraternizing with enlisted men; however, we both decided that we would not allow the Army's stringent regulations to stand in the way of our friendship. I had undergone a severe, life-threatening, assault from two racists youths from Georgia, in my college days. But through my relationship with Ken and Peggy, I learned that stereo-typing is a dangerous, slanderous lie. I believe that God allowed this couple to enter my life in order to demonstrate the contrast between the children of light and the children of darkness; and that evil, bigotry, and racism were not the wholesale attributes of the white race nor any race, but rather the choosing of these hellish traits by individual persons within any race.

Ken and Peggy chose to live a life free from overt racism and prejudice. Their abilities to live such lives, proved that their characters were not determined by the color of their skin; nor their culture; nor even the place of birth; but rather by simple choices they made. Although, I believe that they, like many other whites, had been taught to socialize only with their own kind, they made personal choices on their own to broaden their experience and get to know us. It was rather easy, because we liked each other so very much. Like us, they were surprised to find that we had many things in common. These included the facts that we were both pharmacists; while his wife and my former wife were both school teachers. On the lighter side of life, we were alike also. We both had a great love for the "god-father of soul," the singer, James Brown. Ken even tried to do the famous "mashed potatoes" dance, and the "side-slide" across the dance floor, which culminated in Ken doing "the Split."

It could be rightly said that they also learned and practiced the Golden Rule, which is to: "Do unto others, as you would have them do unto you." As a matter of fact, when Ken and I were about to finish our tours of duty, he persuaded the Pharmacy Director, Lt. Colonel George A. Sommers, who was the Chief of the Pharmacy Department, to hire me to take his place, as a civilian Supervisory Pharmacist. I was the first civilian pharmacist hired at the time, black or white, and the first civilian to serve as the Supervisory Pharmacist over the Main Outpatient Pharmacy, Brooke Army Medical Center, at Ft. Sam Houston, Texas, a position which I held for around ten years.

The point in this being that it is a tragic mistake to ever make blanket generalizations about any race of people: not every white person is a racist, and not every Jew is in the business of exploiting black people. These are lies which black racists are trying to pawn off on the black populace, in order to draw attention and a following to themselves. I would also say to others, not every black person is lazy, uneducated, and unable to hold down jobs that require mental alertness and responsible decision-making. Every person should be judged on their own merits, and not have to wear the stereo-typical labels earned by others; no matter what their race or lot in life may be.

In these two wonder persons, Ken and Peggy, mentioned above, exist two of the finest, upstanding, and most outstanding persons among the human race, no matter what color. In them, I found the true definition of true-blue, Americans. And, although, they are white, Georgia-born and Georgia-bred, they were and still are the greatest friends I have ever had. Others may call me whatever names they wish for saying so, but I came to know them and to loved them like a brother and a sister. What tops it all off is this: they are truly my brother and sister in Christ.

While on the same subject, I would be remiss if I did not mention yet another former boss of mine at the Dallas VA Medical Center, Russ Montgomery, who happened to be white. I had worked as a full-time and part-time staff pharmacist at this institution; but was working at a civilian pharmacy at the time I came to see him about a Supervisor's position which was being advertised. I had worked only a short time under his management before leaving for the job in Retail Pharmacy in downtown Dallas; but I had always tried to do my very best while I worked for him. I actually worked under the supervision of the legendary, black Pharmacist and Supervisor of the Dallas VA Pharmacy, Mr. Byron Mackie, one of the hardest working, and most patient men that I have ever encountered. Byron was there for over 30 years, from the late-1950s to the late-1980s. To make a long story short, Russ hired me as one of the Supervisory Pharmacists in the Outpatient Pharmacy, because he was impressed with my past perform-ance, the positive interview I had with him; and the confidence I instilled in him that I could get the job done. Incidentally, I was also recommended by Ray Miller, the other Supervisor, who happened to be white. Practically all of the other candidates seeking this same position were white; and all were current employees at that institution, at the time I applied. However, in spite of all the odds stacked against me, I walked away with the job. God is truly amazing!!! And God has good people in every class, race, and nation!

I have discovered over the years that while racism is truly a prevalent monster in the American society; however, in the meantime, I have also discovered that not all white persons, nor Jewish persons, in authority are anywhere near the monsters described by Louis Farrakhan and other pessi-mist like him. In many cases, it is a matter of being prepared and being willing to go after opportunities which become available; while trusting and praying that God will open doors for you. Racism does exist, but this is not the truth in every case. Like everyone else, most managers want people whom they can trust to do the job. This I have honestly tried to do; even though my efforts have been a mixture of some successes and some failures; but I have tried to always succeed.

In all of these persons mentioned above, although there were many more, I knew that love and character were not simply products of culture or race, it went much deeper than that. It was a matter of the heart.

THE SOUTHERN EXPERIENCE:
Tragic Encounter With Racist Death Squad

THE DEADLY ENCOUNTER WITH TWO SOUTHERN RACISTS, DESCRIBED IN THE NEXT FEW PARAGRAPHS, NEARLY COST ME MY LIFE. If ever I had reasons to hate white people and join groups like the black Muslims or Nation of Islam, the following incidents could surely justify it. I therefore relate these events in order to reveal my personal sufferings at the hands of racists; and yet maintain my Christian witness, through it all. In the first encounter, which occurred in my younger years, I learned personally, not only the depths of some white folks hatred for black people, but through the results of this hatred, I looked death in the face.

Death to me, a person who wanted so badly to live, was an ugly, gruesome, and violent intruder in my life. When it seized upon me, it was like a vicious strangler clutching and groping at every part of my body, trying to snuff out the light of life. Then it was like a dark, swirling cloud, just before a thunderstorm. I was enveloped by its darkness, so much so that for a moment, I thought that I would never see the light of day again. Fortunately for me, God had invested His Holy Spirit in me, as a born-again Believer, that when I was at the point of slumping down to death's victory over my life, God initiated hope and a will to fight to keep this precious gift, called "life." Without knowing much hope, yet, I hoped in God, and I prayed: "Lord, Dear God, Don't Let Me Die." The Lord heard my cry and pitied my every groan. I lived; I now live; and realize that by God's mysterious power in Christ, I shall never truly die!

THE NIGHT THAT DEATH CAME STALKING:

The Spring of 1965, had been an exciting time for the nation; as well as for me at school. But before long, when the semester had ended, I journeyed back to my little hometown for what I thought would be a boring summer. In contrast to the excitement experienced at the university, my home town was a very dull place. Even though there was as much injustice there, and the surrounding towns, as in most other deep South places, never was there any organized effort to protest anything.

The beginning of my tragic ordeal occurred in the dusk of early evening, on a typically, hot Saturday evening in my little hometown of Greenwood, Florida. I was gathered with "the boys," my life-long friends, under "the tree of knowledge," at Mr. Frank Ward's community store. Mr. Ward, a very proud, hard working, and industrious man, was the only Black man who owned a store in my little hometown. He had a big oak tree which provided shade from the hot, sweltering, Florida sun. The tree had a bench attached to it which served as a place for resting, community talk, checker games, and the latest area gossip. Almost daily, African-American men and boys gathered there to talk about the day's events and "learn" the latest hot news in and around town, thus the name "the tree of knowledge" was adopted.

THE ATTEMPT TO MURDER ME:

In the early darkness of this unforgettable day, the events which sprang upon me would turn my world upside down. My life would never be quite the same. The tragic events to follow occurred while I was home for the summer break from Florida A & M University, where I was in my third year as a pharmacy student. Earlier in the day I had played in an out-of-town baseball game with my hometown team. Before going home to change into our evening clothes, a few friends gathered under "the old learning tree" to recap the events of the day, and pick up where we had left off while I was away at school.

Many people pass through the main artery of our little town on the way elsewhere. The town offered little, other than gas and a few items for refreshment, for most travelers. Rarely did they branch off into the area where black people lived. This night was different. Two white teenagers, with State of Georgia license plates, drove up and began demanding, in a degrading and condescending manner, directions on their travels. Because of their rudeness we decided that it was best to ignore them, so we went back to our conversations. They interrupted us again, and began threatening to shoot us for not showing them more respect as White people. They claimed to have a shotgun in the back seat of their car.

I was beginning to boil in side with anger. Before long my anger would not allow me to remain silent any longer, and a verbal altercation occurred. They drove off a short distance and suddenly turned and gunned their car toward me. Anger and, as I look back on it, stupidity overcame my common sense, and I stood in the road in defiance. They stopped just before their on-rushing death machine took me out. As I ran to the driver's side and began scrambling with the driver, his passenger plunged a large hunting knife deep into my chest, just a fraction of an inch from the base of my heart (so the X-rays later revealed). My friends (six strong young African-American males), whom I just knew was going to help me put a severe whipping on these two young racists, ran like a bunch of scared rabbits and did absolutely nothing to help me.

After the one white racist stabbed me, I guess that excited a murderous rage in them, for the driver began chasing my friends around the street with their car; attempting to run them over. I was still in a state of shock, standing helplessly there in the middle of the street, watching the gushes of blood pump from the hole in my chest. I stood there totally confused, and dumfounded, watching in amazement, while clutching my blood-drenched chest and clothing, knowing that my life blood was draining out of me. I knew that I was dying, but could do nothing to stop it. Suddenly, an acute sense of being stalked by death again, when I realized that these young fellows had stopped chasing my friends, and had now turned the racing car toward me. They seemed determined to get a sure kill before the evening was over. Now, acutely aware of the swiftly approaching headlights, I now realizing that death was very near, my fright quickly turned to flight. Miraculously, I mustered enough energy and strength to run and climb over a nearby wire fence. After missing the kill, they gave a rebel yell, "yahoo," and sped off to the main highway, leading out of town.

We were left breathless and panic stricken, yet I was so glad to still be alive. However, with my condition worsening, I knew that I would only have a short time to live, if help did not come soon. At that moment, life seemed almost hopeless. I was at the end of my rope; my young life, with all of its hopes and dreams, yet unrealized, were spilling to the ground along with every surging flow of my life blood. There were no 911 numbers to call; as a matter of fact, it wouldn't have done any good because there were no ambulances, other emergency vehicles, nor even a fire station in our little town. Not only that, we didn't even have a police officer; the only bona fide peace officer was one of the sheriff's deputies, who had to come from a town 9 miles away. Incidentally, that was where the hospital was located, also.

After the deadly racists drove off into the night, my friends regrouped enough courage to help me back over the fence. I was becoming a bloody mess, as blood pumped from the gaping wound in my chest, soaking my shirt and trousers. I was growing weaker by the minute and now realized that I was looking Death in the face. I needed to get to that hospital, and mighty fast! Headlights again appeared in the night; and once again fear gripped our bodies. But after careful observation, we saw that it was the late Mr. Terry Smith, an older black man, who owned a juke joint in the community. Even though he had known my mother, my family, and me, all of our lives, as I stood there bleeding to death, he refused to take me to the hospital. He said that he didn't want to get involved, and drove off.

It would be very difficult for anyone to imagine what a devastating blow that was to me then; and it still haunts me to this day. I suddenly felt that death would soon claim me right there in the streets. The only potential help I thought I had rested in the hands of this fellow black man, my "soul brother," but he drove off in the night, not seeming to care whether I lived or died. And that, too often, seems to be the sordid history of the human race, we run from the idea of being our brother's keeper, no matter how serious the condition.

I probably would have died, but by the grace of God, there suddenly appeared the headlights of another car in the night. Fortunately, this car was driven by a young black man named Robert C. Ferrell, who was home visiting his family. When "Robert C" (the name we all called him) learned of my stabbing and saw all the blood, he asked no more questions. He simply scooped me up in his arms like I was a bloody rag doll and put me in his car for a record-breaking trip to the hospital in the nearby town of Marianna. He didn't care about the blood which covered me; he only cared that I got help, as soon as possible. God always has somebody who will go the last mile with you. I thank God that this young man was a black man; for the simple reason that I can now say that not every black person is uncaring, nor will every black abandon their fellowman or woman, who is in serious trouble.

The skilled doctors at Jackson Hospital said that it was a miracle that I was alive. They couldn't figure out what prevented that big knife from penetrating my heart. I'm now certain that it was the grace of God which saved me: both, the mysterious deflection of the knife blade and the sudden appearance of Robert C, who delivered me on angels wings, to the competent care of the emergency room doctors. However, unbeknownst to me, the horror of my suffering was just beginning, although they were doing their very best to save my life.

Due to the severity of my wounds, the said that they couldn't risk putting me under general anesthetics in order to perform the surgical repairs which were necessary. They gave me a few local injections, directly into the gaping wound and went to work. The pain was agonizing, as they probed around inside my chest looking for severed muscles. I listened in agony, contemplating death with every tug on the bloody hole that once was a healthy chest wall. Then there was the additional need of cutting the wound open wider in order to get their instruments into the wound in order to find severed muscles, and clamp them with their forceps. They had discovered that a muscle which was attached to my upper chest wall, and extended into my lower abdomen, had been completely severed by the wide blade of the hunting knife. Now with me wide awake, they took the forceps and probed down into the bottom of my abdominal cavity, between my outer abdominal wall and lower abdominal cavity, till they found the severed muscle. Then the agony intensified as they pried open the gaping wound and tugged with the muscles till they were stretched and pulled close enough to sew them back together again. Just imagine for a moment, being awake during this entire procedure.

In between my screaming bouts, I watched as they carefully sewed the muscle back together. My screams were often so loud till they could be heard throughout the waiting area. Imagine what this must have been doing to my mother, who had now been brought to the hospital, and was right outside the trauma room. I had seen her for just a brief moment as I lay on the table, before the surgery began. I could see the grave concern written all over her face, as she looked on in horror at my blood covered clothing and body. When the internal organs had been repaired, I watched as they finally sewed my chest wall back together. What a horrifying, yet life saving, ordeal. May God bless those surgeons, wherever they might be today; may the blessings even extend to their offspring.

MY PLANS FOR REVENGE:

I believe that the best way for the reader to understand my twisted and raw physical and emotional state is for them to come with me into these events. This one night of awful experiences would forever reshape my life, and my way of thinking. Revenge was my chief thought, as I lay in the intensive care unit, feeling the pain and seeing the awful mess which my chest had become. It was one massive, swollen, jelly-like pile of flesh, with the surgical wires and threads criss-crossing and zigzagging across my body. My whole world was concentrated on this scary-looking, ugly scene. I began to hate everything that was white. I completely forgot about, or blocked out thoughts about the all-white surgical team which had just saved my life! I didn't care, so, while recuperating in the hospital, I began planning in my mind the revenge I would seek against White people.

My mind turned to the violent "god" of vengeance. In my own imagination, I dressed myself as a revenge-seeking maniac. "Rambo" had nothing on me when it came to how I played out how to torture and kill those who had assaulted me. I had every intention of going after white racists with as much violence I could muster. If I couldn't find my attackers, I had planned to take it out on any and all racist Whites whom I had ever heard of doing black people wrong. If I had been exposed to militant black groups such as the Muslims, the Panthers, or the Symbionese Liberation Army, I would have been a prime candidate to join their groups, hoping for chances to kill and torment as many white males as possible. Given my present situation, I couldn't imagine but a few of them worthy of living. I was a mental and physical wreck.

I rehearsed it in my mind how I would collect as many weapons as possible: machine guns; automatic shotguns, pistols and rifles; hand grenades; flame throwers; and other weapons of destruction. I was very serious, and had every intention of carrying out my plans, to one degree or another. I had plans for night raids on homes. I had planned to slip into nearby states and kill a few, just as my attackers from Georgia, had done. I was a very angry young man; with a murderous spirit. I openly expressed my anger and bitter hostility to my mother; as well as my plans for revenge. Mother reached deep within her soul to help relieve me from this evil spirit. I don't know how she did it, but she did.

In years past, when I was growing up, my mother had always taught us that God was able to help us overcome any problem we faced; including racism, prejudices, white supremacy, and every other form of evil. She had taught that there was no form of suffering, trial, or tribulation, which was too hard for our Lord and Savior, Jesus Christ to help us overcome. She taught us to love and respect all people, whether White or Black, yet I had been almost killed, for simply being born black in a white-dominated world. I had every intention of setting aside all of my mother's teachings. I had planned to say "Good-bye" to all of those old good-hearted, Sunday School teachings which let black folks do all the suffering, while white folks did all the grinning and killing. At that time, as I looked at the monstrous looking wound on my chest, with all that pain, and all those stitches, the only grace I was in favor of was the deadly force I planned to relieve some white folks of their wicked lives. I had planned to kill as many as I could; and was not worrying about dying. I had been pushed to the last straw. I had been one of the best kids in our community, and what did it get me: just another, almost dead, nigger victim of the white man's evil. I meant to get revenge!

THE PERSUASIVE POWER OF A CHRISTIAN MOTHER:

My mother stayed and prayed by my bedside during my Intensive Care period. The more I expressed my hostilities, the more she reminding me of my commitment to Jesus Christ. As she prayed with me, she also brought to my remembrance the Word of God, which says that vengeance belongs to God. She began talking about love and forgiveness. She told me that I couldn't fight evil and hatred, with hatred. She left a Bible by my bedside; asking me to pick it up and read it sometimes, when I was alone. At that time I didn't want to be a Christian; I wanted to be a justified killer, shooting, cutting, and maiming some white folks. I just wanted justice, even if it came in the form of revenge. Mother never stopped soothing my wounds with her love and her words from the Bible. In so many words, she reminded me that Christ's love extended beyond class and color. She reminded me of Jesus' suffering and death; she told me about the suffering; and eventually the victory of Job, and the Lord Jesus. I tried to listen to mother, but it was very hard. It was hard because I knew that these criminals never would be caught and brought to justice. And, incidentally, they never were apprehended. The sheriff's office sent one deputy out to interview me, a few days after I had been discharged from the hospital. I frankly told them that I didn't expect them to find the culprits, in that they waited almost a week before seeking an interview with me.

As I look back over these events, I must give my mother credit for her great wisdom, and the intelligent and highly effective plan of action which she formulated for me in order to correctly handle this matter. I suppose much of it came from wisdom teachings at home and at the University. You see, in earlier years, she also had attended Florida A & M College (now, University), for 2 years. She had learned that the pen is mightier than the sword; therefore, she encouraged me to tell my story in writing to the entire community and the surrounding areas. This, she said, could be best accomplished through the local newspaper. However, since the newspaper was White-owned, I felt that the white owners would never print anything negative to be published that another white had done to a black person, no matter how evil and unjust it had been. Although I felt it would be useless, I followed my mother's advise.

From my hospital bed, I began writing down the details of that horrendous and bloody night, while they were still fresh in my memory, and while the blood yet oozed from the sutures of that grotesque-looking wound. It was awkward, as well as painful, as I attempted to write the story. However, when I thought about the awful crime that had been done to me, I wrote on. I would write until write until I was hot with anger; which seemed almost to boiled the tears which formed in my eyes. These tears seemed to boil over into unforgivable, revengeful hatred. When for the tears and the exhaustion, I could write no more, I would drift off into narcotic-induced sleep, from the prescribed pain medication. During waking periods, I kept to the task till it was completed.

When I had finally finished the stinging article, my mother took it to the editor of the local newspaper; and to the surprise of everyone, except perhaps, mother, the editor not only published it, but gave it front page coverage!!! Then another unbelievable thing happened, the white editor also joined my cause by adding his own sympathetic editorial decrying the evil act which I had suffered. For some reason, which I didn't quite understand, given all of the negative racial situations which black people faced, mother, seemed to know that my story would be published. We were also joined in this project by Mrs. Guy Long, the local, black Extension Agent for our County, for whom mother was working at the time as Secretary and Journeyman. I began to learn that more can be accomplished through prayer, and by working within the "system" than working against it. Once again I was reminded of the great benefit of having a wise, Christian mother, which also was a woman of great faith.

FURTHER INSULTS AND INJURY

Even today, I can't help but wonder how many black victims those young white racists, and others like them, have murdered, just for kicks; and have gotten away with it, "Scott free." I am thankful to God that I was one of the very blessed ones; for it was only by the miraculous hand of God, that I survived the attack. Many other black victims, most likely, did not. I know this to be a fact, if only by accidental hearing the sordid story of another white racist who worked for me years later, as a Registered Pharmacist. Let me tell this little story: In the early 1970s, while serving as the Supervisory Pharmacist at the previously named US Army hospital at Ft. Sam Houston, Texas, one day while sitting in my office, I overheard a disturbing conversation between enlisted Registered Pharmacists, who happened to be white. These guys often ventured over into Mexico, to have a little wild fun. They would all relate whatever exciting exploits they experienced or heard of, both sexual and otherwise, when they returned. One of them told of hearing of a Mexican national being found murdered, floating in the Rio Grande River, which separates Mexico from the USA, in that region. The dead man was found with his hands tied behind his back, indicating foul play. In the excitement of the moment, an immediate reply came from one of the pharmacists from the State of Georgia. With a chuckle and a deep Southern drawl, he said that it sounded "just like a hog-tied, dead 'nigger,' they used to find floating down the river in Georgia."

I was so shocked, I came out of my office in a flash. Now, knowing that I had heard what was said, they were all flushed red in the face and embarrassed. I jumped right in his case, his reply was: "Mac, I'm sorry; I didn't mean anything. I never thought about you being one of 'them.'" I asked "what do you mean, by 'one of them?'" He said, "Well, you know, colored; you're different." I was mad (not angry), I was so mad until I was speechless. I could have choked the bastard with my bare hands. Seeing my growing anger, he retreated out of the door of the pharmacy. I walked back to my office and plopped down in my chair, just dumbfounded and emotionally drained.

After a short while, several of the white pharmacist came into my office and said how sorry they were; and that I should fire him, or see that he was fired. They were very apologetic. I reminded them all that what's inside of a person would some day come out. I couldn't think clearly. I was angry, I was mad, and I was so disappointed. I had gone to many parties and affairs with these fellows. We ate and drank together. We played group games together, and our department went bowling and on picnics together. Yet, in an unguarded moment, one of them revealed just what they really thought about black people; and of this group, I was, undeniably, a member.

Later, when the culprit returned, I called him in my office to talk. I wanted to hit him; I wanted to do something which would make a lasting impression: most of which were violent and illegal. He began to pour out his sordid history of racism being taught in his home; of racist activities among his peers; and how, finally, he had sworn off using racist language, when he came into the Army and had to be around black people. All this, he mixed with tears and sobs. While I was very angry with him, at the same time, I felt sorry for him. I told him I would have to think about what disciplinary actions I would take against him. To make a long story shorter, I later decided not to do anything! The only thing I asked of him was to think about the hurt and embarrassment he had caused to me, to his co-workers, and to himself. He thanked me and said he would be forever grateful for my leniency. My relationship was never the same with this group, for I did not want to subject myself to their sickening patronizing, knowing that deep down within most of their hearts, I was simply another "nigger."

After this event, my former wife and I attended a Christmas party at our new Service Chief's home (not Lt. Col. Sommers!). It was attended by many of my fellow pharmacists and their wives, plus a few technicians. As the party grew old, and much whiskey had been consumed, the group headed to our host's piano. They began singing and yelling to Dixie war songs; the war cries were extremely loud and with great passion. I told my wife that we had better get the heck out of there before it got real ugly. I went to the host and told him of my decision to leave and why. He was highly embarrassed and asked the celebrants to sing Christmas songs, since it was a Christmas party. He was very patronizing, telling me how he had never experienced this kind of thing where he came from in South Dakota. I decided to leave anyway, because I felt this heavy antagonistic emotion hanging over the party atmosphere. I never attended another function with this group.

The elders have often said that if you hang around a person long enough, his or her true colors will eventually begin to show. Countless numbers, like myself, have had to learn this the hard way. White co-workers often wonder why their black co-workers do not show up for many after-work activities, and most often it is because of the embarrassing, and intimidating experiences they have already encountered in dealing with white people in these situations. Most would rather not go through the agony of it all.

As for the fellow pharmacist, who uttered the racist remarks, today, without any further degrees, he serves as a Chief of Pharmacy Service, at a VA Hospital in Texas. I, on the other hand, am still a Pharmacy Supervisor, several years his senior in years of service, and possessing both Master's and a Doctoral Degree, and even though my graduate and post-graduate degrees are in another discipline, that still is not a valid excuse. This is the way life events most often happen in a world where there are ceilings for blacks, and "the sky is the limit" for whites. But, you see, I knew this when I let him off. I knew that one day he would most likely be in a position of authority, simply because he was white. I knew that at the time of my leniency. Yes, I could have had him fired; but, by leaving him to his own conscience and with memories of the kindness which I had shown him, I felt that one day his conscience might be pricked and he might be prompted to help some black brother or sister in need; just as I had helped him. I, therefore, took the idealistic path of instructive living, in hopes of future rewards for others, though they would be unknown to me. On the other hand, I also know how the "system" often cushions and protects white males, no matter how blatant the offense. I suppose, too, I didn't want to risk adding insult to injury by bringing charges against him, and then having them dismissed by some other white male.

Many others who knew of the situation thought that I was crazy for not going forward, but I stuck with my decision. Then, too, I figured that if Christianity was real, and the teachings of Jesus were to be applied to daily living, then this certainly was a test case for me. Was this the kind of forgiveness which Jesus expected from His disciples? I thought that it was, therefore, I held to my decision. Whether he ever returned the gracious act, and helped another black person, I will probably never know. I planted the seed, perhaps somebody else watered it, but only God can give the increase (1 Cor. 3:6).

I believe that it was only through the persuasion of my dear mother that I did not carry out my hate-filled plans of vengeance after my stabbing. I had every intent to do violence to whomever I encountered whose words and actions reminded me of the white monsters who attempted to take my life. However, out of the respect and honor, which I had for my mother, I deferred my actions and yielded to her wishes. Our mothers have a powerful influence over most of us and play significant roles in shaping our lives. I believe that if Christian mothers would follow the Bible in rearing their children, resisting every urge to teach their children revenge and counter-violence, this would be a much better world for all. I also believe that if governments, local, state, and national, would allow parents to raise their children, according to biblical principles, which includes physical whipping where needed, our police wouldn't have to beat and shoot them later in life!!! I received many such whippings, including leather straps and even a board, by my old Agriculture teacher, and I'm the better for it. It's strange that we allow the fraternities to beat on young men for the fun of it; the police to beat them, and say that it was justified; yet the very people who bring these children into the world, the police will put them in jail for doing with a leather belt, what the police do with a Billy-club. Something is dreadfully wrong.

Thanks mom and dad for raising me like the Bible said. I didn't like the corrections, the restrictions, and the whippings, but you made me a better man!!! Again, I say that the purpose of the stories above have been to show that if anybody has reasons to hate white folks, I certainly do. Yet, I have chosen to live above race hating. I was told from childhood that one who hates others, lives in the valley of scum; and when you hate another person, made in the image of God, your value as a human being is no higher that the scum you live in. I have met many whites who have been hypocritical and filled with hate, but I have also encountered, or have learned of countless numbers of concerned white Christians, who lived the faith that they talked about, and reflect the truth of Jesus Christ. I still refuse to give up Christianity or Christ for the lies perpetuated by Louis Farrakhan.

CHAPTER TWO

THE CIVIL RIGHTS MOVEMENT COMES TO TOWN!

The months and years preceding this traumatic stabbing event, in which I was almost murdered by those white racists, were characterized by Civil Rights boycotts and protests, all over the nation. Before I arrived home for the summer, I had seen many Protest Marches, and had participated in a few myself, while a student at Florida A&M University, in Tallahassee, Florida. At first I had been afraid to get too involved because I didn't want to go to get arrested and go to jail, as had happened to many of my friends and fellow students. At the time, my thoughts only centered around my personal goal of finishing Pharmacy School, which was a chance of a lifetime experience. I had been accepted into Pharmacy School, at the University and didn't want to take a chance on anything blocking me from completing my education. I had known all too well the limited and meager existence available to black men who had little education. As a Pharmacy student, I had a golden opportunity to make something of myself by becoming a Registered Pharmacist. I wanted this too badly to risk it by going to jail as a protester. However, I soon learned that great ideas such as freedom cannot be delayed for personal advancement. Thoughts of the possibility a broader experience of freedom had engulfed the University, and eventually I, too, was drawn into the Struggle.

I remember one occasion, in which Stokely Carmichael was scheduled to speak in Lee Hall Auditorium on our campus. The administration had closed down the University because of fear of unrest and had refused the protesters access to the auditorium, which also housed the Administrative Offices. But when Stokely arrived on campus, there was such excitement and electricity in the air till one super energetic male student, scaled the walls, like Spider Man, then opened an upper story window to gain entrance into the building, in order to let this mad crowd in. Stokely and the other speakers, made it well worth our while, as they poured on their fiery orations. Those were exciting times, which spurred us all on toward this goal called "freedom." This might sound strange to Americans; however, until one has personally experienced oppression, with all of its ugly baggage, one really can't understand the magnitude of its detrimental effects.

MY EXCITING ADVENTURES IN THE CIVIL RIGHTS MOVEMENT:

Soon after my near death, stabbing experience, and release from the hospital, I began hearing talk of a Civil Rights group coming to my town. I didn't know what to think. In my bitterness, I experienced many hope-filled expectations of someone finally challenging the Jim Crow, racist system. The chance would soon come for me to take a stand, to either put up or shut up.

One sunny day, as I walked from my home headed for our usual gathering place in our little town, under the "tree of knowledge," a strange car approached and came to a stop. An even stranger array of youthful people were inside, which include a young white male and female! Now, in our town, and in that part of the country, this was very unusual; as a matter of fact, heretofore, unheard of. I suddenly remembered the nightmare of a few weeks past, when the two white racist drove up, which began my nightmare. I was put at ease when they introduced themselves as representatives from the Civil Rights organization called CORE (Congress On Racial Equality). They had recently come to our town and had set up operations, for civil protests. After having read my story in the newspaper, they had come looking for me. When they asked me to join their Civil Rights protest effort, soon to be launched in our area, I was all too happy to join them. I still had much bitterness in me and I had to do something about what had happened to me; and to make life better for other black people. Even though there was as much injustice there, and the surrounding towns, as in most other places in the deep South, there never was any organized effort to protest anything. Much of the group was from out of town. I cannot remember where the young, white male was from, since he didn't stay long; but I do remember that the young, white female was from Wisconsin. Her named Julia, and she was a senior at Stanford University in California. She had a warm, friendly smile; which also helped to entice me to join up with this group.

This group seemed to me to be the perfect media for venting my anger in a positive way. I would also soon learn about the warmth, compassion, and tender heart embodied in this young white female, who risked her life, along with us as we struggled to throw off our oppressors, and find dignity in an undignified society. However, being a young white female, she increased the risk factor among us. It was truly a very dangerous and volatile situation for us all; but we knew that life would never get better unless we were willing to fight, and possibly die, if need be. However, in spite of the obvious risks, Julia was a dedicated fighter, and hung in there with us. As we got to know each other better, she would do much to help relieve my hurt and anger, as well as, soothe the emotional and psychological injuries I had suffered at the hands of those racist white males.

DISCOVERING SOME ORIGINS OF RACIST ATTITUDES IN AMERICA:

During our many conversations together, Julia and I discussed how she and other white children, especially females, were thoroughly indoctrinated on hating and avoiding black people. She told of her father teaching them the most vile stereotypes concerning blacks; and that black males were to be regarded as the scum of the earth. She told me that she would be completely cut off from her family, and regarded as if dead, if her father ever knew that she became involved with a black male. I was baffled by all the hate lessons she had been taught. Given the fact that many Southern white males had been having clandestine affairs with and sexually abusing black females to settle anything from debts to keeping their jobs, this was truly baffling.

Although, ashamed of this sad part of her past life, Julia seemed relieved to be able to vent it with someone she had been taught to hate. She was blond and blue-eyed, but her heart was warm and tender. I found her to be a far cry from the "blond, blue-eyed devils" described by the late Malcolm X and the Black Muslims. We did many things together in order to mock the system which had set us up to hate each other. In later years, I discovered that these same type of hate-teachings were very wide-spread, often being confirmed in conversation with other white females, whom I came to know: Julie from the south side of Chicago, Illinois; Nancy from Minnesota; Linda from Missouri, and there were others from the North and the South. It appears to be a national thing, this "home-schooling of hatred" against blacks, being taught behind closed doors in the homes of many white Americans. Almost to a person, these women revealed lives of being indoctrinated on the inferiority of black people, and abhorring black males, who had been described in the worst of terms.

I thought it quite funny and ironic that these families, especially the fathers, had spent so much time teaching their little girls how to avoid "black, nigger males," only to have them seek out these same individuals for companionship. I likened their willingness to talk about these things to a sort of spiritual and mental cleansing. They all wanted to "get it out of their systems." Julia talked openly and sometimes with great embarrassment about the two sides of her father. He was a strong, family oriented man; yet he had this dark side when it came to black people. Thus, there was the side of him which she loved and then there was the side of him which she literally hated. She would go over some of the hate lessons he had taught, which she and her siblings had to sit and listen to. At the time, she didn't know any black people in a personal way; therefore, she could only assume that he was right. It was only after she had left the prison of her home and had come face to face with the "beasts" that her father had described, that she discovered the lie.

This young woman admitted that it was really something else that her father, and many other white males, had worried, and were almost consumed by: the notion and the mystique surrounding black male sexuality. She admitted that her mother and other white females she had known had talked very guardedly about it. This notion has prompted more myths, cost more lives to be snuffed out, lies to be told, and prompted so many needless fears, concerning black males, than has anything else in black-white relationships. It was funny in a way, as I listened to her stories; but it was very sad and hurtful when left all alone with my private thoughts. I had to ponder the question, "Why, in the name of God, are black people so deeply hated, by so many white folks; these people that we don't even know?" Only God knows the answer.

MY EXCITING AND DARING LIFE AS A CIVIL RIGHTS WORKER:

Nothing as exciting and daring as the Civil Rights rallies and meetings had ever happened in our area. Our team worked very hard getting people involved and educated about the movement, as well as, getting people registered to vote; for many, it would be their first time. There were sit-ins, boycotts, and marches going on all the time. We were constantly being stalked by the police. Soon the local paper began publishing dirty smear stories concerning the young, white female, troublemaker who was running among the "nigras." They spread many vicious lies and rumors, reporting that she was pregnant; overflowing with venereal disease, among other things. There tactics were designed to infuriate the white populace, to incite them to mob action to do us bodily harm, and/or run all of us out of town. There were also reports that the Ku Klux Klan was planning an action against us. We knew that there was great danger, so Julia was offered the opportunity to leave. The young white male did leave, but Julia decided to stay and fight it out with us; no matter what the costs. We all hung in there together, marching and protesting; holding rallies, boycotting the bus company and supermarkets, and negotiating with the white "godfathers" at the city and county levels. Such actions had been unheard of before. We were really on the move; however, tragedy would soon strike among us, like a deadly viper, with such a devastating blow that almost killed our movement.

THE TRAGIC DEATH OF A YOUNG CIVIL RIGHTS WORKER:

There were many planning meetings in which we mapped out our strategies, assessed, reassessed, and revised our plans. We went about our activities with youthful enthusiasm and without much outward fear. Most of our plans were falling into place quite well; therefore, we felt unstoppable, even while operating in a hostile, racist environment. However, early in our activities, a great tragedy occurred; in which racism helped strike a death-blow among our volunteers.

One of our first major operations planned, other than picketing the local grocery stores, was to conduct a "Swim-In" at a "White Only" recreational area, called "Blue Springs." The area was so named for the bluish color of the water flowing naturally from the underground springs. We had planned for almost every kind of tragedy that Civil Rights protesters had encountered in the past: how to blunt a blow delivered to the body or head by a Billy-club; stick, or brick; how to keep calm when being verbally or physically attacked by racists; how to protect oneself from police dogs, water hoses, and many other survival tactics. However, we had no plans which would help us with the events soon to be encountered. We arrived at the swimming and resort area in a large caravan. It was early on a Saturday morning. The weather was perfect. The sun was out and only a small breeze was blowing. We were wary, yet our numbers inspired a cautious degree of confidence, which ran through much of our group. Our cautious calm and confidence would soon be completely shattered by what was about to happen.

The target area was a beautiful, picturesque, swimming and recreational area which had many naturally flowing underwater springs, along with picnic and fishing areas. This place was simply a small paradise in the midst of nowhere. It reminded you of Gilligan's Island in a way. Of course, it had always been off-limits to black people, since it was reserved strictly for "Whites Only." We entered the area under hostile stares, but without any major confrontations or acts of violence. As a matter of fact, the demonstration was going exceptionally well. The Whites, who for once were greatly outnumbered, had simply withdrawn to other areas when we appeared. None of them produced weapons, or were openly hostile towards us. I suppose that perhaps the article that I had written, and the stinging article by the newspaper editor, rebuking the cowardly act of the racists who attacked me, had produced some calming effect on, at least, a portion of the community.

Our group spread out beach towels and set up picnic baskets, while others headed to the waters to swim in this once forbidden territory. Everybody was having a great time. Both children and adults were splashing about in the water, happily screaming and playing . We had been there for a good while when suddenly there were frantic screams that a small child was drowning. He was spotted by one of our 15 year-old youth volunteers, who swam toward the child and attempted to save him. The child was fighting and thrashing around wildly, with arms and feet. Before too long, not having any training in water rescue, the 15 year, soon found himself in trouble, and began struggling. With his frantic grasps and gasps, it was clear that he would not be able to save the child, because his own life was in danger.

Then, suddenly without hesitation or concern for her own safety, or concern about the blackness of the victim's skin, a courageous, young white female, who had been standing on the other side of the swimming area observing, dived in and sway with swift and powerful strokes toward the frantic group. She swam across the spring expertly and confidently, until she located the young child. She grabbed him and began bringing him to shore; then a few others joined her in her rescue attempt. The small child was brought to the safety of the shore; where she administered emergency resuscitation procedures. Without her efforts, that young child, most certainly would have died. I still can't figure out why all of those swimmers in our group could not, or would not attempt to save the child. I later learned that this young white female, this angel of mercy, was a visitor from the neighboring state of Alabama, where the avowed segregationist, George C. Wallace, was governor.

In the meantime, in the midst of the mass confusion, the 15 year-old, would-be-rescuer, had sunk below the water. I had seen him thrashing about and gasping for breath, only to inhale copious amounts of water, as his head bounced above and then below the water. With all of the people around him, and remembering the gallant rescue efforts of the young girl, I just knew that some of the experienced swimmers would go to him and rescue him. I suppose they were all in shock; however, the boy was drowning. Somebody had to do something!

I had not brought swimming gear to the event because I was still weak, and slowly recovering from my stab wounds. However, I just couldn't stand there and watch the young man die, without even trying. Since nobody else made a move toward him, without thinking, I kicked off my shoes and dove into the water in an attempt to try and save the young man. As I searched under the water, I could not locate him at all! What had been perceived as crystal clear water when viewed from above, was now opaque and impenetrable to my vision while submerged. Realizing that I had been under the water too long and was quite weak, I surfaced and attempted to make it back to the dock. My water-logged clothing seemed as heavy as lead, and I could feel them beginning to drag me down. I knew that I was in big trouble. It was at this point that I felt that I was once again staring Death in the face. I could see the looks of fear on hands outstretched out toward me, urging me to keep coming. Fortunately, I did keep struggling until I was close enough to the dock for those above to reach down and grab my frantically outstretched hand, and literally lift me up on the dock to safety. It seemed that I had no strength left in my body; I had been completely at the mercy of my friends, as well as a friendly God.

By the time I regained my composure, and was again standing and looking back down into the water, once again, I located the teenager. I could see that he was no longer moving, but was now floating, with outstretched arms, below the surface of the crystal clear spring water.

Looking from the dock above, his lifeless body, looked like one of the laboratory specimens I had seen at college, suspended in crystal. He was being driven further from the shore by the strong underground current. Still hoping for his rescue and revival, I ran as best as I could, in my fatigued condition, to the keeper of the supply store, who was an elderly white man, who sat unmoved in a chair watching. I begged him for a rope or a pole to try to drag the drowned young man in. He simply gave me an icy stare and said: "Y'all should'na been down heah in the furst place!" With that he looked away and kept rocking in his chair. Someone drove to find a telephone to call the "Rescue Squad." We waited and waited; then called more times. Finally, they showed up almost an hour later!!! We all stood around numb, dazed, and in silent shock as the divers dragged the boy's lifeless body to shore. In a foolish hope for a miracle, as they went through the motion of resuscitation, I hoped that God would let his life return to him again! There would be no miracles that day. All of us could clearly see that the boy was dead. The quest for freedom had taken another black victim; as well as taken its toll on the rest of our group.

We left the swimming hole drained emotionally, physically, and spiritually. It was a tragedy that none of us had been prepared for. Nobody talked much about inner feelings, but I know that many were thinking that we could have better dealt with him being killed by a hate-filled racist; than by this beautiful spring water. After all, we had come looking to find a measure of freedom as we dived into its depths and frolicked, and splashed at its edges. The man-killer had been one of the natural elements; it was so hard to be angry with it. You wanted to be angry with God; but that too was useless. Yet, at times like these, we do ask God, "Why?" "Why did you let this happen to him?" "Why do you let black people suffer so much?" There were no answers, just silence. However, the major part of our anger and dismay was not at God, but at the calloused and unconcerned nature of those who could have helped, but refused to do so. This incident would test our desire and commitment to pursue this elusive dream of freedom.

There was a sense of hopeless despair that gripped most of our lives that afternoon. I asked "Why could the old man, or anybody, be so cold and hate-filled? For these White people to see a young boy drowning and none, except the brave little girl from Alabama, did anything to help!!! However, another cold truth gripped me: none of the young blacks who could swim, dared to venture below the water to try and rescue the young man, either. In a small way I relived how my so-called friends had run off and left me alone when I was being attacked by the two white racists some weeks earlier. To this day, I am pretty much a loner, because I have know the deceptive, as well unreliable, ways of so-called "friends," all too often.

At the funeral service for our brave friend, we celebrated his short life, remembering that, not only did he die in the pursuit of freedom, but he also died trying to save the life of an innocent little child. It was the greatest sacrifice: to die for a friend. The words of Jesus exalted the young hero to the level of martyr:

"Greater love has no one that this,
than to lay down one's life for his
friends" (St. John 15:13).

We were encouraged to continue the fight for justice, for we were told by his close relatives that this is what the deceased young man would want us to do. We were, therefore, determined not to let this young martyr's sacrificial death, be in vain. Many tears were shed and much sorrow was poured out, but we were strengthened by the encouraging services, and we made a commitment to fight on.

The rest of the summer campaign was carried out with more intensity and enthusiasm. I never shall forget the strong words of encouragement from the very elderly black citizens. We walked from house to house in the cities and towns; and down country lanes and dirt roads in the rural areas. Almost every where we went, we were encouraged to never give up till we had the victory. They would say things like:

"I wish I was young again, and I'd go with you.' But these old legs

done wore out; you keep up the fight; we'll be praying' for you.'

Then, these old soldiers would wave us on as they watched us walk toward the next distant neighbor. We knew that they would be praying for us; and this encouraged us to keep going.

WHITE INSIDE INFORMANTS KEPT US AWARE OF RACISTS' PLANS:

There is a well-beloved gospel song which was written performed by the late, great gospel composer and singer, Thomas A. Dorsey, which has encouraged thousands upon thousands, of past generations of my oppressed brothers and sisters. The song is called "The Lord Will Make a Way Somehow." The first verse and chorus delivers the message:

Like a ship that's tossed and driv-en, Bat-tered by and an -gry sea,
When the storms of life are rag - ing And their fu - ry falls on me,
I won-der what I have done That makes this race so hard to run,
Then I Say to my soul, take cour-age, The Lord will make a way
some-how.

*The Lord will make a way some - how, When be-neath the cross I
bow; He will take a-way each sor-row, Let Him have your
bur-dens now; When the load bears down so heav-y The
weight is shown up - on my brow, There's a sweet re-lief in
know-ing, O The Lord will make a way some - how.* **3**

The title of this song, "The Lord Will Make a Way, Somehow," has
become a standard saying among black people of the Christian persuasion.
It literally came true so vividly for our protest group. We had been protesting
and making demands upon the white leadership in the city and county
governments; but we seemed to be making very little headway. They were
always a few steps ahead of us. Our luck changed about the time that they
finally decided to meet with us. There was this wonderful white couple who
befriended our group. They had seen the injustices which existed in our town
and decided to secretly help us. These two unsung heroes, working behind
the scene, risked their lives and professions in order to keep us abreast of
what the white leaders were planning. Being white, they could sit in on
important meetings with the city fathers and local racists. They would
apprise themselves of the white folks strategies in dealing with us; then they
would meet secretly with our trusted core group, and apprise us of just what
they were planning. They begged and pleaded with us to keep our rendez-
vous, and their names, secret; further advising us to discuss the intelligence
we received from them with only the most trusted members of our group.

THE GREAT CEMETERY DEAL

Sometimes what our spies reported about the behind-closed-doors
sessions of the white council was down right hilarious. In our early
negotiations, the white council had met to map out a strategy. Our informants said that most of city fathers and county leaders were at the meeting.
They had planned to offer us a compromise. They were going to offer us
the grand privilege of letting us bury our dead in the same cemetery as
whites; however, the space picked for us was way in the back of the
cemetery, near a wooded area!!! We laughed for a long while. Needless
to say, we were able to beat them at their own game.

THREATS OF VIOLENCE AND ECONOMIC OPPRESSION

I remember one secret meeting, where they wanted to warn us of some
planned violent action against our group, as well as against some of the
blacks who were activist in the town and nearby communities. Through

their warnings those targeted in our communities were able to take evasive or creative actions which neutralized their threats. Not one member of our group, or the people in the community were every harmed physically. However, several were put under heavy economic pressures in order to dissuade them from helping the cause. Nevertheless, all were too deeply involved, too sold out and committed to the movement, to turn back.

With the new information we received from our informants, we would re-vamp our plans, and devise counter measures and proposals in order to neutralize their strategizing. We always pretended to be very surprised by what they offered us; never letting on that we knew beforehand their useless proposals. Having previously rehearsed our responses, we were able to carry out the charade without a hitch. We realized that without the intelligence we receive from this friendly white couple, we never would have been so successful.

We all knew the risks, and they openly expressed fear of physical violence against their family, themselves, and the loss of their professional standing in the community (I still do not feel at liberty to even reveal the nature of their professions, for fear of adverse reprisals against them, even at this late day. Although, I doubt if they are still in the little town). In spite of all the risks, this courageous and bold young white couple, who had nothing personal to gain, and so much to loose, decided that it was their moral duties to help us in any way that they could. I can't remember their names (and perhaps, that too is a blessing), but I salute their unforgettable efforts; for they were true Americans, in the purest sense of the word. I say to them, "May God bless you my friends, wherever you might be!!!" I submit similar salutations to the memories of all of our good friends: whites, blacks, Jews, Christians, and many other races and groups, all over the nation, who risked life and limb to challenge America to live up to its declaration of "liberty and justice for all." God forbid that I should ever cast all white people in the same lot as the young racists who stabbed me; or the David Dukes; or the Bull Conners; or other racists and bigots of this world.

Through the help and courageous sacrifices of many highly diverse groups from the mass of humanity, on local and national levels, we were able to keep up our efforts until the wall of oppression came tumbling down. Our songs and growing numbers encouraged us. We sang songs like, "Lord, I Won't Turn Back," and "Before I'll Be A Slave, I'll Be Buried In My Grave, And Go Home To Live With My Lord." Most of us were ready and willing to die for freedom. You see, once a severely oppressed person gets a taste of liberation, it is very difficult, if not impossible, for him or her to ever accept anything less.

On the local level, our group worked hard and tirelessly. We were greatly rewarded for our efforts. Instead of joke compromises, like "the great cemetery deal," as proposed by the city and county officials, we began seeking economic improvements for our people. After much protesting, boycotting, and marching (we were peaceful and polite, although we had rehearsed for the worst), our persistence began to pay off. The little city bus line, with its Jim Crow policies, was eventually closed down, permanently. Then, when the merchants saw our resolve and began to feel the devastating effects of economic sanctions, after a few weeks, we began seeing black clerks at the grocery stores. Black folks were being served in some department stores, in the order in which they came to the checkout counter, instead of having to wait till white folks were served. Many of those blacks which had criticized our initial efforts, began to see the positive effects of persistent, organized protests.

A NEARLY FATAL BLUNDER

It was a long, hot summer. There were many good times, however, there were many scary times. Many times we were closer to death than we realized. One time in particular, was one Saturday evening when we all decided to relax and take in the local night life. This usually consisted of going to one of the local little night clubs, which most folks called "juke joints," to dance, drink your favorite beverage, and just relax. There was one particular time that Julia took a big chance and went with us. It would turn out to be a foolish mistake, which nearly cost me my life; and we should have known better. We had been followed, either from a distance, or tracked down, by the deputies from the sheriff's office. They wanted us real bad.

I started out like a really great night on the town. For a few hours it looked like we could forget all of the stresses and anxieties of leading protests, strategizing, and organizing. After everybody was kind of situated at this one club, Julia and I decided in our youthful enthusiasm, that we would venture on the outside, by ourselves. I suppose that we were in search of adventure, in that we were drawn to a small, dark cabin right next to the little club. This would prove to be a very stupid idea! The little building had one way in and one way out.

In the darkened cabin, we held on to each other. But, before our eyes could adjust to the darkness, the whole area was crawling with sheriff's deputies! What in the world were we going to do? We heard the people softly yelling out that they were there, just as they were pulling up. It happened too quickly for us to run out of the place. We decided to scoot down as low as we could, and to stay hidden in the darkness, and wait to see what happened. It scares me right now, to think back on what could have happened to me that night.

When the deputies got out of their cars, they began questioning the people on the outside about the whereabouts of our group. I'm sure that someone on the inside told the other members of the group about the danger we were in, so they, too, came outside and began talking to the deputies. I felt at that moment, that this would be my last night on earth, alive. They were right outside the cabin; and there was nothing to prevent them from coming inside. If they had come inside, I knew that I would suffer a horrifying death. I was certain that they wouldn't shoot me and get it over. Like others who have been lynched, or tarred and feathered, I just knew that they would take me to an isolated place; beat and torture me; cut off body parts and stuff them in my mouth, like I had heard they had done others. Many horrifying thoughts went through my head.

Luckily, for us, or should I say, I believe that it was by the grace of God, that some of the attendees at the club spotted them before they found us. They, and members of our group, intentionally engaged them in a conversation; and must have convinced them that another part of the group, which included the white girl, had left for home. I was too scared to remember all that was even said. However, these good old boys were interested in one thing: whether that white girl was out and about with those civil rights trouble makers. Julie and I heard most of the conversation; even if we didn't understand all that was said. I was simply listening for one thing: whether or not that door opened. We were hiding in the dark, afraid to breathe too heavily. Where could I go? I couldn't run out without running over them; or past them. If they had found us together, I would have been one dead fellow. Fortunate for me, the detractors successfully led them away from our hiding place. It was then, and only then, that we breathed the greatest sighs of relief.

When the deputies drove off, we hurriedly got out of that death trap, gathered our group together, and fled that place as if it had the plague. That night had to be one of the scariest times of my entire life. I was even more scared than on the night that I was stabbed. I felt that I was headed for a horrifying night of excruciating suffering, terror; and an awful death. We escaped our tormentors only by the grace of God. We never pulled a public stunt like that again.

A STRANGE AND AWKWARD GOOD-BYE:

As it has been said around the world, "all good things must one day come to and end;" and as the saying goes, so did our summer of protest and adventures, finally come to an end. However, another condition, which had been brewing in our national office, also helped speed up Julia's departure. We had heard that for several months there had been brewing a strong antagonism against the continued presence of white volunteers and field workers in our, and many of the Civil Rights organizations. Whites were being strongly encouraged, or asked outright, to leave many of these organizations. The national leadership felt that this was best for the progress of the Movement; therefore, each unit had to comply, sooner or later. Watching the newscasts in which these statements were being made was especially painful, with Julia in our midst. We all felt really bad, but we had no control in these matters.

Anyway, the summer was almost over, and the majority of us were college students, and we all knew that we must leave soon, in order to go back to school. Julia and I had become very closely attached to each other, and there was also a very strong camaraderie and sense of oneness among all the members of our group. After all, over a two month period, we had all shared some very precious times of our lives together. We had sacrificed our free time, for a great cause. We spent some of our time together at our "Freedom House." Therefore, we shared in cooking, cleaning, shopping, and just being together, never knowing when or whether we would be bombed out or shot down. The fear of death was always present. When we were not in the field, much of our time was spent at one of the black churches in Marianna, or the Mark's home, which was situated midway between the two towns, Greenwood and Marianna. Their home was always under the threat of violent reprisals; however, they remained unwavering in the commitment of their home to the cause of our freedom movement. These things gave us all that sense of being bonded together in a manner which is seen among soldiers banked together in the same fox hole on the battlefield. And, like battle tested soldiers, our lives and fates were intertwined and co-dependent in the tense environment which we shared. I shall never forget these individuals.

The last sense of terror gripped us when we had to take Julia to the

Greyhound bus station to catch her bus back toward California. When we took her to the bus terminal, we were rudely awakened to the fact that, in spite of our protests and small victories, many old vestiges of segregation, racial prejudice and the Jim Crow system were still standing tall and strong. Big signs announcing that there were still the "White Only," and "Colored Only," sections at the bus station. The angry looks of the crowds there reminded us that we needed to stay in our places.

Julia decided to try this system until the very end. Since it looked too violent for us to sit in the "White Only" section, she chose to sit with us in the "Colored Only" section. Our section consisted of a small rectangular area, with a big wall separating the two sections. There were two short rows of seats facing each other, which was nestled right next to the restrooms. It you wanted something to eat, you had to go to the side door and ask. Somebody would finally come to you after they had finished serving all the white customers. There were no dining tables or booths, like the much larger "White Only" section, where travelers or the locals could eat or sip their drinks in comfort. Whatever you got, you had to bold in your lap and eat. It was in this wonderful section that we all sat down.

The silent question was "Who was going to sit next to Julia?" We all knew that it was risky for the males; and most sat opposite her. Being a risk taker, and having been so close to her, I decided to sit with her. After all, she had risked her life time and time again for the sake of our freedom, when she clearly didn't have to. Nevertheless, it wasn't long before there was a parade of peering and piercing eyes of angry white folk, who began taking turns walking by and gazing at us like we were wild animals at the zoo. Before long, the little bus station had filled up with other white locals. I was going around to peer in the White Only section, but was met with such hostile stares that I retreated to my "unfortunate" seating arrangement. Julia, some of the others, and I tried to make small talk, but the atmospheres was charged with such hostility and fear till it was almost impossible.

What we did say didn't make much sense. It's hard to concentrate when it looks like somebody is about to shoot or lynch you. Pretty soon the police and sheriff's deputies began showing up. We didn't know what to think, or to do. We just sat there hoping that Julie's bus would hurry up and come, before somebody got lynched. There was a very large, and very old oak tree in the town square in front of the County Court House, and legend has it that it was called "the hanging tree." In decades past, it was said that a mob of angry whites had taken several black men there and tortured and hanged them. I didn't want these good old boys to activate that tree using me.

One of the fellows with us named Gerald, sat opposite us. He was literally terrified, wearing his fear like an old overcoat. In other words, it showed all over his body. At first his knees were knocking together, then his whole body started shaking violently; like a person with very severe Parkinson's Disease. He couldn't control his feet, his legs, or even his hands; he was trembling all over. I had never seen anything like it before in my life. But just when things got real bad, they called Julia's bus. We hurriedly got her bags and went out for her to board. Most of us made sure we didn't get too close to her. As she was boarding the bus, I wanted to, and I'm sure, all of wanted to hold her hand, hug her and say "goodbye," like normal folks do, but the fellows dared not touch this white girl in public. We were being watched by the angry and curious crowd; which seemed like hungry vultures, circling overhead, looking for prey. At some point, I even felt like varmint, waiting to be shot down. One of the young black female teenagers in our group, named Cookie, at whose home June had stayed, did for all of us what we couldn't do ourselves: She went over and hugged and kissed Julie, good bye!!!

I could see the hurt in her eyes; but I couldn't prevent or change what fate had so ordered. I also felt the hurt that was in my own heart, as she sat looking out the window at me, with those beautiful, but very sad eyes. However, I began to feel the ambivalent emotion of being both sad and glad, at the same time. I was sad that she was leaving, and we probably would never see each other again; but then I was glad that she was leaving, in that she was taking with her this forbidden zone of white womanhood, which has caused so many black men to lose their lives. This ambivalence of emotion declared me both a coward and a self-preservationist; however, the latter of which allowed me to live to write about the experience. You see, there is no greater fool than a dead fool! After all, What good is a dead fool, for had he used common sense, he could still be alive; waiting for a new day to dawn.

With our jobs done for the summer, each of us would soon return to our private lives, which we had before we met. However, through our multiplicity of experiences, our lives would never be the same. Never again could I ever accept complacency and injustice, without getting involved and working toward the noble goal of liberty and justice for all. Also, never could I simply hate all white people because of the evil of just a few. I was truly glad that our paths had crossed and intertwined; however. they would never do so again. Soon, she was gone, but she has never been, nor will she ever be, forgotten.

CHAPTER THREE

THE ISSUE OF CHRIST AND CULTURE

"Who shall separate us from the love of Christ?"

Romans 8:35

Those familiar with the Holy Bible will soon recognize the quote above as that of the Apostle Paul. In spite of Paul's answer to his own question, in which he said "nothing ... shall be able to separate us from the love of God, which is in Christ Jesus our Lord," **4** it is hard to say that this is the case within the black Christian community, today. With Louis Farrakhan's recent invasion, and seeming capture of, once off limits segments of the black community, there is a real question as to where many Christians stand in regards to Christ and Farrakhan's call for greater loyalty to things black. He has equated the Christian culture with oppression and has called for the people to transfer their loyalties to him, and ultimately to the Nation of Islam. In all of this, I see a dark force of evil which has penetrated, and is eating away, the very core of the African American Christian Community, which is the love of God in Christ. In some cases, this change is occurring with, seemingly, relative ease.

Mr. Farrakhan has been so effective because of his willingness to address, as well as exploit, the issue of white racism; in addition, in some selected areas, he has made highly publicized efforts at offering some solutions to the social ills within the black community. He does this very effectively, I believe, because he is willing to advertise his activities, by publicizing most worthwhile projects of the black Muslims. At the same time, the public gets the idea that the black Christian church is inactive in many communities because many times we do not advertise the good things that we do; and, also, simply because many churches are "inactive!" While Farrakhan comes across like the man with the plan; the rest of us stand around scratching our heads. His neatly dressed appearance; his keen wit; his appearance of being angry for all of the oppressed. Then there is the impression that he makes of being able to speak eloquently, and very pointedly, to all the evil things whites have done to black people, make him a popular icon for final justice, to many, or shall I say, a growing mass of black people.

Louis Farrakhan is offering the African-American community, and many Christians, an attractive and emotionally charged blend of black racist talk on cultural pride and separatism, and the need for black people to break away from a white-dominated Christian community. He is getting a hearing many areas. Mr. Farrakhan, and other disciples of the Nation of Islam are making some, even if slow, progress in winning converts to the Nation of Islam. What is even more scary, is that he is developing a growing support base from some Christians in the African-American population.

While Mr. Farrakhan supports much of his presentations with concrete proof of White racism in America, much of his arguments offer nothing more than inverse racism, and negative reasoning which dwells on highlighting selected evils of white people. Farrakhan seems to believe that American racism and Christianity, which many in their following has dubbed "the White man's religion," are the root causes of the oppressive conditions under which they live. The antithesis of these conditions, which they are quick to point out, is to be found in the racial unity offered under the umbrella of the Nation of Islam and their liberator god, Allah, and Louis Farrakhan, their "savior."

There is a major battle being waged for the souls of the people of America, concerning the precedence of Christ, or culture. Is it one of the two? Both? Or neither? The ideas and thoughts presented here, reflect on that battle. This battle is not being fought in evangelistic camp meetings, where fiery-tongued evangelists lambaste the evil deeds of the devil, or warn against the destructiveness of sin; or the danger of living without Christ in a sinful world. Neither are we talking about sinners being warned to flee their lives of sin lest they become consumed by the wrath of God. No! The battle for souls among Americans is the war of cultural, theological, and philosophical conflict being waged by racists, both black and white. These extremists purposes include: splitting the America people between racial and cultural lines; winning the allegiance of Americans along racial and cultural lines; and then creating separate nations, particularly black and white, within our nation. Their racially distinct methods seems to embody a two-fold strategic objective, using Christianity, in one way or another:

The black racists seek to discredit and ridicule Christianity, in order to curb its influence in black America; and to bolster and promote their racist causes and organization, as the only right way for black Americans. On the other end of the spectrum, white racists using a distorted and perverted form of Christianity, in an attempt to gain their own credibility, while promoting the white racist cause as the only right way for white Americans. There are many factions leading the white effort. However, I will not deal in depth with this group, but with the black racists. The most prominent leader among this group of black racists is easily identified, his name is Louis Farrakhan, upon whom, much of these writings will focus. Mr. Farrakhan is the outspoken, chief minister of the Nation of Islam, a radical, black power, religious cult, claiming some connection with Orthodox Islam.

Like other racists, they prey upon persons who have become frustrated with the American national life and problems between the races. These individuals seek to divide the races along cultural and religious lines. The biblical quote at the beginning of this section was stated by the Apostle Paul. Paul was certain that "nothing" would separate him from God, and His Christ, but as we prepare to enter the 21st century, judging by what Louis Farrakhan is doing to among black Christians, many are not so sure of their willingness to be committed to Jesus Christ. Mr. Farrakhan, like our political candidates, uses race-baiting to win a favorable hearing. It is as evident here as in the racist rhetoric offered by David Duke and others, who, like these two, represent a growing number of disgruntled and dangerous personalities spreading their poison all over America. Therefore, we can see that the race problem in America is becoming more and more like the land mines hidden in the fields of war around the world, just waiting for someone to make the wrong step. The potential for an explosion is imminent.

On the negative side, racism and race-baiting are as American as apple pie. This is not to say that this attitude is exclusively and American phenomenon. In order to dispel that notion, we can look in places around the globe: In South Africa, the Afrikaners are against the Asians, the mixed races and everyone else is against the native black Africans. In Brazil and many places in South America, the Portuguese and other whites hold disdain toward all the other races. The mixed races fare a lot better than black Brazilians, who are at the very bottom. As always, it only takes a few bad apples to spoil the whole barrel. In another way, American racism is like the "always-drunk uncle," who shows up on major holidays or other family events; and are just as predictable as the bitterness of quinine, in causing disturbances. The issue of race prejudice in America knows no boundaries: from many who have occupied the White House; to the "Gangster Rap" artists; from American corporate board rooms, such as the recently made public, derogatory remarks about blacks, uttered by several executives from one of the world's largest oil companies; to the muggers and murderers who prey on foreign tourists; from Japanese government leaders and business tycoons, who question and insult the intelligence of blacks in America; to mom and pop Korean grocers, who live off of, and then shoot down black customers, in black neighborhoods, as shown on national TV. Race is an unhealthy preoccupation for much of America, and the supposedly, "civilized" world.

These writings focus on my observations and reflections on the teachings and personality of, undoubtedly the most well known of this group of black racists, that fiery-tongued, black separatist and extremist, Louis Farrakhan. Some would ask: "With all of the other racists out there, why pick on Farrakhan?" Historically, Mr. Farrakhan and the Nation of Islam have been the first to "pick on," and be highly critical of, black Christians. He has been known to call Christianity, "the religion of the white man," and therefore, and enemy of the black man, while making every attempt to convert black people to the Nation of Islam. Then too, he uses deceit and blasphemy as he promotes himself as the Messiah; claiming that he is the literal fulfillment of "the prophetic Jesus," which is nothing short of heresy. Therefore, as a faithful and an unwavering Christian, it is my duty as a disciple of Jesus Christ to contend with the enemies of our faith.

In the warfare, I find many areas of serious, and often, irreconcilable conflicts with the theology, and the social, as well as, political philosophies of Farrakhan. His theological positions are untenable both from Christian and Islamic perspectives. Socially, he is a strong advocate for the separation of America based simply on racio-cultural criteria. My intent is to make the truth known concerning his claims, and the claims of the Christian faith; and to appeal to African Americans to return to the strong value systems of our foreparents and to work within this reluctant system to help bring about much needed changes. I have no doubts that much of Mr. Farrakhan's success can be linked to his distortions of truth, and the mixing of truth with error. Using these tactics, he has been able to dupe many black Americans into believing that he is their best friend. He vigorously promotes the gross error that Christianity (which he equates with white racism), and the black race and culture are at odds; and that racism and Christianity co-exist as bedfellows, and therefore as mutual enemies of African Americans; which is a blatant distortion of the truth.

Just like the white racists, Farrakhan carefully mixes a few truths with ,many gross errors and exaggerations, in order to promote race hatred, which is the common denominator among racists. Then, in order to complete the deception and bring blacks under his umbrella of protectionism, he, very methodically, highlights those isolated, yet incontestable examples of gross white racism, and racial atrocities committed against black people. He then works hard at projecting to the black community that America is all doom and despair. Then, once hooked into the deception, he is able to sell himself as the black savior and protector. This illusory atmosphere of Farrakhanian protectionism has been used by him to help create an overall illusion of credible leadership. However, no matter how united and black it seems, it behooves all African Americans to look carefully and critically at the entire message of Farrakhan, before making the plunge. We must all realize that the racial, social, and political "ills" of our nation, are not representative of what true concepts of America and democracy are all about.

It was for the true ideals of democracy and freedom that I served proudly in the Armed Forces of our country, as did many of you. In spite of the setbacks, failures, delays, and procrastinations we have experienced, a fair assessment of the overall situation will surely reveal the many victories we have enjoyed. I remember when we couldn't even go into the front door of the town hall or county court house, not even in shackles. We had to go to the back, or if lucky, there was a side door. The only jobs we had was mopping, dusting, cleaning toilets, and the like. Now, in many places, the persons running the whole show are African Americans. We have mayors, County Commissioners, superintendents of schools, presidents of medical societies, judges, assistant District Attorneys, and have had a governor or two. Yes, things are bad, but a quick step back into the past, reveals that we are in our best years. And if we move forward with positive visions, and spirits of cooperation, I believe that the best is yet to come. Yes, I am the same fellow whom white racists stabbed, then attempted to run over, and then left me for dead. In spite of this, America is still the best country on planet earth!

With the above facts in mind, I wholeheartedly choose to remain a loyal American citizen, ever willing to fight against every type of oppression and tyranny, whether domestic or foreign; either black or white; including the anti-Christian and anti-American rhetoric and actions of Louis Farrakhan. Until the time of the purging of America from all of her ills, we must cling to the hope of a united America, where liberty and justice, will one day prevail, for all. If not realized in our lifetimes, then like the prophets of old, who died still hoping for the coming of God's Kingdom of Righteousness, they will be able to say of us, as they said of the prophets:

> *"These died in faith, without ever receiving all the promises of God,*
> *but having seen them afar off, were assured of them awaiting them*
> *on ahead and were glad" (Hebrews 11:13, NKJV & The Living Bible).*

While I plan to enjoy my earthly life, with all of its vicissitudes, I will never lose my view of that eternal, perfect life in heaven. I have worked hard on earth; I have tried to make a difference; yet, I know that this world is not my home, anyway; I'm just passing through. I will not allow the likes of Louis Farrakhan, nor any other racist, white or black, ruin my earthly sojourn dwelling in an atmosphere of hatred.

THE DISTURBING SILENCE OF THE BLACK CHURCH:

Practically, all of America, has heard of Louis Farrakhan; and most have had some serious thoughts and reactions toward his controversial personality, and his black racist, and hate-filled doctrines. However, I believe that there is too much silence, and too many confusing signals, about Farrakhan and his influence, coming from black Christians. Therefore, I feel that there is one section of American life, which needs to really stand up and be counted: that area is the black Christian Church. It is primarily because of the church's ambiguous and confusing stances on matters of black culture and matters of religion, that Farrakhan is having a "field day" among us; robbing us of our influence; as well as spreading confusion and division among us, as he boldly struts his "awful" stuff (racial poison and hatred), in our midst. Many find his hate-filled messages appealing, therefore, like some cultural pied piper, he has many persons skipping along behind him, headed toward a questionable, and quite possibly, destructive end.

THE CONTINUALLY GROWING PROBLEM:

This book is about the sudden rise, if not in great numbers, certainly in the felt-influence, of Louis Farrakhan and the Nation of Islam; and the threatening collapse of the formerly, overwhelming Christian influence and tradition among African American people. The primary mover in this anti-Christian movement is Mr. Farrakhan, and his attempts to destroy the faith and confidence which black Christians have in Christ and the Christian faith. But, as strange as it may seem, the black Christian Church, at times, seems to be aiding and abetting this religious culprit; first by its own inactivity and lack of concern for matters concerning the black community. And, secondly, by those professing Christian churches and institutions, which invite him to take over the pulpit of Christ, and spew out his racial poison. How this courtesy could be extended to one who is avowedly anti-Christ and anti-Christian, in doctrine and teachings, is beyond me. These writings also seek to call attention to Farrakhan's deceptive tactic of making Christ and Christianity necessary enemies, in black American culture and life. One of my main purposes is to counter the arguments that Christianity is an enemy of the black race and to call for both black and white Americans, especially Christians, to come together; to re-group, re-think, and perhaps, re-direct our spiritual, social, and political energies and actions, toward mutually beneficial solutions to American racism, whether black or white.

THE SUDDEN GROWTH OF FARRAKHAN IN CONTEMPORARY BLACK AMERICA

A question which must be asked today is this: Why has Louis Farrakhan become so popular among many American blacks; even among Christians, and those, who, in times past, would not have given him the time of day? A careful examination of the hot racial and political issues which Farrakhan addresses: the rapidly deteriorating social, economic, and political conditions, adversely affecting the lives of many black Americans, and the growing discord among black and white America, indicate a racial hotbed with explosive potential. Farrakhan, and other racists, realize that their survival depends upon the continued hostilities between the races. Therefore, the majority of Mr. Farrakhan's statements, speak of the ills of American life, perpetrated by white America (white racists do just the opposite, in order to keep whites at odds with blacks).

On the positive side, Farrakhan very cleverly calls for much needed changes within the black community, which most citizens find desirable and necessary. He calls for sexual purity among our youth; he decries youth involvement in gang activities (while his own organization often utilizes strong-arm tactics much like the Mafia or a street gang). He speaks out against the sale and use of illicit drugs; he champions black economic self-development; and then he appeals for black men to become better husbands and fathers. Who can be against such things? However, most of his attention has been focused on black males, and rightful so; but what about the troubled and oppressed black female? Where does she fit in within Farrakhanism?

If we use the Million Man March as a measuring device, we must first note they were completely excluded. This should come as no surprise, because, historically, both orthodox Islam and the Nation of Islam hold women in very low esteem. These attitudes toward them, indicate a superior-to-inferior, and less-than-equal, attitudes toward them as significant human beings. How many black American women, or white, as a matter for consideration, would be willing to put the veil over their faces, and forever cover themselves with head-to-foot wraps, in order to be acceptable in the sight of their men? I doubt that very few would be willing to do so. It might appear that I am grasping for straws, yet, in reality, it appears that most of the activities in Farrakhan's organization relegate women to subservient roles. In that very strict culture, women are often left completely out of any decision making processes, except to have babies and bring sexual pleasure.

JUST HOW BAD IS THE RACIAL CLIMATE IN AMERICA?

Throughout these writings, I have tried to give my honest appraisal of the racial attitudes of other Americans which I encounter. I have certainly given credit to our nation for the fine progress it has made over the last two decades; however, many of our day-to-day contact with other races, especially white strangers, indicate that we still have a very long way to go. In saying this, I would be the first to acknowledge that many things which Mr. Farrakhan says concerning entrenched pockets and attitudes of racism have some degree of truth in them.

Whether we will admit it or not, because of this truth factor, the issue of white racism is among his most potent weapons in his rhetorical barrage, which is very much alive in 1997. Just a few hours before I wrote these words, I stopped at a local Minyard's Food Store after church, to buy a few items for Sunday dinner. I was all dressed up in my double-breasted suit, looking rather dignified, I thought. When I took out my VISA checkbook, debit card, the Hispanic cashier, waiting to punch the right button on her cash register, asked me, "Is it a 'Lone Star' Card, Sir?" This is the name for the Texas WELFARE CARD; equivalent to food stamps!!! The same thing had happened about 2 months ago at a Super 1 Food Store, with a young white female clerk! Both individuals, representing different cultures, made the assumption that I was a welfare recipient; with no other information about me, except that I was a black person. These incidents really disturbed me. I have been a loyal American citizen; my brother,

Charles and I, both served honorably in our Armed Forces. I am a long-time Christian; never have been arrested, or served time in jail; have successfully avoided being trapped in the drug culture; have been gainfully employed in one of the most highly respected professions for over 30 consecutive years; have been a minister of the gospel for over 16 years; have always taken care of my family; and have a household income which rates among the top 10% of all Americans. Yet, on any given day, in many different retail establishments, simply based on the color of my skin, when I enter these business locations, I am looked upon as either a thief, or a welfare recipient, or both. Why should I, or any other black Americans, always have to bear the burdens of these assumptions and stereo-types, heaped on us by whites, and even by other minorities? There never seems to be a comfortable position for black citizens of America.

Black people are most often, than not, thought of in negative terms; based on assumptions, simply because they are black. While we do have more than our share of legitimately unemployed; as well as the lazy, those who don't want to be employed; and then there are the criminally minded, who feel that they are justified in taking from the rest of us by force, or any other method is just fine and dandy. However, I can't say strongly enough that the vast majority of blacks are not in these categories. Yet and still, many of our most accomplished black citizens are often treated with such contempt; and are still treated as second class citizens; welfare recipients; and/or thieves, by prejudiced people all over America.. Here I was, with three academic degrees, including a doctorate; having been gainfully employed as a Registered Pharmacist for almost 30 years; yet, being stereotyped as a ward of the state; for no other reason than the fact that I am a black male. An even more recent update of what I have been trying to say, occurred just a few days ago, during second week of May, 1997. I stopped at a local Jack-in-the-Box, to get a few fast food items. I had already placed my order, when my wife entered the store and told me my step-daughter requested that I bring her a sandwich. I placed the second order and waited. In the meantime, the first order was handed to me, and I sat it on the counter while waiting for the second order. Well, I decided to eat one of the tacos in the bag, which I had already paid for. I removed it and went to the condiment bar to get sauce; at which time I was verbally confronted by a second white female employee, so that everyone in the little restaurant heard it, telling me that she couldn't let me get away with my action! When I questioned what she was talking about; she literally accused me of stealing one of the tacos out of the customer's bag on the shelf: the customer who owned the bag, happened to be me! Instead of politely questioning me, or her co-worker, who sold me the items, she immediately went on the attack. She figured that since she hadn't waited, and I was in possession of this fifty cents taco, was black, therefore, I must be stealing. I have no doubt that it was simply because I was the only black person in the restaurant. It didn't matter that I was dressed in shirt, tie, vest, and dress slacks, on my way home from work. This white female saw a black man taking a "taco" out of a bag which she hadn't sold him, and getting ready to eat it, she immediately accused him of stealing. How embarrassing these thing are. None can imagine what we have to go through, because it doesn't happen to them. It's just like the recent incident, when former Governor L. Douglas Wilder was detained and put in a choke-hold by airport security, at the Raleigh-Durham Airport, in North Carolina, for no apparent reason, except for the fact that he was black. The former Governor explained it this way:

"When I went through the airport metal detector check, the buzzer sounded. After taking everything out of my pockets, I went through the check for the second time when it dawned on me that it could have been my suspenders [that set off the buzzer]. When I told the White security man that it must be my suspenders, he literally snapped. He grabbed me, then pushed me and choked me. It was like an out-of-body experience. I just couldn't believe what was happening to me" (Ebony Magazine, August 1996).

Incidents such as these are happening to black Americans, all over America. If this can happen to a former Governor, who happened to be Black, think how devastating and demoralizing this could be for others who are already living under various adverse, and often hardship conditions. To many black Americans, Dr. King's "Dream" of a just American society seem to be slowly fading into another nightmare; while many whites who are diehard conservatives, are determined not to give any black person what even looks like a break. At the same time, these same individuals are perfectly willing to give quite freely anywhere from 1/2 to 10 million dollars to white farmers, who buy exotic equipment, including jet planes, and often file bankruptcy, yet keep the vast farms and lavish personal properties they buy with tax-payers dollars.

If the above situations are not enough to make one sick of hypocrisy, here is more. In the September 2, 1997, edition of "The Dallas Morning News," on page 10A, there was an editorial decrying the many costly and unbelievable agriculture and corporate subsidies being funded by congress. The editorial stated it this way, "Let's call this program by its true name: corporate welfare. At a time when welfare to poor Americans is being sharply curtailed, such largess to profit-making companies is indefensible." "Congress appropriated $90 million in fiscal 1997 to fund the program. And...$90 million...is authorized...each year until 2002."

Although the figures below are not nearly as large as many other "corporate welfare programs," just look at where many of your tax dollars are going, in just this foreign advertising for agri-business programs. The "gifts," given to these for-profit firms, further strain our budget and are a waste of taxpayer resources! Paul Newman received $91,500 of taxpayers money to advertise his salad dressing abroad. Ernest and Julio Gallo received $915,000 to advertise their wine abroad! Tyson Foods of Arkansas received $690,000 to advertise their chicken on foreign shores. The article went on to say that, "Congress funnels huge amounts to the trade associations. For example, in fiscal 1997 the Cotton Council International got $9.3 million, the U.S. Meat Export Federation $8.5 million, the American Forest & Paper Association $6.3 million and the American Soybean Association $2.2 million;" and the U.S. chocolate manufacturers got $721,310 of your money. The defendants of the program claim that such handouts help create U.S. jobs. The question is, why can't they use their own money, since they are the ones benefiting from these markets? Again, we see that our government politicians do just what they please with our tax dollars, and tell us to "Shut up and like it." All the while we're giving out freebies to the rich, government politicians are whining about giving poor black, white, Hispanic, and other needy American citizens, a few dollars to help provide food for them and their children. One writer has noted that:

> In some ways, the dream of brotherhood seems even more distant now than when Martin Luther King, Jr., spoke from the steps of the Lincoln Memorial in 1963.

> "I have a dream," King said in one of the best-remembered American speeches of our time. "I have a dream that one day, on the red hills of Georgia, the sons of former slaves and the sons of former slave owners will be able to sit together at the table of brotherhood."

> It seems so very long ago, because in the 1990s, white Americans hold blacks, and blacks alone, to blame for their current position in American society. "We tried to help," whites say over and over, "but blacks wouldn't help themselves." [5]

As one can imagine, many blacks see the above position as insensitive and less than honest; and just another indication of how deeply steeped in racism our society really is. While there have been some cases of blacks failing to take charge of their lives and take full advantage of the opportunities available to them, this is not the case in general. It has also been noted, and I think with much validity, that the white-controlled media, almost always finds black persons to feature on news specials when "negative reporting" is done on subjects such as welfare, crime, domestic violence, and the like. And of course, there are always enough scandalous cases around to feature, that horrifies even sympathetic blacks and whites. Unfortunately, this type of racially-biased, negative reporting, and slanted journalism goes on all the time.

Given all of the above, one can easily see that it is quite easy for Mr. Farrakhan to pull out many incidents of racism, which many blacks have personally suffered, in this, our dear land. These and other negative incidents which he states so vividly and vehemently, make the blood of his hearers boil with anger; driving many, including Christians, toward his movement. If it were not for the strong spiritual convictions of many of us, the majority of African-Americans could easily turn toward Farrakhan's inviting voice. These are some of the things which make him so popular.

Mr. Farrakhan is having great success in selling many on the idea that through his movement, he can guarantee African-Americans a better life; improved neighborhoods and living conditions; and an existence free from white oppression and domination. His philosophy is, of course, anti-white in nature, and like many white racists, involves racial separatism; calling for the creation of a separate black nation, within America; and the exclusion of Jews and white Americans from our communities. In addition to the above, he is anti-Christian; and this is the area where we differ most sharply. However, I must admit that Mr. Farrakhan is right on the mark concerning some of the social standards which he advocates in his teachings. Some of these include his call for: (1) black males to exemplify respectability in their public and private lives; (2) being willing to punish and hold those black males accountable, who disrespect women; and (3) to weed out of our neighborhoods those who rob, burglarize, and commit other crimes against people.

In many other areas he appears to give a correct assessment of the racial biases in our country; such as, the double-standards applied in the criminal justice system; the exclusion, or limitations placed on blacks in the economic arenas; the refusal of banks to offer loans to black businesses, etc. These good points discussed by Mr. Farrakhan must not be overlooked just because he is considered to be a radical thinker. Many persons considered radicals by others have made great contributions to our nation, and to the world. The list of "radicals" includes such names as George Washington; Abraham Lincoln; John F. Kennedy; W.E.B. Du Bois, Martin Luther King, Jr.; and Ralph Nader.

By most standards, Louis Farrakhan would be considered a radical, and an extremist. However, given all of the negative situations many African Americans face each day, I believe that it is safe to say that a great deal of his radicalism stems from his frustrations in dealing with a racist system, which is reluctant and highly resistant to dispensing justice and equality without respect for race. In a similar, yet limited way his call for equal opportunities for a better, more just, and safer existence in America is much like what Dr. King fought and died for. Yet, I know, without a shadow of doubt, that Dr. King would never have pursued equality utilizing the methods which pervert and corrupt the human spirit, as those promoted by Mr. Farrakhan. I do not believe that life improves when we flavor our existence with racial hatred, bigotry, and isolation from other Americans on the basis of racial and cultural differences. This has been the sad historical legacy of Louis Farrakhan, as well as that of the Nation of Islam (or Black Muslims), since its inception.

MY FIRST MEMORIES OF MALXOLM X:

I was a young teenager when I first heard of the Black Muslims, now called the Nation of Islam. It was at the same time that I also first heard of Elijah Muhammad, leader of the Nation of Islam, and his devoted disciple, known as Malcolm X. Whenever I would see Elijah Muhammad, it was always a picture of a quiet-looking, stern-faced, unhappy-looking, clean-shaven, demure, little man. But whenever I would see Malcolm X on television, he was always like a man on fire. I sat staring in awe, at this baffling sight of this, sometimes clean shaven, sometimes bearded, bespec-tacled, and always fiery-tongued black man, giving white America the tongue lashing many of us only wished we had guts enough to give it.

In those days, the television news would only air those stories where he called white people, "blue-eyed devils;" seemingly in an attempt to enrage white folks. Most often he would also state that Christianity was "the white man's religion," which had been, and was still being used to enslave the minds and souls of black people. The news media would also air those speeches in which Malcolm X encouraged the black man to rise up and take arms, or use other means to throw off the violent, oppressive, white racists; therefore, "by any means necessary," would become a phrase which he made famous. While I knew that some of the things that he said about the racist conditions of our nation were true, at the same time, I felt a strange uneasiness about his call for blacks to resort to violence, taking retributive justices against whites, who outnumbered us almost 85 to 1! It just didn't make sense then, nor does it make sense now. But what troubled me most in those hate-filled speeches, were his calls for blacks to abandon Christianity, and join this Black Muslim, Islamic-related, religion. After careful thinking and pondering these things, I found that most of the things he said was nothing more than reverse racism. In many cases, he succeeded in filling the hearts of many blacks with hate and rage, but failed, just as the broad American system had failed, to supply definitive answers to the pervasive problem of entrenched white racism.

In listening to Malcolm X, I also experienced a strange emotional sense of ambivalence. One the one hand, I felt myself admiring his courage and boldness in speaking out against racial injustice, which most black people experienced; while at the same time, I detested his obviously extreme hatefulness and militancy. Being from the south, I had never heard a black man speak out so openly against white folks like that, during the 1950's and '60's, and remained free and alive. I actually found myself fearing for his life. It's ironic that, years later, it would not be white folks who killed him, but disgruntled black men from the same Nation of Islam, for which he had formerly spoken so vehemently.

I began to compare Malcolm X's approach for addressing the racial problems in America with that of Dr. Martin Luther King, Jr.'s. Malcolm strongly leaned toward black separatism; while preaching violent reprisals and hatred toward whites. His strongest appeal seemed to be among prison inmates and parolees; those in trouble with the law; those who had a deep hatred for whites because of some extremely traumatic experience with white racists; and those with a perpetual chip on their shoulders. On the other hand, Dr. King spoke most often about Jesus' teachings on love and forgiveness, which extended even to ones enemies. In contrast to Malcolm X, He appealed mostly to black Christians; blacks espousing moderate and liberal political and social philosophies; and black college students. I knew within my heart and from biblical Christian teachings, which I held very dear, that Dr. King's approach made the most sense; as well as, required the most courage. Furthermore, Dr. King was a Christian, and so was I. Both Elijah Muhammed and Malcolm X had spoken very negatively about Christianity and Christ. For them it was up with the Prophet Muhammad, and down with our Christ. I knew then that we could never walk in the same shoes. These men were calling for black people to make race and culture synonymous with religious beliefs; and I knew that this was wrong. For me, it could never be race and culture over Christ; but rather Christ above all. This indeed is the point of departure between the Nation of Islam, a black race-based, heretical off-shoot from Islam, and Christianity, which advocates universal inclusiveness in scope and practice.

THE COMING TO POWER OF LOUIS FARRAKHAN

After Malcolm's death in 1965, Louis Farrakhan suddenly rose as the star of the Nation of Islam. And with the subsequent death of Elijah Muhammed, he eventually became the chief minister and chief spokesperson, for the Nation of Islam. Farrakhan has continued the teachings of Elijah Muhammed and has adopted and even improved on the fiery zeal of Malcolm X. At times he has attempted to present himself as a "softer" version, hoping for a broader appeal. With the worldwide exposure he has been afforded lately, it appears that Louis Farrakhan has become increasing more attractive as a spokesman and leader among many African Americans, as to be consider a major factor in both politics and religion. However, his popularity appears to be growing in direct proportion to the resurgence of white racism and the declining influence and respectability of the black Christian church. These conditions have indeed facilitated his rising popularity.

Some of the events which I believe have allowed Farrakhan a more prominent position among African Americans are these: (1) the resurgence of anti-black, and anti-poor activities around the country; (2) the seating of ultra-conservative, state and national Congresses, as well as the Supreme Court; (3) the reversal of Affirmative Action programs by Congress, which were designed to create a fair and equitable playing field for blacks; (4) the rise of white-Supremacist, militia groups, neo-Nazis, Skinheads, Klansmen, and the like; (5) the Rodney King and O.J. Simpson cases, which further polarized the nation; and (6) the sudden and alarming rise in the burning of black Christian churches by white racists; over much of the South, and a few cases in the North. Knowing that these hate groups, named above, would care more for ants at a picnic, than for black folks, Louis

Farrakhan has the African American community caught in the middle of a highly volatile, emotional dilemma. They are being challenged to choose between a white-dominated, hate-filled, and oppressive system, or to join up with Farrakhan and his black nationalists. Farrakhan claims that he is the only right choice for black Americans when it comes to selecting a leader to usher in a brighter and hope-filled future.

There is no doubt that our nation is suddenly going backward, instead of forward, in the area of civil and human rights. These sudden changes, especially the attack on Affirmative Action programs; the growing white militia groups; and the burning of churches, have been startling to many devoted black Christians; while at the same time, these have destroyed the confidence of most black Americans had that our nation ever truly intended to grant full equality to all of its citizens. These shocking events have caused some alarm among truly concerned white political and religious leaders, since they have always quietly depending upon the black church to maintain the status quo in the black community. Without the stabilizing influence of the black Christian church and their leaders, we could be headed for unprecedented chaos, if Louis Farrakhan, and the even more radical disciple of his, Khalid Mohammed. However, we must recognize that we got into this predicament because the churches, black and white, and the nation as a whole, have been surprisingly quiet, too tolerant, and in many cases, have even participated in, the activities of the black and white extremists. And, as seen with increasingly hostile and violent white militia groups, it does not help, when the whole US Government can be held at bay by a few, white, domestic terrorists.

When blacks see how patient our government before taking action against these anti-government groups, there seems to be a definite double-standard. Although, it ended in horror, our government's patience was severely tested in its encounter with the Branch Davidians at Waco, Texas. In contrast, people have not forgotten how quickly the Philadelphia city government, acting with obvious approval from state and national governmental bodies, dropped those fire bombs and burned to death the 6 adults and 5 children, members of the black militant group, called MOVE, who were held up in their row house on May 13, 1985. The question can be easily asked, "Why hasn't the government acted in stronger measures against these white extremists, as it has done with black ones?" All of these issues create a favorable atmosphere from which Mr. Farrakhan can win and influence more and more black Americans toward his cause.

Being a powerfully persuasive, perceptive, and charismatic orator, Mr. Farrakhan, reads his audiences well. He says just what he knows they want to hear. He is astutely aware of the oppressive and impoverished conditions under which many black Americans live. He knows that there is a growing, and increasingly disgruntled, underclass in America, which is decidedly black in proportion, therefore, he is assured of captive and empathetic audiences, when he lambastes our nation's sordid history of racism, in the past and now here in the present. Now, with virtually no activity, little opposition, and perhaps a degree of admiration from the black church, he is now boldly taking over as leader and spokesman for the black community, as he presents himself as its savior.

I am not against Louis Farrakhan simply because he holds different philosophical and religious views, from me. However, I do have some serious difficulties with a sudden "savior," when he, and the rest of the Nation of Islam, exempted themselves from joining in the Civil Rights Struggle, during its most difficult and dangerous times, in the 1950s and 60s. The real truth is this: There were more Jews, more white people, in general, and white Christians, in particular (both Catholics and Protestants), who marched, and even died in the Civil Rights Movement of the 1950's and 1960's, fighting for the rights of black people, than all of the Nation of Islam, or Black Muslims, combined!!!! Secondly, there was a strange absence of Farrakhan, himself, Malcolm X, and those so-called, "brave warriors," associated with them, when other blacks, whites, and Jews, were marching, and protesting, being beaten with Billy-clubs, bitten by dogs, blasted with fire hoses, and even dying, sided-by-side, in "the struggle" for the freedom of African Americans!!!

The sad fact is that the only violence these tough guys commit is against one another, or against other blacks who speak out against them. I am in more danger, as a black man (as was Malcolm X), of being attacked and assaulted by them for writing my opinions about them, than from any bigoted and violent white man or groups of white men, who, along with their ancestors, have hung, shot, mutilated, burned and done violence to black people all over this country. The history of the Nation of Islam reveals that it is truly a religion of violence, but only against other blacks!

Nevertheless, Mr. Farrakhan's daring and caustic speeches against white racism, combined with his subtle, anti-Christian ranting, make him a favored hero, among those who have an ax to grind. He has been able to convince many itching ears that all white people are devils, and thus, inherently evil; that black people are Divine; and that to embrace Christianity, is to embrace the devil, himself. For those whom he knows are not quite ready for such strong rhetoric, yet who have been, or who still are, victims of the oppressor, he very subtly plants the idea that to be Christian in an oppressive Christian world is to be in league with those who oppress them.

This man is a clever and adept artisan at the craft of mixing "hot items" of blatant racism with his ambitious religious, economic, and political agendas, in order to win support and influence. He did this with "The Million Man March," (which should have easily raked in over $10 Million); with his trips to the Middle East (reportedly received a $1 Billion pledge from the international terrorist, Col. Kadhafi of Libya), and with his "Day of Atonement and Reconciliation," in October of 1996. And because of his charisma and clever craftiness, his popularity is growing in leaps and bounds. His followings now seem to include many who profess to be Christian. For the first time that I can remember, Farrakhan and the Nation of Islam, seem to be driving a wedge between African Americans and the Christian church.

THE LEADERSHIP "VOID" IN THE BLACK COMMUNITY:

If one outstanding characteristic could be chosen which black Americans have been known for, it would likely be that they are very religious, and very loyal to its religious leaders! And in the majority of cases their religious preference has been one of the mainline Christian denominations; which, in the past, was the source from which community leaders emerged. There is a major battle being waged for the souls of black folks in America; which is being led by other than Christian leaders. I believe, that unless the Christian church and its leaders change the way it approaches social problems, it might find itself losing many souls who are desperately searching for meaning and hope, to the Nation of Islam and other cults which speak more directly to human needs and real problems people face each day!

Many individuals who have turned from the Christian church feel that it plays no significant role in their day-to-day lives. The concept of Christianity embraced by our ancestors is being challenged as ill-serving the modern day needs of black people, in a highly sophisticated and technologically advanced age. Black people are being told that the Nation of Islam has what they need.

Dr. Martin Luther King, Jr., was one of the strongest Christian leaders of this century. It would do our leaders well to follow many of his philosophies in today's struggle. He did not give in to the black militant influence, but successfully challenged the church to get involved and write its own history of involvement in solving those human problems which needed addressing; but our "King," has long since been dead; felled by a white-racist, assassin's bullet. His "dream," once so vibrantly alive in the hearts and souls of many black Americans, is being bashed by a growing anti-Black sentiment around the country. The current, "would-be," black leaders often can't lead because many are engaged in in-fighting, petty jealousies; and a lack of a clear vision as to where we need to be focused. Consequently, Dr. King's dream is now slowly fading into a seemingly unrealizable "mirage," in the lives of so many, who have given up hope. Hope for many, now means nothing more than surviving another day; of being able to keep the lights, gas, heat, and air on another day or week; of making another soup line; or, if real lucky, making another day at some "temp" agency.

These desperate struggles are going on in cities and townships all over America, even as we hear echoes from the voice of the Rev. Jesse Jackson, pleading for America to "keep hope alive." Jackson, too, is fading. Once the dominant and prominent leader of black people in America, he is slowly being jointly swallowed up by strictly "bottom-line" agendas of giant corporations; the insatiably, hungry national political machinery, and the Washington, DC, in-crowd, which, like some giant, voracious octopus, wraps up and consumes, even cannibalizes, all who get caught up in its giant tentacles. Then, too, even though Jesse Jackson has done many positive things, such as influencing large corporations to invest in black America; bartering for international trade which include blacks; attempting to bring peace between warring black gangs, and the like; however, his confusing remarks, indicating support for the ridiculous suggestion by black representatives on the Oakland, California, School Board, to recognize "Ebonics" as a legitimate black language, suggests that his wisdom is highly suspect in this case. Certainly, he never promoted this kind of language as being acceptable for his own children. The puzzling question becomes, why would he even hint at legitimizing something so horrible as this, for other less fortunate, and often, misguided black children? It makes one question his motives, as well as his ability to make intelligent and informed decisions about the future of our children.

With Jackson virtually neutralized, and Rangel, and others too localized, most of black America, are like sheep without caring shepherds. Many feel that they have been led to, but now abandoned, at the very pool of social and economic opportunities. Many who came expecting to have their economic thirst quenched and to share a piece of the American economic pie, are discovering that it will not happen anytime soon. The masses who came with unprepared minds, having been disillusioned by the lingering spirits of the "free-gifts-and-no-training" politicians of yesteryear, are suddenly discovering that America has reversed its racial and socio-economic agenda.

Many who stayed on welfare too long; or who shied away from the challenge of meaningful training programs, while on it, or those who were duped into thinking that integration really meant equal opportunities for all, are now facing unexpected, revolutionary changes in the political and economic thinking of the white infrastructure. There appears to be a mad rush toward reversal of all of the equal rights and Civil Rights legislation enacted under Presidents Kennedy and Johnson. The majority of Congress, since the time of President Ronald Reagan, seem obsessed with a resolute, "do-or die," mentality to dismantle all existing legislation which used "creative" methods, such as Affirmative Action, in attempting to reverse the damages done by past discrimination and to create a more fair playing field for blacks, women, the elderly, and other traditional victims of institutionalized racism. Therefore, many of these once-familiar programs, such as "Affirmative Action;" special set-asides and quotas for minority businesses (most of which were still going to white businesses, which qualified by merely having white women figureheads as owners) are rapidly disappearing. Gone too, or soon to go, are the special entry procedures in colleges and universities; the national Welfare Program; Medicaid; Head-Start Programs; and other programs created to bring about equality. Subsequent to these changes, many black Americans being left "up a creek without a paddle." In this swirling stream of change, many are drowning, instead of drinking deeply, in the pool of American opportunity.

While much of black America was being duped and doped, into a senseless stupor, thinking that equality and fair play was the ultimate goal of America, there has been a watcher in the shadows, waiting for the right chance to come forth. This stalwart opportunist has now seized that opportunity. He has come forth, daringly and boldly, in these latter days, to claim the spoils of the wars of others. Seeing the hostile environment in America, and knowing the desperate struggle for survival by countless numbers of black Americans, the man in the shadows, with great wit and confidence, stretches forth his hand to the desperate masses, in a gesture of salvation. Many are reaching toward, and grasping, this unfamiliar, but welcomed hand. The man on the end of the hand appears as a caring friend, for he has elevated their hope in the hour of their desperate need. The hand belongs to the man called Louis Farrakhan.

Nobody had foreseen, nor had the slightest premonition, that we needed to plan for a such a powerful resurgence of the American cancer called "white racism," as we head toward the 21st Century. This wicked idea had ruled our lives like a violent king, for centuries, until our "black Moses" came along. This unrelenting, eloquent, untiring leader came in the person of Dr. Martin Luther King, Jr. Under Dr. King's leadership, and with the help of the masses, who were too tired of waiting on true freedom any longer, took their cause to the inhumanely cruel, enemy and to the world-at-large, with unabashed bravery and fortitude. Many went forth in "the Struggle," fully aware of the grave possibility that they might suffer an untimely and violent death; however, nothing would dissuade them from the CAUSE: the illusive dream of "freedom."

Many among this unarmed army, eventually and inevitably shed blood and died, including Dr. King, himself. In their dying, we had all hoped that the violent, and vicious American infatuations, racism and White Supremacy, were believed to have died in America in the 1960s and the 1970s, on the blood of these martyrs. Many thought they were dead for all times; therefore, many spent their time only eating, drinking and making merry." The unwise didn't even take time to pray, nor to give thanks to God for bringing them out of bondage; neither did they think to teach their children the tragic, yet rich history of their past.

It seems that the cancer of American racism was only in a sort of congressional and court imposed bondage. Having been temporarily shackled by the guilt and shame of having the whole world had watch the bloody, savagery of American racism. America seemed to have developed a conscience, even a moral resolve to repent after the world watched in horror as the bomb-ravaged, dead bodies of the five little girls being brought out of a bombed out church in Birmingham, Alabama; the dog-bitten behinds of old men and women; the bloody, Billy club-swollen heads of black folk of every sex and age group; as well as, the death of many martyrs. The murder victims of American racism included, the five little Black girls in Sunday School, who were victims of a church bombing; Emmett Till, the teenager hung in Mississippi for allegedly whistling at a white female; Medgar Evers; Dr. Martin Luther King, Jr.; Viola Liuzzo; Michael Schwerner, Andrew Goodman, and James Chaney; President John F. Kennedy; Senator Bobby Kennedy; and many, many others who may or may not have made national headlines. These were either shot, mutilated, burned, hung, decapitated, bombed, drowned, or combinations of the above.

Please note that the last 5 names given, with the exception of Chaney, were all white. Two of these persons, Schwerner and Goodman, were Jewish Americans, the group that Farrakhan loves to attack, who gave their lives, sacrificially, in order that black people might move closer to justice and equality. There were many other white victims, some Protestants, some Catholic, some Jewish, and some claiming no particular faith, at all. These all died in service to their fellow citizens, the black people of America, who were victims of the twin evils of American oppression and racism. The violence and blindness of white racism has claimed many victims, from many, many races and classes of people. But, unlike Farrakhan and his bunch, these were not directly affected by the evil, as they decided to lay their lives on the line to help. May their memories never be marred by those who contributed nothing but criticism.

In the book, I have shared my own horrifying, and literally, blood-curdling encounter with white-racist, nightriders, who did their damnedest to end my life. I shall also share personal eye-witness accounts of other lives which have been forever damaged, ended, or changed because of white racism. Racism is one monstrous anomaly which must be eradicated if ever America, and the world order, hopes to find lasting peace. However, had it not been for the outbursts of racist savagery, of subsequent rioting, and killings, captured by television cameras and broadcast world-wide, I truly believe that we would still stuck in the Jim Crow, segregationist atmospheres of the early 1960s (and South Africa would still be ruled by Apartheid)! America, which had condemned Hitler's barbaric slaughter of the Jews; and Communist Russia's onslaught of Czechoslovakia and other nations, lost much of its world clout and respect, when the world learned first-hand, of its own savage and barbaric treatment of its black citizenry.

We all must admit that some real and positive changes did come to the black population in America. Many new and unheard of opportunities were suddenly made available to those who were willing to prepare themselves to take advantage of them. Unfortunately, a large segment of the population only took advantages of the "freebies," which prepared them for nothing but future disappointment. While a large group of irresponsible black persons were basking in its new-found, "take-all, give back nothing- freedom," some folk were planning.

First, the leaders of the old white regimes were slowly planning and meticulously establishing a sounding board for the resurgence of a more sophisticated race-based system. They began building a sounding board for the return of ultra-conservatism, many years ago. This careful program was disguised, very ingeniously, using the funny racism of "Archie Bunker;" Morton Downy, Jr.; the case of Bakke v. University of California, in 1978, which struck one of the first major blows to Affirmative Action, where the Supreme Court struck down the use of quotas for admission to a state medical school. Then came the Rev. Jerry Falwell and his "Moral Majority," numbering in the millions, and lobbying against every perceived liberal and moderate idea which did not reflect ultra-conservative, old South ideals. In more recent times, this push has been continued by ultra-Conservatives, such as Rush Limbaugh, Pat Buchanan, and Newt Gingrich. Most of these persons have served to give this new conservatism, which, in many cases, is viewed as nothing short of modern racism, a sense of respectability. It has been reintroduced as a more subtle idea, but it has the same vicious effects. Even more frightening, the new movement or revolution is funded by PAC (Political Action Committee) dollars from large corporations fearing retributive legislation if they don't come up with big bucks, or from those seeking to buy favors.

This new racism, which is growing in popularity, has been showcased with a new twist. At times it seems funny; is presented as "the only right way" to win back America; it uses terms such as "The Moral Majority," and "Contract with America." It dresses in nicely tailored 2 and 3 piece suits, like the Senator David Duke, former Grand Wizard of the Ku Klux Klan in parts of Louisiana; like the out-of-control, Speaker of the House, Newt Gingrich, who seems to be doing all he can to return our nation to the pre-Civil Rights, racial chaos of the 1940s and 1950s. There are many others, much more subtle, and deadly serious, than these two. Secondly, there has been one among African American people, who did not miscalculate the pernicious nature of American racism, even in the least bit. That individual is Louis Farrakhan. It seems that all racists, no matter what color, tend to know how other racists think.

Mr. Farrakhan realized beforehand that the intoxicating effects of American guilt and shame would soon wear off, just like most intoxicants do. He knew that this utopic marriage, this mass racial miscegenation in America, was only a temporary affliction, which White America would soon throw off. Farrakhan knew that it wouldn't be long before the white power structure would look with affectionate memories toward an old friend, the notion of white racial supremacy, and release American racism from its shackles, once again. He knew that it would strike with a vengeance, leaving many wounded, helpless, and hopeless victims, in its wake. He seems to be like the old singer who crooned, "I'll be around, to pick up the pieces, When somebody breaks your heart, Like you broke mine." Louis Farrakhan is doing just that, in the black community. I believe that he observed that the Christian church would be slow to respond to the needs, and the prevailing sense of despair among many blacks. Therefore, his idea to become the leader and savior of the black community, has met with little resistance, and even help, from the church, which seems lackadaisical and theologically uninformed, in many instances.

IS FARRAKHANISM SIMPLY AN IDEA WHOSE TIMES HAS COME?

History tells us that one the most powerful force on the earth is an idea whose time has come. It does not seem to matter whether it is in the minds of sinner, or saint; a gentle scientist, or raving madman. The power is to be found in the idea and its corporate effect upon the masses. It was an obscure Alsatian chemist, named Charles Frederick von Gerhardt, who, testing an idea, "first synthesized acetylsalicylic acid in 1853, at his laboratory at the University of Montpellier" in France. [6] Later, known around the world as "aspirin," it became the most widely used painkiller and anti-inflammatory drug in the world. It began as an idea. And so did the first automobile, the electric light, and air conditioning (thank, God!).

Great nations, like America; and great ideas of social privilege, such as "freedom," both began as great ideas in the hearts of men and women. Even the great religions of the world had their beginnings in ideas. Christianity, for example, began with the idea of the lostness of man and their need for a Savior. God, the Creator of the universe, had a very unique idea about how this was to be accomplished. Desiring to save humanity, the highest of the created order, God sent His only Begotten Son, Jesus Christ, into the world to die on the cross for the sins of the world. God's requirement is summed up in these words: "Whoever believes in Him, should not perish, but have everlasting life" (John 3:16b; NKJV). This was the beginning of the Christian culture; Jesus Christ would become Savior of all mankind; irregardless of race, class, or culture. Christians believe that God's sacrificial love makes Jesus Christ supremely above race and culture, always and forever. This unmerited, unexplainable love which God had for fallen humanity, is founded in the Divine idea called "grace."

The Divine idea concerning love extends to the human race in this challenging statement:

"Beloved, if God so loved us,
we also ought to love one another" (1 John 4:11).

This revolutionary idea has been slow to catch on by the human family. While we have many good ideas, the bad ones often overshadow them. As a matter of fact, some human ideas, such as democracy, freedom (religious and social), and justice, sometimes seem to soar toward the very heavens themselves. On the other hand, some human ideas are embellished with such great evil, that they seem to come up from the depths of hell, itself. A few such ignoble ideas include nuclear, chemical and biological warfare, racial supremacy, racial hatred, and bigotry.

While American democracy and freedom, both began as wholesome ideas in the hearts of men and women; it was reserved for a select few. We cannot deny that America is the greatest country on the face of the earth; I truly believe that. Since the days of Slavery, we have made great strides toward liberty and justice for all. Think about the accomplishments of black Americans such as A. Phillip Randolph, Adam Clayton Powell, Gary Hatcher, Coleman Young, Dr. Martin Luther King, Jr., Barbara Jordan, General Chappy James, General Colin Powell, Andrew Young, Ron Brown, and many other outstanding black Americans, too many to be numbered. America is still the place where impossible dreams have come, and are still coming, true.

Unfortunately, in these modern days, we see in America a nation torn with racial strife and social unrest. And if we do not see significant changes in the near future, this tyranny of racism and counter-racism in America, more than any other element, threatens to eventually tear her apart. Our land, better known as "the land of the free and the home of the brave," is overrun by bigots, racists, and cowards of every kind and persuasion. If America is to remain the land of the free, and the place where impossible dreams still come true, we who love America and the concept of freedom must band together in denouncing bigotry, racial prejudice and hatred on every level, and in every quarter. All true Americans, and especially Christians, must all resist, reject, and dissuade bigots of every kind and persuasion, whether black or white.

Like it, or not, Louis Farrakhan had a tremendous idea on how to draw black males together, and ultimately, how to draw attention to himself and to his cause, increasing his appeal and influence around the world; as witnessed in his highly successful "Million Man March." Much of our discussion shall focus on the actions and influences of Farrakhan, this man who seems driven by his personal ambition to become the most powerful leader among black Americans, in general, and also of furthering the cause of the Nation of Islam. Additionally, he has opened himself up to be used as a front man to promote traditional Islamic interests in America, at the bidding of Libyan President, Col. Kadhafi, the international terrorist and avowed enemy of America, who has pledged $1 billion to promote this cause. It is widely held that this man is still hiding the terrorists who planted the bomb on Pan American Flight 103, killing 107 American citizens. Farrakhan's buddying up to this terrorist, almost has the rotten smell of treason. Fortunately, Congress has honed in on this little deal and brought it to a screeching halt.

However, I am quite disappointed in the fact that Congress can zero in on this deal, and can't seem to do much about white terrorists, such as the Ku Klux Klan; violent, white Militia groups; neo-Nazis; and other right wing groups, many of which are financed by international, as well as, good old American dollars. Then there are the most pervasive terrorists of all, the drug lords. How I wish Congress and other government bodies could be so keen when it comes to these latter groups, as it has done with Farrakhan. Certainly, if they can send the military into the little country of Panama Canal Zone, and arrest its leading citizen, even the top general and President, certainly it can go into the ivory towers here in America and make some key arrests. Why hasn't our nation had a desire to do so? I have some thoughts, but it might take me too far from my subject.

While I have my ax to grind with this man, I am not totally unawares that America is often very selective in how it pursues certain law breakers. This is an area which I am praying that our nation will clean up its act.

America has many faults, but it was, and still is, too great of an idea to be ruined by Louis Farrakhan. We have come a long way from the pre-Civil Rights days. We all enjoy such great freedom, that we take much too much for granted. What nation in the world would allow one of its high profile citizens to go on foreign shores and call our nation, "the great Satan?" This is the thanks that Louis Farrakhan offers to his country, where he lives like a king, at the expense of the poor who support him. Had he been a citizen of one of those Islamic nations where he uttered these treacherous words, when he returned home, he would probably be facing a firing squad. While

America has many serious racial problems, I do not feel that her citizens should go on foreign soils and lambaste her, as this man has done.

Furthermore, it is my sincere belief, that Louis Farrakhan, in spite of his immense popularity and cultic appeal, does not offer any real, in-depth, solutions to the race problems in America. I am convinced that for me to join him is to subjugate myself to just another violent gang leader, delving in hot rhetoric, and goon-type tactics, in an attempt too create a reason for his existence. He leads thousands into this whining and complaining mode; speaking about how bad white people are; how bad Jews are; how bad "uncle Tom" blacks are; how bad Christianity is; and how bad conditions are in America. Rarely, or never, have I heard him encouraging his emotionally-charged hearers to expand their visions; or to open their "race-covered eyes," and see the mountainous array of opportunities spread out before them; which, with determination and diligence, they, too, can have them if they choose to go after them. However, he refuses to do so for it would be an admission that all is not wrong with America as he contends. Then, too, Farrakhan and his followers, cry often and loudly about the violence of white people, while glossing over the epidemic array of "black on black" violence! Nor, will he acknowledge the cold-hearted, Gestapo-like tactics and violence, perpetuated by his own black troops, the Nation of Islam, directed exclusively against other blacks! He quickly justifies their actions, such as the murder of Malcolm X, as a necessary evil. Farrakhan, "the Great," has publicly stated that Malcolm X deserved to die, because he was a traitor, a "Benedict Arnold," to their movement. If they did this to Malcolm X, a national figure, just think what he will do to others who dare to speak out against them? Such power must not to be granted to men like Farrakhan. Black America needs to wake up before it's too late! I am committed to sounding the alarm concerning this dangerous man and his dangerous movement.

It has never been my intention to handle Mr. Farrakhan with kid gloves; for just as he tells it like it is, I choose to do the same. If we were facing each other today, I'm sure he would have some choice, ear burning, hair-raising, words for my ears. I also recognize that it would be too simplistic, as well as unfair, to make these strong charges against Farrakhan, without bringing to the forefront the equally satanic evil of white racism, as well as, the religious hypocrisy often found among many mainline, white Christian churches. Neither must the black Christian churches be rendered guiltless, for it has often been its own lack of concern and love toward those who suffer among us, that the tide of economic and social progress is in a state of chaos and regression. How can we expect others to show love and concern for the growing underclass among us, when we don't show love ourselves?

A NEED TO TIGHTEN UP ON CRIMINALS AND LIGHTEN UP ON THE POLICE:

While the majority of black Americans are law-biding citizens, it is only a small percent of the criminally-minded, who give our communities bad names.

Black people must get involved in their own communities, and begin cleaning up and keeping their neighborhoods clean and free from blatant criminal activities. We must get rid of drug dealers; the lucrative business of underground merchandising of "hot" (stolen) goods; run down buildings, which house crack houses, and other criminal activities. We must return to the old value systems of yesteryear, which taught our children to respect their elders; and to "do unto others, as you would have them do unto you." It is all too easy to blame everybody else for our troubles, and never see the glaring faults among us. All of these issues must be addressed, when we consider problems which contribute to this downward trend in black communities.

I have personally seen, bloody headed, fear struck, hard-working black women, after being mugged by young BLACK MALES; mind you, NOT WHITE MALES, BUT BLACK ONES!!! Most of the serious crimes against black people, are not at the hands of white people, but that black, criminal element, who would rather not work, but prey on other black people, who do work and try to provide for their families.

Most of the outlandishly high costs of maintaining and staffing our Emergency Rooms and Trauma Units, are a direct result of the brutal crimes many black, career-criminals, commit against other law-abiding black people. We need to do some house cleaning! We need to stop yelling "Police brutality", EVERY TIME the police are summoned into our neighborhoods and have to forcibly arrest some crazy-acting, irresponsible, black terrorist; and that's all that they are. They are not "brothers," who do these crimes, they are low-down, criminals, who need to show that they can be rehabilitated, or be put away, forever. Enough is simply enough! When are the masses of black Americans going to get angry enough to take a definite stance against violent black males? We should all join together in this effort. For either we discipline our own, beginning in early childhood, or it will be left up to the police authorities, who will thoroughly whip their heads or shoot them down, in the streets.

The African American community must show that it's willing to support, as well as MONITOR, our police agencies: monitor because there are still problems with police brutality; but support because the police, many times are our only line of protection from the black terrorists in our neighborhoods. Unfortunately, mainly because of past police abuses, there has been a great reluctance on the part of the black community to give the police, the much needed support they deserve. I once wrote a weekly Sunday School column for a black newspaper; and when I stated in one of the articles that we, as black people, needed to be more supportive of the local police and stop bashing them all the time, unfortunately that newspaper completely edited out that section; and did not print, what seemed like good, common sense observations. Yes, I know about police brutality; and it still goes on in many places. I know about Rodney King, and others. These vicious acts were inexcusable, and totally unacceptable. But I do not believe for one minute that every act of police restraint can be judged as police brutality, when some people decide to act belligerent and become dangerously out of control. If the police are willing to risk their lives to protect ours, they deserve our respect and support.

We also realize that much damage has been done to destroy the confidence black people have had in the police because of a few police of low character and integrity. We must remember that the police come from among us; they are our children, at varying degrees of maturity. There will always be some bad ones mixed in with the good. It's the same in families, what makes us think that the police will be any different? However, it is not time to give up on them; nor to become anti-police. We must make a conscious and determined effort to fix, or repair the problem areas; because sometimes the only thing standing between us, and a state of total anarchy, are our police departments.

THE SCOURGE OF CRACK COCAINE: WHO BENEFITS?

As practically everybody knows, that the greatest social disorder which plagues our society is the scourge of illegal drugs. One of the lead drugs in this group is "crack" cocaine. The quick profits and ease of addiction, serve to destroy much of our cultural life , as we once knew it. This problem is so pervasive till it touches almost every aspect of our community life. It will require a courageous commitment from people in high places, in order to really fix this colossal problem. The task will not be easy because we are talking about huge profits margins, profits so large that they rival, or even outdistance, the Gross National Product of our entire Nation. Any thinking person can see that it requires individuals with vast fortunes in order to be able to finance these hundreds of thousands of dollars, and even multimillion dollar deals, being transacted. It doesn't take a rocket scientist to figure that one out! This is a multibillion dollar business. What small time hood can you think of who can operate and finance these massive undertakings? The news media most often feature small time drug busts where blacks and Hispanics are involved. Small time black hoodlums might share the "peanut" profits from this gigantic undertaking, but it's the "big boys" who own these operations.

It goes without saying that many powerful white men, and some South American drug lords, are running the show. You see, in order for this thing to work, you need to own banks, savings and loan institutions, shopping centers, and other money laundering schemes. Think about this also, we constantly see documentaries or feature stories on the television news showing how airplane pilots who fly their illicit cargo into our nation from South America and Mexico can afford to ditch, sometimes, brand new airplanes, costing from tens of thousands of dollar to several hundred thousands of dollars, when pursued by police, without giving much thought to the loss. They don't worry, because in a few weeks, they can pay cash for another plane, from the huge profits involved!!! If that much profit is being made, it follows that there is a huge, almost insatiable demand, for their life destroying goods. Another unfortunate result of this clammy mess is that pastors and funeral homes are kept busy also; for we have to bury the dead of drug wars and overdoses. Most of the victims turn out to be teenagers.

This is one of the major reasons that the church must regain its strength and begin to reach the many casualties of this plague. In this area, we must take our hats off to Louis Farrakhan for his efforts in helping young men get out of this lifestyle. Some of our Christian churches are also sponsoring drug "Rehab" programs, but we can clearly see that much more needs to be done.

IS FARRAKHAN'S ASSESSMENT OF THE JEWS, FAIR AND OBJECTIVE?

In these writings, we shall also look into why Mr. Farrakhan continually lodges so many accusations of racism against the Jews. We want to know why he, nor those who led the Nation of Islam, before him, have ever mentioned the atrocities millions of African people suffered at the hands of marauding Islamic invaders on the continent of Africa. He has blamed most of black America's problems on the Jews, when in fact, in times past many Jews were our most ardent supporters. All of us must realize that there are some bad apples in every barrel, why blame all on one group, for the actions of a few? With this in mind, I would like to challenge him to respond to the blatantly racist and inhumane past actions of Islamic Arab raiders of North Africa., who committed some of the most vile acts of violence against black people over the past several centuries. The reader will be shown that Islam has indeed had a major influence in the lives of black people of African descent in years past; but it is certainly not what you might have thought. Most will be quite surprised that the wicked influence Islamic Muslims had over black people for many centuries, was as some of the most aggressive stalkers of black victims for the African Slave Trade! We shall make this connection in the next few chapters.

My major purpose, however, is to explore the phenomenon and mystique of Louis Farrakhan, who is perhaps the most prominent, popular, powerful, and profane, among an ever increasing class of black racists. One among Farrakhan's chief aims appears to be to win the support of black Americans, and then to separate them from the Christian faith, which it declares to be nothing but a tool in the hands of racists, determined to keep black people mentally enslaved. He proposes that the only way to successfully fight white racism is to join his army of warriors. All others who resist his proselytizing are viewed as "Uncle Tom's" and enemies of his movement. This group is usually dealt with punitively, through overt violent means; either to teach an unforgettable lesson, or to eliminate completely.

I am reminded of the story told me by a young African American male, college student. He was an eye-witness to some strong-arm activities by members of the black Muslim, Nation of Islam, student group at Morehouse College. It appeared that a member of the group, his personal friend, had made the mistake of mentioning some of the "secret" activities of the group (all their internal actions seem to be of a clandestine nature). For this error, he was savagely beaten by his "brothers," to such a degree of severity that warranted hospitalization. The beaten down brother said that he had made the mistake of breaking their "code of silence" concerning some of their activities, and this was his punishment. This sounded more like "La Cosa Nostra," or a street gang, or prison-yard retribution, rather than a religious group.

THE INFLUENCE OF THE NATION OF ISLAM AT BLACK COLLEGES:

We hear of all the college students who have established Nation of Islam chapters on many campuses, however, we must keep this sobering fact in mind: the Nation of Islam has never established a major college or university; nor have they donate any significant sums of money or other resources to already established black institutions of higher learning. Yet, like leeches, they come and take all they can get from colleges and universities, like Morehouse, which were established by Christian Churches; which are sustained by private dollars from major corporations; generous benevolent Jewish and white foundations; and private donations from black, Jewish, and white individuals and groups. Then they drain them of their strength, by destroying their support bases, by creating environments hostile to the very persons who support these much needed institutions. They sell their bean pies, newspapers, and other paraphernalia, while supplying nothing but confusion in return. But, what can you expect, look at Farrakhan and his Million Man March. It is reported that he charged each individual $10.00 to attend; and had influence, or a controlling voice over some of the concessions; but has anyone ever heard of him contributing any of this "easy money" to these needy black institutions? If you have, please inform the rest of us. I say, so goes the leader, so go the followers. Like Farrakhan, his young disciples usually gather just enough of a following to disrupt the normal operation of these fine institutions; heaping criticism upon criticism on those who supply needed funds.

Like many young radicals in the past, Eldridge Cleaver, H. Rap Brown, Stokely Carmichael, Bobby Seale, and others, these young people represent raw, brilliance in the making. It's too bad that they are so misguided. However, like most idealistic and highly zealous, young people, and especially black youths who have seen, or felt the ill effects of oppression, they easily fall for the Black vs. White rhetoric, void of the principles of critical thinking. Like the young zealots before them, these usually result in chaos and disaster. It was many years later, after maturity had set in, that Cleaver and others came back to the media to extol the greatness of our nation, in spite of her flaws. Many idealistic brothers abandoned America and went off to Africa, seeking a link with the "motherland." After only a short stay in many of these places, these seekers found only widespread chaos, more crime than can be found in America, and wide-spread black-on-black genocide. The same kind of slaughter is going on today.

In the March 25, 1997, issue of The Dallas Morning News, page 1 of Section C, in an article written by Staff Writer, Thomas Huang called Black On Black, he explores some shocking revelations uncovered by the black Washington Post correspondent, and now author, Keith B. Richburg, in his new book, "Out of Africa: A Black Man Confronts Africa." The article goes something like this:

> The dead kept coming, floating down the river, tumbling over a waterfall. Hundreds upon hundreds of bodies, some with hands and feet bound, others mutilated beyond recognition. This was in Tanzania in 1994. From a bridge over the falls, Keith B. Richburg watched in silence. The Washington Post correspondent considered the massacres in neighboring Rwanda that had created the horrific parade. He was struck by the anonymity of death. How a life, ten thousand lives, could be snuffed out without record. . . He could have been among the anonymous dead, had it not been for an ancestor who had survived the journey from Africa to America 400 years ago, he says. Therein lay Mr. Richburg's painful and controversial admission. He could never justify the evils of slavery, he says. Still, he was glad that his ancestor had made it to America. As a black American in search of his roots, he concluded that he did not belong in his ancestor's homeland. He had, in fact, come to hate the brutalities and injustices he saw there.

While much of what Mr. Richburg says is controversial, what he says seems so glaringly true. However, we must not forget that Africa is not the only place where mass killing is taking place. You will find some semblance of this is taking place, or has taken place, in places like Bosnia, Ireland, Lebanon, China, Vietnam, and other far away places. Nevertheless, many have gone to Africa seeking this utopic solution to their sickness with American racism, only to find that America is the only cure for what they discovered while abroad. America remains one of the most desirable places on the face of the earth, where one can live out their lives. Sure there are exotic places around the world, but after the newness wears off, most people want to come back home. So it was with the young radicals of years ago.

However, let me make this point crystal clear, Cleaver, Seale, and most of the others had every right to raise their voices against the gross injustices and inequalities which they faced. The unfortunate part of it all was the they, and sometimes the "too-eager to make a story," news media, often distorted what they said and did for greater popularity. Furthermore, these young black activists, being denied equal access to the justice system, took advantage of the only avenues available to them, which usually consisted of street protests and the mass media.

In our study, we will continue to explore Louis Farrakhan's bold attempts to separate black people from Christianity and elevate black culture above Christ, and we shall also explore the super-hype surrounding Ron Karenga's created holiday, called Kwanzaa, and its inherent competition with the Christian holiday of Christmas. Karenga states that his holiday was not religious, nor was it intended to compete with Christmas. However, the facts, which we discuss later in the book, suggest otherwise. For instance, why did Mr. Karenga superimpose the pre-Kwanzaa preparation activities, as well as the holiday, itself, over the period before and after Christmas? He even went beyond New Years Day! To me, this is very strange, rendering his motives highly suspect. Who ever heard of a harvest festival in the dead of winter? Come on Ron, you can do better than that! While Karenga does offer many positive principles in this celebration, yet none of these can ever surpass this teaching of Jesus, "Thou shalt love the Lord thy God with all thy heart, and thy soul, and thy spirit, and thy neighbor as thyself."

Unlike Karenga, who tries to side-step the issue, Mr. Farrakhan, on the other hand, is known for his strong denunciation of Jesus Christ as the Son of God. He has also made past calls for an exodus en mass by black Christians from Christianity. Realizing the difficulty of getting true Christians to turn from Christ, he is now carefully veiling his appeal under the umbrella of cultural and religious solidarity. What he is leading us to turns out to be his unorthodox version of the Islamic faith.

While I admit that, given the present and proliferating conditions of blatant racism and the growing number of anti-Black, anti-Jewish, and anti-government, White Supremacist militia groups, as well as the burning of black Christian churches, in 1996, all over the country, there has not been a greater time or need for African American racial unity since Dr. Martin Luther King, Jr., led the Montgomery Boycotts in 1955-56. The noted black scholar, Professor Manning Marable, states that,

> With the vast social destruction of our central cities today, with 23 per cent of all African-American males between the ages of twenty and twenty-nine currently in prison, on probation, parole, or awaiting a trial, Malcolm X [and now, Louis Farrakhan] personifies the ability of an individual to overcome the worst circumstances to achieve personal integrity and leadership." [7]

Even though Louis Farrakhan has found an appeal among many blacks, because I am a Christian, to follow him would necessitate the denial of Jesus Christ and His rightful position as the Eternal Son of God; therefore, I could never be a follower of Louis Farrakhan, who by word and practice, possesses the spirit of anti-Christ. To follow him would amount to nothing less than apostasy, as well as spiritual and religious suicide. I, therefore, submit this personal declaration that in the midst of American racism, oppression, black and white cultural elitism, racially motivated violence, hatred, deception and theological meandering and compromising by black and white Christians, I am, and shall remain, unashamedly, unabashedly, and wholeheartedly Christian. Such a declaration is by no means fool-hardy, for, like Paul, "I know in whom I have believed, and am persuaded that he is able to keep that which I have committed unto him" until the day of Jesus' return. [8] I am a Christian because of my relationship to God through faith in His Son Jesus Christ, and not by my relationship to any earthly being. I will not allow Louis Farrakhan, nor any other racist, whether white or black; whether mother, father, sisters, or brothers, none shall take this precious, and priceless gift away from me.

Black, as well as all other Christians, must come to realize the Church of Jesus Christ is under attack. There are many individuals, who are under the influence of spiritual principalities and powers, rulers of darkness of this world, and spiritual hosts of wickedness in heavenly places (Ephesians 6:12), who are doing all they can to turn black Christians away from Christ. If God has truly made of one blood all nations of men (Acts 17:26); and if He has redeemed us by the blood of Christ out of every kindred and tongue, and people, and nation; And has made us unto our God kings and priests (Revelation 5:9), then all Christians must come together for the preservation, defense, and ongoing of this kingdom, in which we shall live and rule!

Another very important goal is to warn the black church of the contradictions in the essential doctrines of Christianity and the Nation of Islam (and Islam). While we hope to be candid and objective, we also reserve the right to speak as frankly, and at times critically and openly about the illogical continuum of white racism; African-American apathy and violence against each other, and, especially about the unacceptable doctrines of the Nation of Islam, much as its representatives feels so free to openly criticize and slander Christianity and our Lord and Savior, Jesus Christ. Christianity's point of departure, and incompatibility with the Nation of Islam is found in the doctrine of Jesus Christ, the Son of God, and our only Savior. Finally, we shall propose that Jesus is not a destroyer of African-American Culture, but the preserver of the same. With these goals completed, each person can choose for themselves, whom they will follow.

CHAPTER FOUR

PROPHECY AND EXPERIENCE: THE GREATEST TEACHERS

In that experience described in Chapter One, with my co-worker, and Muslim friend from Newark, New Jersey, I saw how people use race and culture to sway people toward their causes. People often use religious and social causes to promote their own selfish agendas. Most recently, take the case of the famous boxer, Mike Tyson. Facing accusations of rape, he turned to the Christian faith, was baptized in a highly publicized ceremony, and claimed that he was now a born-again believer, a follower of Jesus Christ. Unfortunately, that didn't help him, which I suppose he thought it would; so, off he went to prison. While in prison, he suddenly decided that he would become a follower of the Nation of Islam, which is diabolically opposed to Christianity; in fact, they are mutually exclusive. What happened? No doubt, he became a very angry man: angry with the system, angry with the White jury and lawyers which put him behind bars. It also seems that he was angry with his new Christian God, who did not deliver him like others in the Bible. So often, people get the idea that God can be manipulated to get what we want. God is not some magical genie which we can summon by rubbing our little lamps.

It is no secret that a major portion of the converts to the Nation of Islam, especially in earlier years, were in prison or in trouble with the law. We learn that it is behind bars where many African-American men join the Black Muslims. The disciples in the "pen" seem to do well in planting seeds for the Nation of Islam. Isn't it amazing how many African-American young men get converted to the Nation of Islam in prison! It seems to be a religion of anger and retaliation; therefore, it has enormous appeal to those who are incarcerated. No doubt Mike Tyson, with all of his millions, was deemed a prime candidate for the "Nation's" highly effective, prison yard proselytizers, who easily delivered him into Mr. Farrakhan's hands.

The strategy of using high-profile, very rich athletes as drawing cards is basic to the American economic and social institutions. Retailers of shoes, clothing, cereal, cars, and other commercial ventures, as well as colleges and universities, employ these tactics in selling their products. Think of the shameful practice of most major universities in using student athletes to earn millions of dollars from television networks for televising games to expose advertisers' products, yet harshly penalize these same student athletes, if they accept a few free dinners or a wrist watch. The Nation of Islam, under the leadership of Mr. Farrakhan, has learned the this lesson well, from the best of exploiters. Unfortunately, like a Pied Piper, he is leading many who are honestly seeking a better way of life, down the road of spiritual destruction. He is conveniently aided in his efforts in proselytize young Black males by the flagrant evils of American racism and prejudicial Christianity, American-style.

While any clear thinking person in America, whether black, white, or otherwise, must admit that Mr. Farrakhan touches on a number of good points, such as Black men acting responsibly and caring for their families; staying away from drugs and other debilitating substances; owning businesses, and the like. These are very good, very positive ideals, and should have always been pursued by all decent and civilized persons, with diligence and perseverance. However, when it comes to my faith in Jesus Christ, I believe that it is the truth and the whole truth. Therefore, I refuse to surrender that which I believe, without a shadow of doubt, to be authentic and undeniably factual; for that which is simply a counter religious movement, created in the minds of men to spite white folks.

This faith, aptly called Christianity, is based upon historical fulfillment of many prophetic utterances of prophets and wise men. Many such prophecies concerning the coming of God's Messiah were recorded throughout the Holy Bible, beginning in some of the earliest writings, and continuing until the actual coming of the Messianic Person of Christ. In the earliest writings, there were many covert intimations spoken and written down up until the overt fulfillment, recorded in later writings, covering the death, the resurrection, as well as, the ascension of the risen Christ, back to heaven. These actions occurred during a period covering several thousands of years; while on the contrary, the establishment of the Nation of Islam as a religious entity began c.a. July, 1930; when a white, Arabic man, Walleye D. Fad Muhammad, started this movement in Detroit, telling the disgruntled people there that he was their "brother from the East." This was only about 67 years ago!!!! (I will say more on this later). Today, they claim that he was many things, from the Messiah to Allah (God), in human form. Is there anybody out there, who has become involved with this organization, who is really in search of truth?

It would be foolish for me to give up the Christian faith, which contains incontestable verities, and proven prophetic utterances, covering thousands of years, for uncertain, unproved doctrines developed in an atmosphere of racial hostility, that which is merely fragmentary religious scraps, collected from various contestable sources. The religious doctrines of the Nation of Islam, seem to have been sewn together, in piecemeal fashion, using worn out threads of race-hatred and cultural biases. What am I talking about? I am talking about the manner in which Walleye D. Fad created "the Lost Nation," from various sources, which they now call "the Nation of Islam." We shall discuss this in more detail later.

As far as black Americans are concerned, it was the Christian faith which brought our forefathers and mothers through some of the worst conditions of oppression and physical and mental abuse, during the years of their enslavement. For those who had been touched by the Holy Spirit, were able to stay with Christianity because they were able to see beyond the polluted Christianity brandished by those hypocritical whites, who said they were Christians, yet sold fellow humans, like animals, in the slave market. It was the same "so-called" Christians who worked and abused our ancestors till they literally wished for death, even more than they cherished life. By the hands of "Christians," many were beaten into bloody, pulpy, masses of flesh in order to "put the fear of God" into any of the "darkies," who even "thought" about rebellion. Some were maimed in order that they might not run away; and others were mutilated to show the power of these, so-called "Christian," owners over their lives. The Nation of Islam, and others who are all too happy to point out the hypocrisy of Christianity, use these glaring examples to help make their point.

In spite of the dehumanizing treatment by white Christians, they knew that God's grace was truly amazing. This is why they sang with heartfelt zeal and with passionate tears this line from the much loved hymn, "Amazing Grace:"

> *"Thro' many dan-gers, toils and snares I have al - read - y come;*
> *'Tis grace hath brought me safe thus far, And grace will lead me*
> *home."* [9]

Our ancestors were strong Christian men and women. They faced much greater troubles and trials than we ever will face. They were blown about in far stronger winds of racism than we shall ever get caught up in. However, they were sustained by the love of God in Christ Jesus. They knew nothing of the Nation of Islam, nor black Muslims. Therefore, in loving memory of their tenacious and unfeigned faith in Jesus Christ, as their Lord and Savior, against the greatest of odds, they didn't give up, and I won't give up either.

Another significant point of departure is this, I surely won't give up Christ for unbelievers who pit Christ against my culture. Any people, whether Black or White, who put their culture, nation, clan, or even family above their god, has no god but have made a god of that which they hold in highest esteem. For me, culture is not God, for there is only one true and living God: the Triune God, manifested in the Persons of God the Father, God the Son, and God the Holy Spirit. I look not to my culture nor any other source to save me from sin or the vicissitudes of life, I look to my God, for only God can be trusted to remain faithful in every situation. [10] You see, not only have I been oppressed and abused by some White folk, I have been deceived and deeply hurt even by members of my own race and culture. Evil is not isolated to one race or nation. Unfortunately, it has manifested itself within the church, as well as down at the local honky tonk. Only God is consummately good; only God is perpetually faithful and true.

In view of the above facts, I cannot write truthfully and freely without being granted the freedom to be critical of the various camps: blacks and whites; Christians and Muslims (Nation of Islam); true and false prophets; and other categories as they may apply. I also reserve the right to respectfully use interchangeably the terms "African-Americans," "black," and "Afro-American," for as Harry V. Richardson has said, " we might do well to heed the word of Henry Highland Garnett, a great militant, spoken over a century ago:

> Let there be no strife between us, for we are brethren, and we must rise or fall together. How unprofitable it is for us to spend our golden moments in long and solemn debate upon questions whether we shall be called "Africans," "Colored Americans," or "Blacks." The question should be, my friends, shall we arise and act like men, and cast off this terrible yoke?" [11]

If we lose our focus on working to gain full access and participation in the economic and political future of America, there is the greater danger of getting hopelessly sidetracked on the trivial. I am afraid that this is where the African-American liberation movement finds itself today, when we are so desperately in need of an enlightened focus and those displaying undaunted courage to make happen this elusive dream called "freedom."

Let it be also known that freedom involves more than economic, social, and physical liberation. Freedom also involves responsible and active decision making in which we resolve to become intellectually competent, in order to compete in a free society (if there is such a condition on earth). Close observation and analysis of all societies reveal that there has existed, and probably will always exist, the mental and social disorders such as racial biases, bigotries, and elitism. However, these can become increasingly self-limiting and debilitating when we fail to recognize them as mental disease states of the biased ones, and when we accept these sub-standard attributes as our own.

Now, I must admit that there are many white Christians who test, and strain to the breaking point, every remnant of toleration and love in one's body. Some of the greatest white preachers and leaders of many of the largest of Christian churches and denominations, were well-known racist and separatist, in the not too distant past. One such man, is one in whom I consider one of the greatest preachers of this era, and a well-known, now-retired, pastor in Dallas, Texas. Many native black Dallasites, confide that he did not change until he was really, involuntarily, carried along with the many changes brought on by Civil Rights legislation. This man, an avowed Southern Baptist, has often boasted of being an ardent admirer of the great 19th Century, British preacher, Charles Haddon Spurgeon, who openly detested and spoke out against the inherent evils contained in racism and the enslavement of fellow human beings. Spurgeon did what he could to help his hearers establish moral and spiritual precedences against Slavery, which eventually was dismantled in the 19th Century, during Spurgeon's time. Yet, in contrast, to Spurgeon, who was also Baptist, this man, was regarded as a friend to, and one who clearly embraced the evil system of legislated racial segregation. Some have laid the cause of his position on "the times in which he lived," or "the instinct of survival," and "the racism which existed within his congregation and Convention," I still contend, that as a Christ-ordained, Christian leader, he was put in a place of great responsibility, much like Queen Esther found herself in, as recorded in Esther Chapter Four. Realizing that the survival of the Jews held captive in the Persian Empire depended on her utilizing the position which

God had miraculously elevated her to. Queen Esther took this courageous position in Esther 4:16c:

"I will go to the king, which is against the law; and if I perish, I perish!"

Those in whom God entrusts to a position of prominence and power; are put there in order that they might make a great difference for right. For the longest time, this man, who had such great influence and power (and there were many others like him, across the nation) did nothing, even seeming, at times, to lend support to this evil cause of the oppressors of African American people. History reveals that more men are driven by a desire for personal aggrandizement and fame, than are often driven by Holy Spirit-inspired goodness and justice.

Since I was not reared in Dallas, nor the state of Texas, I had no knowledge of the negative past and influence this great pastor had with African Americans. I was introduced to his preaching through Christian radio; but one of the greatest moments for me was when he came to speak at one of our chapel programs, when I was a theology student at Dallas Theological Seminary. His preaching revealed a great love for the Bible, which he and I, both regard as the Word of God. It was because of this that on many Sunday mornings, I would go to his 8:00 AM service, at that great church in the heart of downtown Dallas, before going to my own church. I never encountered any problem while going there, therefore, I had no idea or indication of racist inclinations in the past. What I would learn later would, of course, be quite surprising, and I might frankly say, quite hurtful, to me.

So many times I have listened to his impassioned and fervent preaching of the Gospel. I shared his great emotion as he shed tears while relating to the suffering of Jesus. I stood in awe of his theological diatribes exalting the glory of Christ; as well as his fluent use of Greek in exegeting his texts. I listened with great anticipation at his enormous and unending quotes of Paul's doctrine of grace. He was some kind of preacher. He was my hero.

It was during the 1980's that an interracial and interdenominational council selected him to be the preacher of the hour, at our church, in the predominately black area in the South Oak Cliff area of southern Dallas. The silver-haired old man, preached that day with great fervency and power. I have seen men with less of a message and with less power, cause his hearers to stand on their feet and urge him on; but that didn't happen with him that day. Many of the older black preachers, who are normally very vocal in worship services, sat and listened to him politely, but with little show of favorable emotion. I knew then that something was wrong. Later, I questions some friends who were life-long residents of Dallas. It was then that I began to understand the cool reception that this, otherwise, great white preacher had received.

I was told that he had made very negative remarks concerning the black race, in the past, which seemed completely out of character for this great man. I was also told that had given strong support in the fight against integration; even indicating that it was not the will of God. All the things that I heard, just didn't seem to fit my hero. I pray to God that it was just a misunderstanding. Only he and God know for sure.

However, honesty causes me to look at many, even among us, who share a common heritage of being born black. We soon recognize that there are many Black Christians who possess theses same ignominious racist peculiarities as whites. Additionally, there are probably ten times more black people doing violent harm to other blacks than any whites or other groups put together. It is also unfortunate that the small percentage of criminal elements among black people, commit most of the violent crimes against other persons, in all of America. Another black is probably 95% more likely to get mugged, raped, robbed, shot, murdered, or otherwise assaulted, by a fellow black than by all of the other racial groups, combined. Our women, which includes our mothers and grandmothers, are most likely to be disrespected, cursed out in public, mugged, and/or assaulted, by young black males (and sometimes by young females) than any group on the face of the earth!!!

We must first get our own houses in order before we involve ourselves in wholesale accusations against other races of people. With this knowledge at hand, I am forced to ask myself the question: "Why highlight the sins of the whites over the blatant sins of blacks?" I believe that in order for all of us to better appreciate our differences, as well as those we values we hold in common, everything must be put in proper, and fair, perspective. The violent crimes of blacks can never justify the oppression blacks receive from whites. While on the other hand, neither can we declare all whites guilty for the evil and oppressive actions of a small percentage of whites. At the same time, we realize that because many whites tend to benefit from the oppression of blacks, they are less likely to protest this injustice done to black citizens. These are tragedies which we all continue to suffer and tolerate.

However, with all of the aforementioned knowledge concerning black-on-black crimes, I do understand the gut reasons behind the prevailing attitudes of oppression and victimization among many Black Americans. In all of our years of living in a so-called integrated society, many white people still do not seem to have a clue as to the extent of poverty, deprivation, and suffering, and thus, feelings of despair, which still exists in the lives of so many black Americans. Most of these individuals are still most likely to end up on the end of a broom or mop. Many are constantly singled out and shut out and dumped upon, simply because of their blackness. And it doesn't matter how poor or rich, how untalented or successful, when there is a close call to be made, in most cases the black individual most often gets shafted. That hurts more than you will ever imagine. It hurts so much more because most black people, having been dependent upon others for so long, are quick to trust people; only to find out that they still live under the shadow of even the most undeserving white person. While this is not universal, it is so widespread till it seems as though that is the unwritten policy of this country, and many other countries around the world.

CHAPTER FIVE

TWO FORCES WHICH DIVIDE OUR NATION: WHITE RACISM AND FARRAKHANISM

THE BIRTH AND GROWTH OF WHITE RACISM:

History reveals that the substructure for the rudimentary, conceptual idea of racism, along with classism, were firmly established in the ancient European system of feudal serfdom. From there they degenerated and evolved into the baneful and amoral system called slavery. The distinguished Harvard scholar, Orlando Patterson, writes:

> The ambiguity in the word serf was removed once and for all by the introduction and rapid spread of a new word for slave, throughout Europe, this being the word all the European languages now use—the root term Slav, originating in the fact that the Slavic peoples were the main sources of slaves at this time. Closely associated with this was the emergence of the word Franc (the origin of the English frank) to mean a free man, not only legally but possessed of the character of this group. Primacy returned to natal alienation as the quintessential quality of the slave: the Slav being the archetypal stranger, who did not belong. Was this remarkably new and rapidly diffused pan-European identification of the natally alienated slave with a specific ethnic group—something that had never happened during the millennium of large-scale classical slavery—the genesis of Europe's most loathsome heritage of racism? This, it should be remembered, was the real beginning of Europe as a meaningful civilizational entity. Racism, the one indelible scourge of this great collective enterprise that is the civilization of Europe, was present at the creation. Alas. [12]

European whites who came to America brought with them, along with their many good and notable attributes, this scourge of an idea called racism. The intrinsic accomplice of racism is the idea of racial supremacy. Although we acknowledge racism among blacks and other racial groups, history reveals that there have been, and still are, more white racists in America, than probably anywhere else in the world.

Many other writers and writings have well documented the above fact, therefore, it is not my purpose to spend much ink and paper on this well-known, and often secret, social malignancy. My purpose was to make a connection between white racism and the rise of a black, counter-racism. I have simply tried to establish that, in a very real way, black racism was conceived in the womb of white racism, which first evolved in Europe, but many of her children escaped to America where they grew up, underwent a metamorphosis, and then rapidly multiplied.

These proto-types of the present day American racists, were sustained across the Atlantic by attaching themselves, like leeches, to European serfs, whom they brought to feed on till better prey was discovered. When they first arrived on the American shores, they began feeding on the kindness of Native Americans, whom they called Indians, until they had consumed most of them with their voracious appetites; then they brought forth African slaves. This reign of the terror, called slavery, was born in racism and lasted for over 400 years, in some degree or another, in America. During the entire course of this reign of terror, the oppressed slaves yearned for the condition which we know as freedom.

Bernard Patterson states that:

> Freedom began its career as a social value in the desperate yearning of the slave to negate what, for him or her, and for non-slaves, was a peculiarly inhuman condition. . . Slavery is the permanent, violent, and personal domination of natally alienated and generally dishonored persons. It is, first, a form of personal domination. One individual is under the direct power of another or his agent. In practice, this usually entails the power of life and death over the slave. Second , the slave is always an excommunicated person. He, more often she, does not belong to the legitimate social or moral community; he has no independent social existence; he exists only through, and for, the master . . . As Aristotle observed, "The slave is not only the slave of his master; he also belongs entirely to him, [and has no life or being other than that of so belonging]." Third, the slave is in a perpetual condition of dishonor. What is more, the master, and . . . his group parasitically gain honor in degrading the slave." [13]

THE SURVIVORS OF AMERICAN RACISM:

The ability of African slaves to endure under the extreme hardships of American bondage and forced labor was found in inner strength of character, was indeed a miracle within itself. Their sheer determination to survive was derived from the inner strength derived from the grace of God. The story of Jesus and His sacrificial life and death instill the hope of survival and liberation into the captive people. Oftentimes, the Word of God was used to transform the slaves into docile, servile creatures; however, that very Word often reached deep within them with unanticipated elements of hope. When they heard the peculiar words of the Apostle John, saying,

> *For God so loved the world that He gave His only*
> *begotten Son, that whosoever believes in Him should*
> *not perish but have everlasting life (John 3:16),*

they took it to heart, and they believed. They felt a new kinship to God; and they hoped beyond hope that they would survive the evil system they were being subjected to. This hope was further fortified by the story of Israel's liberation from Egyptian bondage, by the hand of God, through Moses.

In the Exodus experience the slaves saw hope of their own liberation. They had hoped and prayed for their own freedom experience; but when freedom did come, the permanent stigma of slavery usually followed the slave, to the point that being free, he was yet refused full freedom and equality. This has been the scourge of American democracy. The slave, or servant, label which has been attached to African Americans, and fortified by the distinctive feature of the race, which is our blackness, has helped perpetuate and sustain racism in our nation: a land which prides itself in being called "the land of the free and the home of the brave."

THE COMING OF LOUIS FARRAKHAN:

In my estimation, Louis Farrakhan has to be one of the most dangerous, anti-American, and anti-Christian personalities of our time. I say this because, not only does he cuddle up to the avowed enemies of America, such as Col. Kadhafi of Libya and Saddam Hussein of Iraq; he attacks many of our friends, such as Israel; the Jewish people, in general; President Mandela of South Africa, and the list goes on. As a matter of fact, he seems to have little respect for few black leaders, at home or abroad. Think for a minute on these remarks, reportedly made concerning Nelson Mandela, in a speech in Dorchester, Massachusetts, on May 22, 1994:

> "Mandela sold us out ... Mandela's the biggest clown in the big top
> ... I say give 'em [whites] 24 hours to get out of town. If they don't,
> kill every white in sight. Kill the men, kill the women, kill the children,
> kill the blind, kill the crippled. God damn it, kill them all."

These super-evil remarks came from a man in whom many fine and decent black people have begun putting their trust. The above remarks reveal that this man is a man of blasphemy and of great wickedness. It seems that he and Adolf Hitler were cast from the same ungodly mold. If this man is leading black America, then it would seem it would be only because he has been able to thrust himself upon the people in the face of an inactive and unconcerned church. It is always a dangerous situation whenever the Christian church acquiesces concerning its duty to provide moral and social leadership, in addition to spiritual leadership, for God's people; for it leaves the people open to many false prophets. The evidence seems to support the idea that Louis Farrakhan falls well within this category. However, we find that biblical history is replete with examples where God permitted evil rulers to rise up and enslaving His rebellious people for the purpose of purging them from their sinfulness. Eventually, the wicked were destroyed; and the people returned to God; however, the people suffered greatly under these conditions. Could we be headed for such a condition? I pray that the church will recognize its failure and return to its proper place of leadership. In the meantime, Farrakhan is "having a field day."

In addition to the depraved position he stated concerning Mandela and the killing of white South Africans, here are some other strange positions he has taken: First on the list is his referring to Adolf Hitler, that monstrous dictator of Nazi Germany, during W.W.II, as a great man; knowing that Hitler was ultimately responsible for the massacre of millions of Jews during the Holocaust. And, if things had gone his way, black folks would have been next on his list for extermination. The second strange position was the warm reception given those Ku Klux Klansmen on a national television show, even joining them in calling for a segregated society, based solely on race. After all of the terror, lynching, and bloodshed caused by these avowed, anti-black, domestic terrorists, all over our nation, I found Farrakhan's rather ridiculous and insensitive. It was all just a little too strange for me. At times he seems to cuddle up too closely with those who, historically, have been our strongest and most troublesome enemies; while launching many fervent attacks against those who have actually been our friends and supporters, which includes many Jews and whites. Could this be some kind of hidden fear, courting the bully, while taking out ones frustrations on those who appear weakest, because they are less likely to strike back in a violent manner? Or, is this some master plan which he intends to reveal later? Remember, after the Million Man March, he asked the US Government to set aside a separate black nation and for them to give him $25 Million to run it! I don't think so! It seems like the only master plan he has is to enshrine Louis Farrakhan as the new king of the African American race. But when all things are considered, he just doesn't fit the bill.

What is most troublesome to me, however, are his attacks on the Person of Jesus Christ, and the lies concerning Christianity, and its position in the history of the black race. His highly obvious attempts to pit the black race and culture against the culture of Christ, which he has construed to be synonymous with white race, and thus with racism. On many occasions, Mr. Farrakhan peppers his fiery racist-laden tirades with out-right and outlandish prevarications, false teachings, and faulty theology concerning the black race 's association with Christianity, the white race, the Jews, and many other ridiculous assertions. Following the bizarre teaching of Elijah Muhammad, he, too, postulates that a mad "black scientist/god by the name of YaKub made the white man," [14] as an evil being; who must eventually become subject to his creator, the black man. In addition to this weird position, he has even failed to get his own theology in sync with orthodox Islam, which states that Allah, the god of the Muslims, never appeared in any physical form; yet the Nation of Islam claims he appeared as Master W. Fad Muhammad, then Elijah Muhammad; and now, Louis Farrakhan. [15] Where will it end? Now, it doesn't matter to the world what their claims are; however, it seems that they would want to be consistent with the doctrines of the parent religion, upon which they claim their religion is based.

While I guardedly agree with some of what Farrakhan has to say about the tens of millions of African slaves and African Americans who have perished due to slavery and its aftermath, this does not in the least bit diminish the horrendous evil which Nazi Germany did to the Jews at such death camps as Auschwitz, Dachau, and Treblinka. In these, and in other such horrible places, an estimated 6 million human beings, including women and children, whose common "crime" was being Jewish, were systematically slaughtered. No race of people, or nation on the face of the earth, which claims to be righteous, should ever forget or belittle such a horrifying crime against humanity.

However, Farrakhan's comments about the Holocaust should not be surprising, given his own acrid remarks about the Jews, in general. Nevertheless, that's his own private argument with and concerning the Jews. However, another of his strange actions, among his many, was his exclusion of all women from the Million Man March, indicates his insensitivity to the issues of women, as well a propensity toward distorting reality, given the enormous problems faced by black women in today's society. From all indications, his primary purpose seems to be personal aggrandizement, and gaining enough power in the black community, in order to be considered "the big cheese," the godfather, among African American political and religious leaders, in our nation.

History records that oppressed people look for a hero, a rescuer, who will bring down the oppressor and established the oppressed. This was the case in point with the Jews, during the times of Jesus Christ. Their expectation concerning Him, if He was truly the Messiah, was to destroy Roman rule over them, and re-establish the glorious Kingdom of David, in Israel. Like the Jews of old, African American people keep looking for their deliverer. Keeping this in mind, we can see that it is simply because of the racist, oppressive world in which we live, that any black person who shows himself bold and radical enough to stand up against the oppressive, white racist system, and to inflict upon it a verbal barrage of charges of racism, injustice and insults; is quick to get an easy audience of fervent, radical followers. This is never too difficult to do, in that, black oppression is still very much alive in so many areas of American life. Here it is over 100 years after the end of Slavery, after Brown vs. the Topeka Board of Education; after many Civil Rights Laws, and we still find many black people who are still waiting for true freedom. This is the very sentiment which Mr. Farrakhan has been so adept at feeding upon, and pretty much keeping the nation divided along racial lines.

FARRAKHAN'S BATTLE FOR THE SOULS OF BLACK PEOPLE:

One of my intentions has been to show that true Christianity, in spite of Farrakhan's charges, is not race-based, nor anti-black, as claimed by him and the Nation of Islam. It is strictly because of the many false charges made by Farrakhan against the Christian faith, that I have committed to the task of seeking to expose the real truth about Farrakhan's deceptive charges, and all others, who attempt to deceive black Americans and turn them toward their religious lies. His most effective tool have always been the emotionally charged issues of loyalty to the black Culture and Race, and the evils of white racism, as reasons for rejecting Christianity, as if these are mutually exclusive.

He would do well to clean his own "doctrinal house" before trying to teach on the ills of Christianity. For, in spite of Louis Farrakhan's claims of being Islamic, those who profess orthodox Islam, wholly reject him and his religion as impostors of the real thing. This is discussed in more detail, later in this chapter. Farrakhan, like those before him, seems to have used this religious faith only to further his own cause. Therefore, it seems obvious that instead of promoting world brotherhood and sisterhood, and the complete liberation of black people in America, I believe that Louis Farrakhan is more interested in swelling the ranks of his lean organization. There is great need for this move by him, because most reliable reports state that in spite of his high profile position in America, it does not by any means reflect the actual number of members in the Nation of Islam. They are actually hurting for members; therefore, the major battle currently being waged by Farrakhan is more for the controlling the allegiance, and hearts and souls of black people in America, rather than fighting for their betterment.

This battle for the souls of black people is not taking place in evangelistic camp meetings, where fiery evangelists lambaste the evil deeds of the devil and the darkness of sin, or even the danger of living without Christ in a sin-filled world. Neither is it emotionally charged sermons warning sinners to quit their lives of sin or face the wrath of God. No! The battle for the souls of African Americans is a tactical war of words, using fiery racial darts, which is being skillfully led by the highly charismatic, sometimes eloquent, and always keen witted, orator, minister Louis Farrakhan of the Nation of Islam.

However, let the hearer be forewarned, that many men, given the right time and under the right circumstances, are capable of uttering great and profound words. Those who are more highly skilled in oratory, as Mr. Farrakhan most certainly is, are quite capable of inspiring, or exciting men to action, as he did in his Million Man March. However, even these great motivators or instigators, are not necessarily the embellishments, or symbols of truth. Real truth is able to withstand even the most rigorous investigations of history and of higher criticism. Christianity and the Gospel of Jesus Christ has met and passed all of these challenges. However, upon closer observation of many of his charges concerning the extent of racism in this country, it seems that Mr. Farrakhan is a masterful alarmist, and has, in many cases, grossly twisted the truth for his own purposes. It seems to me that he is more concerning about continually perpetuating an adversarial relation between the black and white populace in the nation. He also realizes that one of the major obstacles standing in his way is the Christian church; and he is doing all that he can to discredit it, and, thus, neutralize its effect on the lives of black Americans. Consequently, he and other Black Muslim leaders can be found denouncing the Christian church as the black man's enemy. Judging from the content of his rhetoric, and his questionable theology, this man will only lead us from the slavery of oppression to the slavery of race hatred; neither of which is acceptable. His continued distortion of the facts about conditions in America tend to further divide of our nation into black and white factions.

As a matter of fact, when it comes to the facts, Louis Farrakhan seems to fall within the same modus operandi of most racists, such as his Klan friends. Their methods, and his, seem to be to purposefully stir up antagonism between the races, in order to create racial tension, and thereby justify a need for their unseemly and sick politics and social actions, or, in many cases, their publicity grabbing antics. Some of Farrakhan's antics are to stir his audiences into hand clapping, foot stomping frenzies, by constantly harping on the injustices of the American way of life, and the coming demise of white folks and Jews. Through these tactics he keeps black people upset with white and Jews, never allowing them to observe the bustling opportunities all around them.

Anyone who has been half way alert concerning the past and the present social, political, and economic conditions in our nation, can easily discern that much has changed for good in America since the beginning of the Civil Rights Movement. Not only have things changed, but many groups and races have participated in bringing about the changing demographics of black folks within the American way of life. While at the same time, on the contrary, many individuals and groups which are highly vocal now, did nothing, or very little, in helping to bring about these changes. As a matter of fact, history reveals that more credit is due to our many white, Jewish, Labor Union, Corporate and foreign friends, in helping bring about economic and social changes than any who embraced the Nation of Islam, and its hate-filled teachings. While this wide variety of multicolored, and multiracial freedom protesters, consisting of laborers, housewives, national and local politicians, students of every variety, clergy persons, and everyday people, sacrificed their time, efforts, and lives, in the Civil Rights Protests, Farrakhan and the Nation of Islam stood by doing nothing to help. So many of these persons were often insulted, brutally beaten and some even made the ultimate sacrifice, that of death. While this variegated mass of humanity, vowing never to quit till victory was won, put all on the line, the entire population of the Nation of Islam, which included Elijah Mohammed, Malcolm X, and Louis Farrakhan, sat on their hands, and watched us, the real Freedom Fighters, from the comforts of their homes. Oh, yes, they made a lot of hot and fiery speeches; but these were most often from the protected corridors of Muslim mosques, and in all-black neighborhoods. Therefore, we can see that when we needed real soldiers in the struggle for freedom, they refused to join in. Now that all is safe, and the major battles won, Mr. Farrakhan comes to declare himself, our savior and our leader! Few who have full control of their logic and common sense will ever fall for such nonsense; for any length of time.

We consistently find that historical facts have been utterly discarded and neglected in many of Mr. Farrakhan's assertions. For instance, while he continues his unrelenting attacks on those Jews and whites, who did involved themselves in the African Slave Trade, he never mentions the leading role that Arabic Muslims played in this dastardly practice, even centuries before the other groups became involved. As a matter of record, the Hadith, which contains sacred writings about the life and teachings of the Prophet Muhammad, reveal that Muhammad, himself, was a keeper of slaves; and that Muhammad used very derogatory and demeaning words when referring to black people. These and other startling historical evidences and facts about Mohammed's and the Muslim's sordid interactions with black people in past centuries, which included the massacre of thousands of black African Christians who refused to accept Islam, have been well documented. In a similar fashion, the Nation of Islam often uses intimidation to quell criticism of its tactics and wayward theology, which includes acts of violence.

FALSE CLAIMS CONCERNING ISLAM AS REVEALED BY FOLLOWERS OF ORTHODOX ISLAM:

In spite of the hype surrounding Louis Farrakhan's highly published trip to the Islamic countries of Libya, Iran, and Iraq, most serious students of Islam do not regard the Nation of Islam as Islamic at all. The opinions expressed in the articles in the paragraphs below are from the best experts, those who best know the fundamental beliefs and practices of Orthodox Islam. These experts, wholly reject Louis Farrakhan's brand of Islam, stating that even the name itself, "The Nation of Islam," was definitely the result of misnaming Farrakhan's religion, by confusing it with Islam. That is pretty strong evidence. The experts have spoken, it's up to the hearer to make their personal choice.

In a published brochure by The Institute of Islamic Information and Education (III&E), which states that it is established for the sole purpose of disseminating true and correct information about Islam and taking corrective action for the removal of misinformation and false perceptions which exist in the American society about Islam and Muslims. In Brochure Series, No. 19, we find the following contrast between Orthodox Islam and Farrakhan's religion:

COMPARISON BETWEEN ISLAM AND FARRAKHANISM

ISLAM, and so-called "NATION OF ISLAM," are two different religions.

The only thing common between them is the jargon, the language used by the other. "The Nation of Islam" is a misnomer; this religion should be called Farrakhanism, after the name of its propagator. The religion of Elijah Muhammad and W.D. Fad died with their death because their officially and popularly elected successor, W.D. Muhammad, integrated the community with the Muslim community at-large, following the Qur'an and Hadith of Prophet Muhammad and gave his pledge of allegiance to him after Elijah Muhammad's death; he later rebelled and broke his oath with impunity, or without any expiation, and restarted "The Nation of Islam."

Examine the following comparisons between Islam and Farrakhanism with regard to the belief or practice in each:

BELIEF/PRACTICE

1. GOD/ALLAH ALONE

ISLAM: One unique, never appeared in any physical form; hence, no physical representation is possible. He is recognized through his 99 names.

FARRAKHANISM: ". . . Allah (God) appeared in the Person of Master W. Fad Muhammad, July 1930; the long awaited 'Messiah' of the Christians and the 'Mahdi' of the Muslims."

2. PROPHET/MESSENGER

ISLAM: Muhammad (S) is the last Prophet and the last Messenger. No messenger or prophet will come after Muhammad (S).

FARRAKHANISM: Elijah Muhammad was a "messenger of Allah." Are there any more messengers or prophets to come? Not clear.

12. THE QUR'AN

ISLAM: It was revealed to Prophet Mohammed (S) between 610 and 632 C.E. It is the last revelation of Allah to mankind.

FARRAKHANISM: Contradictory beliefs. On one side, ". . . BELIEVE in the Holy Qur'an and in the scriptures of all the Prophets of God," and on the other side, "We, the original nation of the earth . . . are the writers of the Bible and Qur'an. We make history once every 25,000 years . . . it is done by twenty-four of our scientists." "Both the present Bible and the Holy Qur'an must soon give way to the Holy Book."

12. AUTHENTIC HADITH

ISLAM: An indispensable source of Islamic beliefs and practices, the only source after the Qur'an. Indispensable for the understanding of the Qur'an itself.

FARRAKHANISM: Ignored, if not totally rejected by Farrakhanism. However, the leadership, including Farrakhan himself, may invoke Hadith if it suits their purpose to fool gullible Muslims.

In addition to the above differences between Islam and the Nation of Islam, most writers point out the NOI's false teachings concerning the brotherhood of all humanity. While orthodox Islam teaches equality of all races, and that there is no difference between black and white or other races. This is one of the major reasons why Malcolm X finally broke away from the Nation of Islam; changed the name given him by Elijah Mohammed; and began practicing orthodox Islam. The Islamic world wholly rejects the religion of Louis Farrakhan, calling it un-Islamic and contradictory to the Islamic beliefs introduced by the prophet Mohammed. If, then, the Islamic world rejects the Nation of Islam as a false religion, why would any sane individual embrace it and entrust their eternal salvation to a religion which was just created, or made up, just a few years ago? Does not this fit the pattern of many modern day cults and religious sects? Think about it.

CHAPTER SIX

ISLAM, CHRISTIANITY AND AFRICA

One among the other great prevarications perpetuated by Louis Farrakhan and the Nation of Islam Muslims, is that Islam is the historical religion of continental Africa. Nothing can be farther from the truth; for the Gospel went to North Africa very early in the First Century, AD. Before this time, much of Africa was polytheistic. We must not be fooled by any of these persons who use our African heritage to get us to buy into their twisting of history. History clearly reveals that the Gospel story concerning the life, death, and resurrection of Jesus Christ, entered Africa not many years after Jesus' death and resurrection. Therefore, it follows that in those lands where Christianity was embraced among African people, they too, embraced the idea of the Incarnation, and Virgin Birth of Jesus Christ, as the Son of God. We must also remember that the Gospel went to Africa before it was taken to Europe, by the Apostle Paul and later disciples!

Most astute and meticulous students of African history will readily refute the preposterous declarations that Islam was the religion of the black man in Africa, as false and unscholarly. While the Islamic faith has made tremendous strides in Africa, it came very late to the continent, and advanced mostly through violence and intimidation. It was a long, long time, after the advent of Christianity, before the Islamic faith was established; and even longer before Islamic raiders invaded the African mainland and began hawking their religion. The very birth of the prophet Mohammed, himself, came some several hundred years after Christ's death, resurrection, and ascension!

HISTORY CONFIRMS THAT CHRISTIANITY WENT TO AFRICA MANY CENTURIES BEFORE ISLAM:

The good news of Christ went to Africa, during the early Apostolic Age. In Acts Chapter 8, we learn that Paul, who was still known as Saul, was persecuting and consenting to the death of Christians, when God the

Holy Spirit, decided to plant the Gospel in Africa. Philip, one of the original proto-deacons of the early church, was selected to evangelize, baptize, and teach an important citizen of Ethiopia about Jesus and the Christian faith. The recipient of Philip's preaching and teaching was a notable citizen of north Africa, the very Treasurer of Ethiopia, a eunuch of great authority under Candace the queen. The story relates how, after he was converted, he declared:

"I believe that Jesus Christ is the Son of God."

He was then baptized as a Christian. The writer concludes his story with these simple words:

"The eunuch . . . went on his way rejoicing."

The "way" of his travel was back to his country of Ethiopia in northern Africa. The Bible testifies that after his inspiring experience, the eunuch went on his way back to Ethiopia, in AFRICA, rejoicing and telling the good news.

This event occurred between AD 31 - 33. The preacher of this good news was Philip, the evangelist. It is inconceivable to think than he had no testimony or influence when he returned home. Given the rich history of Christianity in north Africa and Egypt, it is obvious that he helped lay the ground work for its warm reception and tremendous growth. For it was the Ethiopian eunuch, who, after his conversion to Christianity, returned to Ethiopia with the Gospel! It is most likely that he began a small Christian community.

Additionally, it has been well documented that the Christian Coptic Church was established during the reign of the Roman emperor Nero in the first century, just a few years after the ascension of Jesus Christ. This makes the Coptic Church one of the oldest churches in the world. History further reveals that it was not till almost six centuries later that hostile, Islamic raiders invaded the African continent, killing off many Christian martyrs.

The Ethiopian Convert Becomes Evangelist: The Apostle Paul was not even converted to Christianity until AD 34, long after the African traveler had returned to the motherland and spread the Word. The Pulpit Commentary states that "Eusebius . . . . speaks of him [the Ethiopian eunuch] as the first Gentile convert, and as the firstfruits of the faithful in the whole world. He adds, as Irenaeus before him had hinted (iii. xii.8), that he is reported to have preached the gospel to the Ethiopians, by which the prophecy of Ps. lxviii. 31 was fulfilled. Later traditions speak of Candace [the queen of Ethiopia) as baptized by him." **16** Whether these assertions are fact or near facts, the truth of the matter is that Christianity in Northern Africa, predates many "great" church bodies in Europe.

Early Christianity in Africa: Religious history confirms that the Ethiopian Coptic Christian Church is one of the oldest churches in all of Christianity. Christianity in northern Africa predates that of, even, the Roman Catholic Church, in the so-called "holy" city of Rome. Even more so, it predates the establishment of the Islamic faith by more than 580 years!!! The prophet Muhammad, founder of Islam, was not born until AD 570; some 540 years after the death and resurrection of Jesus Christ. By the time of Mohammed's birth there were great cathedrals of the Coptic Christian Church already established in Africa. The Christian heritage of Black people long predates that of many white, European nations. Hopefully these facts should put to rest the notion of Christianity being a "White man's religion," and/or open up more objective thinking concerning our religious heritage.

The shame of these findings is that few white historians of the Christian church hardly ever mention the great contribution made by the Ethiopian eunuch. In searching many church history books, aside from the brief comments in "The Pulpit Commentary," I could find only this one sentence in the late Dr. Robert H. Gundry's book, A Survey of the New Testament, which states that, "The story of the Ethiopian eunuch foreshadows the Gentile missions of Paul." The Holy Spirit's efforts in directing the gospel to a whole continent is summed up in that one sentence! It just so happens that the continent is black-Africa, and not white-Europe. The shame of white America, as well as the White Christian church, is their failure to recognize the contributions made by black people around the world. Black people are wounded daily by this failure; and the open wound is not about to be healed. This has been one of the sordid contributions of racism.

CHAPTER SEVEN

THE PROPHET MUHAMMAD AND HIS BLACK SLAVES

The more I research the subject of Islam and its influence among black people, the more startling things I find. If I am able to find so many startling and revealing things in my research, it seems that others could easily do the same. Yet, given the things which I have found, it becomes obvious to me that either Mr. Farrakhan has done only a limited amount of research on the prophet Muhammad and the Islamic faith and, therefore, knows very little about them, or he knows the whole truth and is withholding it from his followers. If the latter is the case, he then becomes one of the world's greatest deceivers.

It would do well for all black persons who are followers of Islam or the Nation of Islam to read the teachings of Islam and the prophet Muhammad. I have taken time to really look at the life and teachings of the prophet Muhammad, and, as a black person of African descent, I have discovered some disturbing things concerning the prophet's relationship to black people. Obviously, Mr. Farrakhan, himself, as well as his followers, need to do further research in order to discover how the prophet Muhammad really felt about black people.

Practically all persons familiar with Islam, know that the two books which are regarded as the sources of Islamic law are the Koran, the holy book (similar to our Bible), and the Hadith, the teachings and words of the prophet Mohammed. If, then, these two documents are sacred to the Islamic faith, it, then seems logical that all who are practitioners of this faith, should regard the words which it contains as truth by which to govern their lives and faith. With that said, I have been enlightened by the historical scholar, Dr. Robert Morey, who discovered several racist and derogatory remarks concerning black people contained in the Hadith. For instance, in his masterful work, "The Islamic Invasion," he has made the following quotes and observations:

Black People —Raisin Heads

As to the attitude of Muhammad about black people, he referred to them as "raisin heads" in vol. 1, no. 662 and vol. 9, no. 256.

Throughout the Hadith, black people are referred to as slaves.

If this is not insulting enough to black people, Muhammad felt that if someone dreamed of a black woman, she was an evil omen of a coming epidemic of disease (vol. 9, nos. 162, 163). [17]

Next, we find this little gem of interesting information concerning the great prophet's relationship to black people, from the same author:

Muhammad: A Slave Owner!

In Hadith no. 435, vol. 6, when Umar bin Al-Khattab came to the home of Muhammad, he found that, a black slave of Allah's apostle was sitting on the first step. [18]

Dr. Morey continues:

From this and other references in the Hadith, it is clear that Muham-mad was a slave master and that he owned black slaves.

As a matter of fact, in almost every instance in which black people are mentioned in the Hadith, they were the personal slaves of Muham-mad! This was in stark contrast to Jesus of Nazareth who did not own slaves but came to set men free. [19]

The evidence concerning the Prophet Mohammed's low estimation of the value and personhood of black people is rather overwhelming. The quotes above, were taken from one of the most sacred books among orthodox Islam, the Hadith. The facts from the life of Muhammad clearly reveal that he believed in the slave system; and, that he, indeed, kept black slaves for his own personal use. The evidence is not found in Christian writings, but in Islamic writings; therefore, it cannot be construed to be something created by Christians to denigrate Islam, or the Prophet Muham-mad. All true Muslims hold the Hadith in high esteem; just as Christians regard the Old and New Testaments of the Bible; and indeed the entire Bible.

It would be unthinkable, and highly embarrassing, for me as a Christian, to have to tell the world that when Jesus was in the world, our Savior had attending Him, His own black slaves, who waited on Him hand and foot.

Then it would add insult to injury, to know that He used scornful terms, such as "raisin heads," to describe them. The Holy Bible reveals that Jesus did not come into the world in order to enslave people, but to set them free, both physically and spiritually. He said in Luke 4:18, that,

> *The Spirit of the Lord is upon me, because he hath anointed me*
> *to preach the gospel to the poor; he hath sent me to heal the broken-*
> *hearted, to preach deliverance to the captives, and recovering of sight*
> *to the blind, to set at liberty them that are bruised (KJV).*

I would like to invite all readers to know for themselves what our God has revealed, concerning His relationship to us all, through the teaching of Jesus. His words reveal that he does not set one culture or race over another; nor does He hold prejudicial thoughts concerning the people of the earth. As a matter of fact, the Apostle Paul, one of the most zealous preachers of the Gospel of Jesus Christ, writes in Galatians 3:28,

> *There is neither Jew nor Greek, there is neither bond nor free, there is*
> *neither male nor female: for ye are all one in Christ Jesus (KJV).*

In contrast to Christ, the liberator of the enslaved among humanity, the Prophet Muhammad was a slave keeper, just like the white slaveholders in our nation's past.

CHAPTER EIGHT

ISLAM AND THE SLAVE TRADE

█t seems that within most cultures there resides that desire which other men have to rule or lord over other men or their culture. This is found to be rather handy when economic benefits to the slave owner is added to the great convenience slaves add to the lives of their masters. In the rather new American frontier, the claiming and clearing of farm land took high priority, especially in the South. Farming became one of the chief sources of income and thus a means of providing prominence among the Southern settlers. The idea of slavery was nothing new to these white, European settlers; for it had existed in one form or another in Britain, and a few other European countries. In Europe, slavery had seemed rather successful and, quite acceptable. According to Susanne Everett, who authored the revealing book, "History of Slavery," Aristotle fully accepted the institution of slavery. In the following statement, she records his thoughts and the conditions which existed in medieval Europe:

> "From the hour of their birth, some are marked out for subjection, others for rule." Medieval Christendom was influenced both by the classical tradition in which Aristotle featured prominently and also by St. Paul's acceptance of the institution of slavery in the Epistle of Philemon. Yet that same epistle, by its accompanying request to Philemon, the owner of the slave Onesimus, to liberate him or at least treat him kindly revealed an incipient anti-slavery message in early Christianity. The compromise of the medieval Church was in effect to accept the institution but to urge good treatment of slaves and, on occasion, the liberation of captives, especially those of one's own skin color. [20]

In America, the agreement was to purchase African slaves, through the slave market. Apparently, there was no serious opposition mounted against the institution of African slave trading on American soil. In order to satisfy the new American demand for slave labor, the "new Americans" resorted to "the transatlantic trade that brought 11 million slaves from Africa to the Americas in the course of 300 years;" according to Susanne Everett, on the cover sheet of her book, "History of Slavery." [21]

In the book, Mrs. Everett notes that "the slavery which existed in parts of the Mediterranean basin in the Middle Ages and which was principally fed by the ISLAMIC MERCHANTS' [capitals mine] trade route across the Sahara from the interior of West Africa." [22] Consequently, History reveals that the first major influence Islamic or Arabic people had over black or African people was in the slave trade. Mr. Farrakhan often mentions the Jewish influence in trading of African slaves, yet he never mentions that one of the earliest, and greatest traders of black African slaves were the Arabs, of the Islamic faith.

After the decline and collapse of Rome in the early 5th century, it is reported that slavery in Europe declined. However, a revival of slavery "occurred in the 8th - 10th centuries, when the Germans captured hordes of Slavs. The equation of nationality and status in Germanic languages gave us the very word 'slave.'

The next great revival in the institution of slavery resulted from the spread of Islam in Africa. By the middle of the 7th century the crusading followers of the Prophet Mahomet [Mohammed], who had 'submitted themselves to the will of Allah' were marching from Arabia to conquer Syria, Palestine and Egypt. From there they looked across western desert to the fertile lands of Tunisia, Libya and Morocco. The Arab conquest of North Africa was, however, a long and tortuous affair, fiercely resisted at every step by the independent Berber tribesmen. Although the Berbers finally succumbed to the faith of Islam and, in fact, joined the Arabs in the conquest of Spain during the 8th century, they never lost their separate identity.

The Berbers of the Tunisian plains and the coastal belt of Algeria and Morocco had already tapped the greatest future source of slaves: West Africa. . . .

Beyond the Sahara lay the vast savanna belt that the Arabs called the Sudan, or 'the country of the Black People,' stretching from the Atlantic to the Red Sea. By the 9th century, great merchant camel caravans were traveling from Tripoli and Ghadames to the oases of Fezzan and even further south, beyond Lake Chad into the kingdom of Kanem, carrying black slaves for the households of the Arab palace city of Qairwan, on the

Mediterranean." [23]

I think that the point is well taken that Islamic Arabs were one of the major exporters of African slaves. As a matter of fact, it was not until 1448, that "the Portuguese had arrived in the Senegal and the Gambia, the Arab monopoly of the trans-Saharan traffic in slaves, which had existed for so long, had finally been broken." [24] The Islamic Arab traders did not desist from slave trading when the Europeans entered the market, they simply became fierce competitors among others who had entered this lucrative flesh market. Mr. Farrakhan would do well to include a redress directed toward his Islamic predecessors for these past atrocities which they inflicted upon our forefathers and mothers, and brothers and sisters of yesteryear; just as he has so openly done toward Jews.

The American connection to this is that, it was from this African slave market that the new settlers in America purchased their black slaves. By so doing, those who were once oppressed and persecuted, became the oppressors and the persecutors. Then, to assuage their guilty consciences, as well as escape the hard work and high costs involved in building a new nation, they declared the African race an inferior race. With this declaration, our black foreparents were doomed to servanthood, and many were worked and abused, literally, to death. Those slaves who questioned their masters or were considered troublemakers, often suffered having limbs chopped off, eyes gouged or burned out, tar-feathered, hung, and many other atrocities. These past horrors inflicted on our helpless forefathers and mothers, have left many bitter, almost beyond repair.

THE CHURCH AND THE GOSPEL: THE SLAVES' ONLY HOPE:

In times past, it was always the church and the gospel of Jesus Christ which provided the oppressed slaves with coping skills in order to endure the arduous conditions of slavery. These gave them enough faith and hope to make it through the hostile environment they now found themselves in; which included severe and unexplained beatings, which often included mutilations; separation from family members; loss of a sense of manhood, womanhood, and personhood; and then there were the awful feelings of hopelessness and despair, resulting from being under the complete control of another, foreign, hate-filled person. However, in spite of these negative situations, black people have always found a way to hang in there and survive; always hoping beyond hope that there was a brighter day ahead.

They would sing songs like:

Father I stretch my hands to thee, No other help I know;
If thou withdraw thyself from me, Ah, whither shall I go?

The black preacher helped his hearers endure by pointing to the sufferings and persecution of Jesus Christ as being similar to the black experience. Jesus had been persecuted by His own people, which prompted Him to say in John 15:25c:

"They hated me without a cause."

This has long been the experience of black people in America. Forced to acknowledge that there seems to be a global hatred of black people, they often looked mournfully at their debased condition and sang emotionally, this Old Negro Spiritual and sorrow song:

"Nobody knows the trouble I see, Nobody knows my sorrow;
Nobody knows the trouble I see, Glory hallelujah!"

"Sometimes I'm up, sometimes I'm down, Oh, yes Lord!"
Sometimes I'm almost to the groun'; Oh, yes, Lord!"

In essence, the words of the Bible verse above and the words of the song give neither rhyme nor reason why Jesus suffered and died on the Cross, nor why blacks in America have been so brutally and shamefully mistreated. In the past, black folks took upon themselves the burden of Jesus' suffering and cross-bearing; but a new day is dawning; many are not willing to "bear their burden in the heat of the day," any longer. Long gone are the days of Dr. Martin Luther King, Jr.'s urging the black masses to love evil and bigoted white men in spite of their evil ways. He once preached that,

"Love is the only force capable of transforming an enemy into a friend. We never get rid of an enemy by meeting hate with hate; we get rid of an enemy by getting rid of enmity. By its very nature, hate destroys and tears down; by its very nature, love creates and builds up. Love transform with redemptive power." [25]

Even his adversaries must admit that Dr. Martin Luther King, Jr., was the ultimate champion and prophet of non-violent protest. The test of a champion is whether or not he or she wins; and the test of a prophet or prophetess is whether or not what is predicted comes true. Dr. King noted in a speech before a crowd at the University of California at Berkeley, on June 4, 1957:

> From the very beginning there was a philosophy undergirding the Montgomery boycott, the philosophy of nonviolent resistance. . . We had to make it clear that nonviolent resistance is not a method of cowardice. It does resist. It is not a method of stagnant passivity and deadening complacency.

None can deny the incredible results he and his followers achieved during the Civil Rights struggle during the 1950s and the 1960s. However, we are left with the realization that non-violence is a self-limiting concept and its appropriateness must be interpreted in each individual incident, or in each corporate community action. The concept of "non-violence" must be reinterpreted continuously for situational relevancy. However, I believe that Dr. King was absolutely correct in adopting this concept during the Civil Rights Movement. Without his proper interpretation of the conditions of the time and the application of an appropriate plan of action, it seems quite likely that we would still be living in a Jim Crow, segregated, society. It seems that Dr. King made an informed, intelligent choice, which insured the safety of those who followed him, as well as insured the continued progress of the Movement.

Dr. King, and the leadership, knew that mass violence by mobs of black folks, would most certainly bring down the full wrath of an already super-hostile nation. The beatings, the fire hoses, and the dog attacks would have seemed like child's play, compared to what could have happened, had the demonstrators been armed. I believe that the police would have been allowed to use their own weapon of choice on the demonstrators; which could have included automatic weapons, tanks, armored personnel carriers, and the like. If the reader has doubts, think back at what happened to those white demonstrators at Kent State University. They were shot down in cold-blood; and the action was defended by, then President Richard M. Nixon. God only knows what would have happened had he been President during the Civil Rights Movement. For another stark testimony on how cold governments can be toward demonstrators, even unarmed ones, one has only to look to what happened at Tiananmen Square, on June 4, 1989, when, reportedly, hundreds or thousands of Chinese students were maimed and/or murdered by the Chinese Armed Forces. If that doesn't move you, think about the highly publicized, video-taped beating of Rodney King, who was unarmed and crawling on the ground, while being repeatedly kicked and beaten severely with Billy-clubs, and were later exonerated by an all-white jury. Given these incidents, which clearly demonstrates what could have happen, non-violent, peaceful demonstrations, seems to have been the best choice; especially, given the fact that it accomplished what the leaders were after, freedom!

The same crowd which cried out against non-violence (yet did nothing themselves), are back today. Once again, they are challenging black people, including Christians, to pull of the robe of non-violence; and to steer clear of love and suffering; and to pick up the weapons for warfare. Many powerful and influential men are teaching that it should not be necessary to love the dog that continues to bite you, so to speak. They're teaching that its time for black people to bite back every time that they are bitten. Black folk are being persuaded that its best to take up the sword of violent confrontation; to separate themselves from their "white enemies," and to follow the racist teachings of Minister Louis Farrakhan, the chief minister of the unorthodox, highly militant, pseudo-Islamic group, calling themselves, the Nation of Islam.

THE FALSE HOPE OF FARRAKHANISM:

Louis Farrakhan is finding much success in leading many away from Christ and Christianity. Most of his teachings are designed to counter white racism; but it also runs counter to Christianity, which he and others of his persuasion, have called "the white man's religion." Farrakhan's movement, and the success of it, is basically black peoples' response to a continued proliferation of American racism and an alarming growth of anti-government, anti-Black, and anti-Jew, far-right, White Supremacist, radical militia groups. In addition to that our Congress has been taken over by right-wing, ultra-conservative, factions which have been viewed as anti-Black, anti-women, and other minorities. In the midst of this hysteria, Mr. Farrakhan has come forth as a powerful, charismatic messenger, with words which challenge the authority and brutality of the white establishment.

Minister Farrakhan has flooded our airways, our churches, and much of America, with his racially charged, counter messages of African American unity, nationalism, and militancy. Strangely enough, his messages often reek with, not only anti-white, but also anti-Jewish rhetoric, much like other hate groups, such as the Ku Klux Klan, the Skinheads, and Neo-Nazis, which he is assumed to be diabolically opposed to. His fiery and bold messages, have touched the "hot button" of many African-Americans, including many who say they are Christians. These black citizens of America are lending a serious ear to Mr. Farrakhan's emotionally charged anti-racism, anti-White counter-racist messages, by the tens of thousands. Farrakhan's immense popularity of late, has made him a major player in the broad arena of American politics and religion. He is causing many black citizens to come to the point where they feel challenged to choose culture and race over Jesus Christ and the Christian faith.

Although, Mr. Farrakhan claims to be religiously rooted in the orthodox Islamic faith, there are serious doubts concerning his claims. Dr. Robert Morey, an internationally recognized scholar in the field of comparative religions, the cults, and the occult, writes that "orthodox Islam does not want to be identified with the black Muslim movement in America, which it condemns as spurious and heretical. Black Muslims are not viewed by orthodox Muslims as true Muslims or as part of Islam." [26] Even Malcolm X, who was eventually murdered by allegedly, fanatical, Nation of Islam followers, denied the validity of the teachings of the Nation of Islam after his own visit to Mecca, the religious center of the Islamic faith. Malcolm X discovered that the teachings of Elijah Muhammad and the Nation of Islam ran counter to true Islam (one of the most recent and highly public figures to abandon the Nation of Islam and convert to traditional Islam is former heavyweight boxing champion, Muhammed Ali, as reported during a special during the 1996 Atlanta Olympic Games).

Concerning Malcolm X's defection to traditional Islam, Robert Morey writes that:

> "After 12 years of devoted service to the Nation of Islam, Malcolm woke up to Elijah's many moral problems, such as his 13 illegitimate children, his greed and jealousy, and the constant strife which filled Elijah Mohammed's life.
>
> These things began to bother him. How could Elijah be from Allah and do all the evil things he did?
>
> It was during his pilgrimage to Mecca that for the first time he clearly saw the heretical and racist nature of the black Muslim movement in America. They were not Muslims at all. The whole thing was a sham." [27]

Nevertheless, Mr. Farrakhan considers himself Muslim and continues to proselytize Black Americans, using cultural solidarity as the hook and White racism as the bait to win a following. Recent developments tend to support the notion that his followings and influence, both nationally and internationally are now beginning to grow at a faster pace.

In the past, Mr. Farrakhan, following in the steps of Wallace D. Fad (sometimes spelled "Fard;" later known as Farad Muhammad), the founder of the Nation of Islam, and his successor, Elijah Muhammad, was quick to associate the evils of White racism with White Christianity. Morey notes that Fad, a white man and "peddler of 'African' clothing . . . claimed to be 'a brother from the East,'" was the first to mock Christianity as "the white man's religion," although, he himself was White [I'm sure it helped him sell more African clothing]. He further states that "it is interesting that black Muslims today are following the religion of a white man whom, like in the days of slavery, they call Master Fad Muhammad!" [28]

Mr. Farrakhan has learned that a direct attack on "Jesus" is counter-productive; therefore, he has very cleverly changed his tactics as he travels around the country, seeking disciples. He now uses language which makes him appear as a friend of Jesus, though he has repeatedly denied, both that Jesus is the Son of God, and the Messiah (Christ). One of his tactics of late has been to point out that the Jews are to be blamed for the crucifixion of Jesus as well as the economic woes of blacks today. That sure gets a lot of attention, because both items push most black folks "hot buttons." Author Susan S. Lang writes that "when covering Farrakhan's speech to a full Madison Square Garden crowd in 1986, the Canadian magazine MacLean's reported:

The black preacher asked the 25,000-strong crowd,

"Who are the enemies of Jesus?" Many raised clenched fists and chanted, "Jews, Jews, Jews!"

This was obviously a rhetorical question anticipating a well-calculated, anti-Jewish response. It has been his custom in the past, that, after demeaning the Jews, to attack Christianity, for it began with a Jew, under the Man, Jesus Christ, God in the flesh. Our only hope lies in the faith of Jesus Christ, and not Farrakhanism.

CHAPTER NINE

WHITES SEARCHED FOR FREEDOM CARRYING THEIR OWN SLAVES

White Europeans in Search Their Own Freedom While Enslaving Others

Religious persecution and the horrors of the caste system in Medieval Europe, made life impossible for those who thought differently from the ruling classes. With the discovery of America, many of the oppressed in Europe, sought a refuge in the New World. When the Pilgrims came to this land, they dreamed of a land free from the tyrannical oppression inflicted by absolute monarchs, from which they had escaped. Oppressed in Europe, many white settlers journeyed to the New World seeking religious freedom, social liberty, and a land where justice was for all. In order to assure this end, the Founding Fathers wrote noble documents declaring blind justice and true democracy as their absolute goal. However, hidden by these declarations of blind justice was a nation that had already bowed to another evil ruler, the concept of white racial supremacy.

Although seeking freedom themselves, many of the settlers, had an inward desire to "lord over" other men, as superiors to inferiors. They, therefore, patterned their lives after European serfdom, and brought with them indentured servants; many, of whom, were white. However, pretty soon, after discovering that the building of a nation required hard manual labor, many resorted to the more oppressive and economically beneficial form of serfdom, which was the evil institution of slavery.

THE GREAT CONTRADICTION IN THE WHITE MAN'S LIFE

The white men, who ventured to the American Continent in the early 1500s, lifted high the virtues of family life and freedom of choice. The last thing they wanted was for the government or their local assemblies to dictate to them concerning these God-given rights. They would rather die than give these up; yet they had no qualms about violating the God-given rights of other men, other families, other nations. This is clearly documented by their vigorous participation in, and active promotion of, the trading of African slaves. And in order to satisfy the demand for slaves, beginning around the early 1500s, slave traders permanently disrupted the lives and families of millions of African people. And in the early 1600s many young African males and females were captured and brought to America and sold as slaves. One can only imagine how devastating these barbaric acts must have been to the African societies when we put in the context of our own contemporary society's dismal view concerning the kidnapping of our children and loved ones today. Through these barbaric acts, myriad's of families were ripped apart, for only in rare occasions were whole families taken together.

In early America, with agriculture and land cultivation in its infancy, there was a great demand for strong, young slaves who could do heavy work, and for young females who could bear many children, over long periods of time. Realizing this preference, the slave traders usually sought young, healthy males and females, because the buyers of slaves considered this group a high-return investment. After their capture, the slaves were stacked like cargo on slave ships for the long and perilous voyage across the sea.

Upon their purchase from the slave auctions, the slave owners began immediately to deprogram and detach the enslave youths from their home-land, cultures, and traditions of the old societies from whence they came. This program was often facilitated by changing their names to names given by their new owners. They would also separate those who spoke the same language, or came from the same village, or geographical area. Whenever it was discovered that there was a commonality between the captive slaves, they were separated from each other. Even mothers and fathers were considered threats to the ultimate control demanded by the slavers. They wanted slaves who were more easily controlled and molded into the kinds of human automatons desired by individual slaveholders, and who were more easily conformable to servitude; therefore, a great majority of slaves were between the ages of ten and eighteen years of age. [29]

BRUTALITY BROKE DOWN MOST OUTWARD DISPLAYS OF REBELLION BY THE SLAVES

Once under the complete control and power of the slaveholder, the de-programming and programming efforts were begun. These were deliberate and vicious actions designed to replace spirits of courage with spirits of fear; and spirits of individualism with spirits of corporate servitude. They further desired to break down all forms of resistance and rebellion, and to reduce their desire to escape the masters plantation, and to keep them productive while they were in the most prolific years of their lives. [30] When this did not work, and there was rebellion or resistance, the brutal slave owners use every imaginable evil method of punishment in order to ensure their return to unequivocal and absolute obedience. Most of the punitive methods often included, but was not limited to, brutal beatings, mutilations and murders. [31]

The strict moral codes and traditions found in the African family system were soon lost after families were torn apart by the slave system. The supply side of slavery required more males, consequently, this excess, according to E. Franklin Frazier, resulted in casual associations for satisfaction of sexual hunger. After the female population increased some relationships developed from purely physical contacts to stable family groups. [32]

The slave trade broke up many family units and affected many slave youth. Charles Vert Willie, noted Harvard scholar, quotes Frederick Douglass. born in slavery in 1817. revealing his first-hand experience with the traumas of slave life which is presented here.

> The reader must not expect me to say much of my family. My first experience of life, as I now remember it, ... began in the family of my grandmother and grandfather. The practice of separating mothers from their children and hiring them out at distances too great to admit of their meeting, save at long intervals, was a marked feature of the cruelty and barbarity of the slave system. It had no interest in recognizing or preserving any of the ties that bind families together or to their homes.

> My grandmother's five daughters [one of whom was my mother] were hired out in this way, and my only recollections of my own mother are of a few hasty visits made in the night on foot, after the daily tasks were over, and when she was under the necessity of returning to respond to the call to the field in early morning.

> Of my father I know nothing. Slavery had no recognition of fathers...

> Old master ... only allowed the little children to live with grandmother

for a limited time; as soon asthey were big enough they were promptly taken away ...

The time came when I must go. ... I was seven years old (Douglas 1962:27-33). [33]

A similar background and story is offered concerning the life of the famous African-American scientist, inventor, and educator, Booker T. Washington, on page 6 of Dr. Willie's book. Such was the life of youths in the slave economy.

Many slave owners used the slave women for their own sexual gratification. These relationships depicted the moral bankruptcy of the slavers, and often resulted in mulatto (mixed) children being born out of these sexual unions. Frazier states that:

There is sufficient evidence of widespread concubinage and even polygyn [two or more concubines at the same time] on the part of the white masters. The maternal family organization, i.e., the family in which the mother was the head and main source of support, was fostered partly by the association between the males of the white race and the slave women on the plantation.

There were white men who acknowledged their offspring and gave them an education and a start in the world.

There were white slaveholders who neglected their wives and gave their affection and their worldly goods to their [black] mistress and their mulatto offspring. [34]

In order to further demonstrate how slavery destroyed African families, Perkins cites this commentary from the writings of A. Leon Higginbotham, Jr., which exemplifies how outrageous and heathen the American slave system really was:

In a 1646 contract, Frances Potts sold a Black woman and child to Stephen Carlton, "to use forever." Another deed records William Whittington's sale of a girl merely ten years old; looking to the future he noted that she was sold along with any issue (children) she might produce for her and her children's "lifetime" and their successors forever. [35]

In America the African slaves were shamefully and scandalously exploited, their family lives were almost completely destroyed. They were drained of their cultural and ancestral traditions, and then banned from all intellectual pursuits, such as reading, writing and arithmetic, in the belief that an ignorant slave was less of a threat than an intelligent one.

Attempts at social cohesion were destroyed by slave owners in that slaves were prohibited from communicating with other slaves who spoke the same language. E. Franklin Frazier wrote that,

> If by chance slaves who spoke the same African language were thrown together, it was the policy on the part of the masters to separate them. . The enslavement of the Negro not only destroyed the traditional African system of kinship and other forms of organized social life but it made insecure and precarious the most elemental form of social life — the family. [36]

However, after the slaves were emancipated, the masters had no legal ownership rights over sex and family lives of the slaves. Compliance with the emancipation order by the masters was insured by the invading Union armies. This new sense of freedom was so overwhelming that many thousands of slaves, with no place of their own, took off in many directions. According to Frazier:

> Not only were the sentimental and habitual ties between spouses severed but even Negro women often abandoned their children. Among the demoralized elements in the newly emancipated Negroes promiscuous sexual relationships and frequent changing of spouses became the rule. [37]

In spite of seemingly insurmountable odds since emancipation, the African-American family has survived; even though many, not-so-well-intending, skeptics have long since predicted its demise. Dr. Clarence James in a speech to youths at the Concord Baptist Church in Dallas, Texas, in August of 1991, stated that:

> The scientists of America declared in 1875, that by 1920, there would be no black people living in this country; that because of the superiority of white folks and the inferiority of black folks, that we could not live in competition with them, and that we would die off. But we are like the children of Israel in Egypt Land; we multiply generation by generation, and now they are saying that there are too many of us! The same thing that the former generation did, the present generation can do. [38]

The African-American family has learned how to cope with, and then rise above, even the greatest of odds. Past generations have miraculously survived all of the vicissitudes and monumental evils of slavery and post-slavery oppression. They did it by trusting in God; by their inner courage and determination to live above their enslaved conditions; by always struggling, never giving up; and by conveying to their youth, through survival stories, their songs, and through their hope-filled faith-practices, that "with Jesus you can make it." The teachings were begun in the family, and fortified by the worship and teachings of the church. Thus, the family and the church worked hand-in-hand in helping to sustain the oppressed, as they waited, sometimes patiently, sometimes agonizingly, for their elusive change to come.

Along with the family, the church played a monumental role in laying a strong foundation of hope for a people who seemed to have so little to hope for. I mean, it takes some kind of risky faith to remain optimistic and expectant about the future, when the experiences of the past have been nothing short of nightmarish and monstrous. How many of us would be hopeful after being snatched away from our native land; violently wrenched from our mothers arms, or having seen our fathers brutally maimed and killed? How many would remain hopeful after being probed in every part of our bodies and then put on an auction block and sold like an animal? How many would be hopeful with a heavy yoke around our necks, or shackles and chains around our ankles? I dare say, not many!

But the amazing story of the African slaves and their descendants, is that many did remain hopeful, faithful, courageous, and daring enough to remain fixed on the notion that "there is a brighter day ahead," even in the midst of the greatest of suffering. The church help fortify and promote this idea, when the oppressed came to worship. They left their troubles and hardships outside the place of worship; for when they entered the "house of the Lord," they came for the purpose of worship and praise. E. Franklin Frazier called the Christian church:

> A refuge in a hostile white world. For the slaves who worked and suffered in an alien world, religion offered a means of catharsis for their pent-up emotions and frustrations. Moreover, it turned their minds from the sufferings and privations of this world to a world after death where the weary would find rest and the victims of injustices would be compensated. [39]

Unfortunately, the legacy of the brutal slave system has affected every generation of youths since its inception. When I was a very young child, I remember the horror stories my mother would relay to us which she had been told by our neighbor, Mrs. Alice Cooper, who had been born in slavery (she was 100 plus years old when she died), and my great-grandmother, Mrs. Hettie McElroy, born at slavery's end (she lived to be 97 plus years old). They told of hearing their fathers and other males screaming from the beatings they often suffered at the whims of slave owners; of slave masters "taking" the young slave girls at their pleasure (referring to forced sexual intercourse, or rape), and many other horrors of the slave system. This legacy of evil is the shame of America; and as painful as it may be, these historical events must be relayed to generations to come.

A NEED FOR NATIONAL REPENTANCE:

America has yet to truly repent for the atrocities done to black people on this continent during the years of American slavery. Many African-Americans still have to contend with the remnants of this system in which many whites have ingrained in their nature a false sense of racial superiority and deep hatred for African-American people; especially those whose descendants fought on "the wrong side" in the Civil War. But African Americans are a people who were brought here in servitude, but have endured and earned with blood, sweat, and tears, more right to first-class citizenship than most other immigrants on American soil!

Although, denied by many, African Americans still suffer for the ill effects of brutal slave system. Those who were not affected by it can easily dismiss it as irrelevant and without merit. You will never hear a Jew saying that the Holocaust, which occurred during a period spanning 10 years or less, was not important for them today. Yet, white people want black people to forget the horrifying slave system, which occurred during a period spanning over 400 years!!! The noted theologian, James Cone, stated in his impressive book, "God of the Oppressed," that:

> Because white theologians were not enslaved and lynched and are not ghettoized because of color, they do not think that color is an important point of departure for theological reflection (p. 53).

However, the oppressed know for a fact that it has never really been fully addressed like it deserves. The noted Civil Rights Activist and Comedian, Dick Gregory, once said that it was a wonder to him that all black men in America were not crazy, because of all the injustice we have suffered.

The Emancipation was the greatest event in the lives of blacks in this country; however, there were no "damage control" programs established to aid the slaves in their transition into a free society. Dr. J. Deotis Roberts addresses this in his book, "Roots of a Black Future," p. 34. He states that:

> Emancipation was a difficult experience for ex-slaves. Blacks were simply turned out into the world ill prepared to shift for themselves. As the plantation system swept away, many became refugees.

American Slavery was a great moral evil and its effects will not easily go away. We must deal with it and not sweep it under the rug; for we are reminded of it each year when black people celebrate two Independence Days. God placed the Christian Church in the world to give leadership in times of moral crisis. However, before the church can minister, where it has been guilty of oppressive behavior, it must first repent. Many denominations, such as the United Methodists and some Pentecostals, offered apologies and acts of repentance to African Americans, as far back as the 1960s and 70s. However, it was not until June, 1997, that the Southern Baptist Convention offered a full apology for American Slavery, which found its greatest support among Southern Baptists!!! This tells us that we still have a very, very, long way to go.

CHAPTER TEN

THE RELIGIOUS ORIGIN OF THE NATION OF ISLAM, OR BLACK MUSLIMS

As previously stated, the Nation of Islam, or Lost Nation, as earlier called, began under the creative imagination of one, Walleye D. Fad, a traveling clothing seller, who was apparently an Arabic white man. However, being dark complexioned and by claiming that he was "a brother from the East," implying that he was from somewhere in Arabia; and by speaking harshly against white people, he gained acceptance from his black customers. He soon discovered that many were disgruntled, discriminated against, and denied equal justice and economic opportunities. It is said that he encouraged these brothers and sisters to give up their Christian birth names and adopt Muslim names.

Robert Morey notes that:

"The source of much of what Fad had to say about the Christian Church and its doctrines came from the teachings of the Watchtower Bible and Tract Society, or, as they are commonly known, the Jehovah's Witnesses. . . The Watchtower's denial of the Trinity and its reduction of Jesus to mere humanity laid the foundation for Fad to introduce his unique brand of Islam. Going from house to house using Watchtower literature, Fad tore down his black followers' faith in the gospel of Jesus Christ." **40**

The next major hurdle for Fad was to convince oppressed blacks that Christianity was the "the white man's religion." This meant that for blacks to participate in Christianity was to participate with their oppressors in further oppressing them and declaring it righteous. This, he knew, would never be acceptable to those whom he had developed a following among. So, this lone white man (call him "a brother from the East," or whatever you like), convinced many black people that white people were "devils," and that black people were divine.

One of his early converts was one Elijah Poole, who had moved to Detroit, Michigan, from his birthplace in Sandersville, Georgia. Under Walleye D. Fard's teachings, Poole, the son of a Baptist pastor, renounced the Christian faith and later changed his name to Elijah Muhammad. After Mr. Fard's sudden disappearance, Elijah Muhammad took over the black Muslim movement. He would advance much of the teachings of Walleye D. Fard and added many of his own. He was extremely successful in developing a following of many fiercely loyal subjects. This can be attested to by their seemingly suicidal attempts to protect Mr. Muhammad; and also by the vast fortune and real estate he amassed through their efforts before his death.

One of Elijah Muhammad's most loyal converts and disciples was Malcolm Little, the son of another black Baptist preacher . When he was converted to the Nation of Islam, he also dropped his Christian last name and replaced it simply with "X." Malcolm X would become one of the most famous disciples of Elijah Muhammad and the Nation of Islam. He became a trusted leader among Mr. Muhammad's disciples and was very successful in establishing new mosques.

Malcolm was very devoted to Mr. Muhammad until he learned of the many accusations against him, alleging sexual misconduct with many young teenage girls who were among his followers, as well as, other alleged moral and personal problems. In the latter years, Malcolm appeared to be a man in search of truth, so he took a trip to Mecca, the center of Islam, in Arabia. There he saw how different the teachings of true Islam was from the highly racist teachings of Elijah Muhammad and the Nation of Islam. Unfortunately, when Malcolm X returned to America, he made the tragic mistake of criticizing his leader, publicly. It wasn't long before he was exiled from the Nation of Islam by Elijah Muhammad; after that his fate was sealed. Before his assassination, he had predicted that he was a marked man; and could be killed at anytime by rival black Muslims. His prediction came true as he was making a speech at a dance hall on February 22, 1965. He was gunned down in an obvious "hit," by an allegedly black Muslim death squad.

The media and other inside sources had noted that Malcolm's assassination was a well-planned, inside job, carried out by fanatical supporters of Elijah Muhammad. It is a well-known fact that Louis Farrakhan, a young lieutenant of Mr. Muhammad's, at the time, had mention that Malcolm X had deserved to die for his statements about the Honorable Elijah Muhammad. While Mr. Farrakhan has acknowledged his hard feelings toward Malcolm, no one has been able to directly link him to his assassination. Recently, in an angry outburst, he likened Malxolm X to the infamous American traitor, Benedict Arnold. In that America took care of Benedict Arnold, Farrakhan indicated that Malcolm X was their traitor, therefore, he got what he deserved. He asked the white world, "What the hell business is it of yours?"

When the assassination hit the news media, black America were once again how dangerous it living among fellow blacks. We all had to come to grips with the stark reality of another violent, black-on-black crime, resulting in the murder of one of its most famous citizens. The Nation of Islam and its leader had been promoted as the savior of the black race, yet it had only proven itself as violent and deadly as the Klan and other hate groups.

Elijah Muhammad, Malcolm X, and Louis Farrakhan, had all spoken of meeting violence with violence when dealing with the white man. Yet, in spite of all the talk, the black Muslims, or the Nation of Islam, have only proven themselves to be a religion of violence, but only against its own people. I doubt that one can find one incident where these "brave" soldiers of the Nation of Islam ever punished a white person for all the atrocities committed against them with the same kind of violence they inflict upon other black people.

It is a sad, but I believe true commentary, that the Nation of Islam under Louis Farrakhan, like his predecessors, have developed a religion based on fear, threats, and violent reprisals directed at members of its own race, whose only crime was to criticize, and publicly disagree with its teachings. Any religion which can not stand the scrutiny of sincere examination and inquiry is afraid of its own doctrines and founding principles. This has been one of the ignoble characteristics of the Islamic faith, in general. In the words of Fatima Mernissi, the highly acclaimed Moroccan sociologist, Middle East thinker, and author of the book "Islam and Democracy: Fear of the Modern World:"

> Islam is probably the only monotheistic religion in which scholarly exploration is systematically discouraged, if not forbidden, since rational analysis would not serve the purposes of the despots.

Mindless obedience and the threat of divine disfavor are the primary enforcers, and therefore, sustainers, of this tyrannical system. Louis Far-rakhan picked up on these self-serving traits very early, by watching Elijah Muhammad's rule of absolute obedience, as well as the code of silence, and he uses it to its fullest. However, as noted above, this atmosphere of silence and unquestioning allegiance was not unique to the Nation of Islam, but the Islamic faith, in general.

THE REAL PROBLEMS IN ISLAM:

Nations and communities within the Islamic faith are ruled by the caliphs or imams. Some are heads of state, such as the late Ayatollah Khomeini, ruler of Iran in the 1970s, and President Saddam Hussein of Iraq; as well as many other leaders in local communities. Judging from all that we have learned about them, we know that they demand and get absolute obedience, especially since they claim to speak directly for Allah. In them lie the power of life and death; therefore, anyone who raises questions concerning their station in life or the state of the nation is subject to immediate death. How can one ever forget the death contract ("fatwa"), or "hit," as the Mafia would say, that Khomeini place on the life of the British author, Salman Rushdie, after accusing him of blaspheming Islam and the Koran, and of mocking the prophet Mohammed. These same individuals think nothing of blaspheming Christ, Christianity, or the Holy Bible; yet they can't stand a little criticism or critical analysis themselves. If Christianity is true, or if Islam is true, or if the Nation of Islam is true, let them stand or fall on their own merits and the tests of prophesy. The test of a prophet, and thus of any prophesy, is whether or not what is prophesied comes true.

The caliph, or imam, uses his, supposedly, divine connections to create suicidal fanaticism, among his followers. He does this, as was the case with the late Ayatollah Khomeini's "fatwa" (or "hit") against Rushdie, by promising immediate eternal life to those who kill others for Allah, or who take on suicide-missions, because they are doing a personal favor for Allah. These bomb carriers are usually mindless, fanatics, who, in their unquestioning ignorance, will do anything for their caliph; much like the Japanese, suicide-pilots in World War II. These individuals constitute most terrorists, and the terrorist mentality.

Some major motivations cause the caliphs and imams to maintain the status quo; never allowing any democratic ideals to be discussed. First of all, they are fabulously, and incomprehensibly rich. Secondly, they have vast harems, consisting of some of the worlds most beautiful girls and women. These could not last in a democracy, because it stresses individual liberties and responsibilities. In these authoritarian states, ruled by the caliph or imam, the only ideal is submission to the will and wants of the imam, or other rich rulers. Thirdly, all of the wealth is in the hands of a very select few; this would not hold true in a democracy; and fourthly, though there are other reasons, these few, elite men control most of the world's oil reserves; and that means world-wide power. Anyone possessing such power, is highly unlikely to give it up.

In her book, "Islam and Democracy: Fear of the Modern World," Fatima Mernissi identifies at least seven fears which the Islamic world have. These are: (1) Fear of the Foreign West; (2) Fear of the Imam; (3) Fear of Democracy; (4) Fear of Freedom of Thought; (5) Fear of Individualism; (6) Fear of the Past; and (7) Fear of the Present. It was particular noteworthy to me that most of the fears highlighted here are the same fears most white racists in America, past and present, have had concerning black Americans. Two of the most prominent in both cases concerns the fear of losing control of their economic possessions and control over their women. These subtle concerns are becoming more and more evident to me, the more I study the cultures of both groups.

Given these sets of circumstances, I doubt very seriously whether there will ever be lasting peace in the Middle East, in the United States of America, or anywhere else around the world.

In contrast the criticisms directed at Islam and Christianity, Christianity stands out as being tough enough to take it. Christianity has been scrutinized and attacked for centuries, yet it has remained firmly intact. Why? Because it is built on a rock: the precious blood of Jesus Christ. I believe that when all others religions and creeds have fallen and crumbled under the tests and scrutinize of a hypercritical world, the Christian faith will be found intact, as strong as ever. For as the noted philosopher, William Cullen Bryant has stated:

> I believe that truth crushed to earth,
> Will rise again.

Jesus, who was crushed to the ground, being crucified and buried, did rise from an earthly grave. He had declared that:

> I am the way, the TRUTH, and the life.

The information gathered concerning the prophet Muhammed came from the Hadith, which is regarded as his teachings and sayings. Any person who is truly as seeker of knowledge and wisdom, could easily research these claims at their local library. I would definitely advise a "personal, and private search," in that putting such queries directed to almost every leader and teacher in either the Nation of Islam, or traditional Islam, would most likely draw the ire, and possibly swift punishment to themselves for ever raising the question. On the other hand, you can, and your are encouraged, to ask any question concerning the Christian faith, and of Jesus Christ, on any issue in which you need further understanding. Biblical Christianity is very positive and is revealed in an atmosphere of certainty and confidence. It was Jesus, Himself, who said:

> Ask, and it shall be given you; seek, and ye shall find; knock, and it shall be opened unto you: For every one that asketh receiveth; and he that seeketh findeth; and to him that knocketh it shall be opened (Matthew 7:7-8, KJV).

Therefore, friends, you can see that the true Christian religion, as revealed in the Bible, the Word of God, is fully open to inquiry. Most true teachers and preachers of the Gospel, would not be offended in an inquiring mind trying to discover truth. I challenge any reader to pray to God, and inquire of Him, as to the person and nature of Jesus Christ. And, since, even the Islamic faith gives recognition to the earthly person of Jesus, then certainly God will not object to a truth seeker praying for further revelation concerning who Jesus is. If God is a God of Truth, then certainly God will reveal to every seeker, just who Jesus is. Are you willing to take the challenge?

CHAPTER ELEVEN

FARRAKHAN AND THE NATION OF ISLAM

According to Newsweek Magazine, Louis Farrakhan, who was born Louis Eugene Walcott, in the Bronx, NY, in 1933, was a fairly successful calypso singer and dancer before joining the Nation. In his early years in the Nation, he began to gain influence in the Nation after he wrote, staged and starred in a play called "The Trial," which decried white racism. He also wrote a song for the play called "The White Man's Heaven Is the Black Man's Hell," which later became a Nation of Islam calypso anthem. He later distinguished himself early on as a man to be reckoned with, through his actions and influences, in dealing with Malcolm X after he made the fatal mistake of, publicly, making uncomplimentary remarks about Elijah Muhammad and the Nation of Islam. That issue of Newsweek reported that:

> Farrakhan also rose by being willing to viciously condemn anyone who dared challenge the prerogatives of the Nation. When Malcolm X renounced the Nation's racist ideology, Farrakhan declared him to be marked for "death." Malcolm was assassinated soon thereafter. There is no evidence that Farrakhan was connected to the killings, but he's admitted to helping create the "atmosphere" that led to the murder. [42]

Mr. Farrakhan since that time has proven himself an expert at creating "atmospheres" of various sorts, most of which are highly controversial. He has created an atmosphere of pseudo-compatibility of the theologies of Christianity and the Nation of Islam. Unlike Walleye D. Fad, founder of the Nation of Islam, and Fard's successor, Elijah Muhammad, who condemned the Bible, Farrakhan has won many followers by quoting carefully selected Biblical texts from the New Testament, and from the words of Jesus Christ. No doubt, when speaking to Christian audiences, Mr. Farrakhan does all he can to soften his image, appearing even to be a friend of Christ, instead of anti-Christ, which he most certainly is, as revealed by his own publicized views of Christ and Christianity. His purpose seems ultimately geared toward producing an increased following to make up for the dwindling numbers in the Nation of Islam.

Robert Morey sums it up in these words:

Elijah Muhammad . . . warned his followers that the Bible was pure "poison" because it had been corrupted by the white man . . . He went so far as to call the Bible a "graveyard of the black man," because it was used by white people to keep black people down.

Farrakhan, however, holds up the Bible as the Word of God and quotes from it far more times that he quotes from the Quran." **43**

The grand deception is revealed in his own words. In the Newsweek interview, the observer states that:

In place of a wedding band, Farrakhan wears a giant gold ring emblazoned with 40 diamonds that form a silhouette of Elijah Muhammad, As the pope is wedded to Christ, Farrakhan says, "I am wedded to this man whom I believe is the Messiah." Pointing to the ring, he notes another detail — "a little tiny diamond where Mr. Mohammed's heart would be. I think that little, little bitty diamond represents Farrakhan."

If indeed Mr. Farrakhan believes that Elijah Muhammad was the Messiah, sent from Allah to reveal truth (a recognition which Farrakhan seems to make for himself, now); and if Elijah Muhammad had such a heinous view of the Bible, then how can Farrakhan now accept the Bible as the Word of God, while still claiming to revere Elijah Muhammad? It is my personal belief that his whole act is self-serving; designed to deceive black Christians, giving the outward impression that he is friendly toward Jesus, the founder of Christianity. Sadly enough, far too many Christians are falling for his grand deception. It is truly the fulfillment of the prophetic words of Jesus Christ, for He said in Matthew 24:24,

For there shall arise false Christ's, and false prophets,
and shall show great signs and wonders;
insomuch that, if it were possible, they shall
deceive the very elect.

This charismatic and masterful orator, has transformed himself into what appears to be an angel of light. Having grown religiously in sociopolitical status in the black community in recent times, which heretofore had been decidedly Christian, he has many believing that he is "a changed man." An elderly lady at the facility where I work made this claim to me, and got real hostile when I suggested otherwise, for she had heard him mentioning the name of "Jesus" during his speech at "the Million Man March."

Mr. Farrakhan came to the forefront during a period of inactivity among black Christian churches; and the shameful in-fighting, mis-focused and poor leadership within our leading national Civil Rights organization, the NAACP, during the term of its ousted, former president, the Reverend Mr. Benjamin Chavis. Like an eagle, observing the valley below for victims to prey upon, Mr. Farrakhan saw the weakness in the national leadership, and was able to seize the opportunity in order to further establish and present himself as the most legitimate, issue-focused, stable moral leader, and spokesman for black people in our nation.

His cause was aided by the chaos and leadership void during the messy affairs in the NAACP national office. Additionally, he was further aided and abetted by the, ever-hungry-for-a-sordid-story, national news media, which fell right into his plans and became his national sounding-board. Mr. Farrakhan, not only became a man to be contended with politically, but was also able to broaden his arena socially and religiously, by cuddling up to the disgruntled, Mr. Chavis, who was still licking his wounds, but still had much residual influence in many places, even after his, highly publicized, ouster from the NAACP presidency. As these two made many public appearances together, Farrakhan gave the appearance of an old, experienced politician, greeting and shaking hands with all the right persons. He had put together a very smooth plan; for with the addition of Ben Chavis to his team, he was able to shore up some weak areas in his program and bolster his acceptance in many other, heretofore, unlikely places. With these preliminary things done, Louis Farrakhan went about working his plan. He went on to pull off the biggest surprise in his career, with the highly successful, Million Man March, in October 1994. Let's face it, the man has charisma and influence; and is not ever to be taken lightly, again.

Being fully aware that the news media's cameras were focused on him, Farrakhan was able to get the nations attention free of charge. On these occasions, he unleashed many "cut-them-to-the-bone" remarks; as well as his constant re-plays on the glaring racial ills in our nation. He also had a plan for winning support from black Christians. He presented a more gentle side to them, often quoting the sayings of Jesus, and familiar passages from the Holy Bible. He played the wisdom clad, fine social gentleman, by calling for black teens to turn from drugs and gang violence. Then, he turned to the older black males, calling them to responsibility toward their families and communities; reminding them of the tremendous problems in our own neighborhoods, all over the nation. Unlike but a few before him, he was able to make many, previously unconcerned, African American men, feel ashamed of how badly they had let their communities deteriorate. But, in addition to the problems in the "hood," he brought to the forefront, and made the nation face up to the shameful level of hidden racism; segregation; discrimination; poverty; and divisions, which still exist in America, and of course, he would never leave out that which exists between the black and white Christian churches.

Louis Farrakhan and various representatives of the Nation of Islam, and/or black Muslims, have long taught that Christianity is "the religion of the white man," in the words of the late Elijah Muhammed, it is, therefore, "the greatest enemy of black people in America." As with other leaders of the Nation of Islam, Mr. Farrakhan is quick-witted and well-informed concerning injustices in America and knows how to light fire to issues of racism and White injustices against Blacks, much as Malcolm X did in his earlier years, before abandoning his racist philosophies. However, Louis Farrakhan has taken it a few giant steps higher by laying claims to having been endowed with a personal touch of divinity to bolster his claims of authority to speak for God.

FARRAKHAN, THE MESSIAH?

Robert Morey writes that "in the 1991 "Savior's Day" celebration, Louis Farrakhan was introduced as the fulfillment of Isaiah 9:6-8. He was proclaimed as the "child who would be born" and the "son who would be given" because he was "Wonderful, Counselor, the Mighty God, the Prince of peace," etc.! Louis Farrakhan has even declared that his "god," called Allah, has sent him to save black people from white folks, whom he identifies as devils. Coincidentally, he and other representatives of "the Nation" state that white people were created by the Black god, Yakub, from his darker side, therefore, making whites products of created evil. Such nonsense pervades much of the doctrinal statements of this misguided bunch.

These aggressive invaders have publicly declare no love for Jesus

Christ, Who is recognized as God Incarnate by Christians. It was also stated at that 1991 "Savior's Day" celebration that Farrakhan healed the sick and made the blind to see, claims previously attributed to the late Elijah Muhammed. It was implied clearly that Farrakhan was now "God manifested in the flesh." [44]

I was astonished at claims he made concerning himself during several video-taped sermon excerpts which were played on the 700 Club television program, on March 6, 1996. He comes on like a fiery, spirit-filled Bible-believing preacher, but his message is to the contrary. In one sermon he meticulously explained the difference between what he called the "historical" Jesus, and the "real" Jesus. He said that the "historical" Jesus born 2,000 years ago was merely a figure or type of the "real" Jesus to come. He said that the "historical" Jesus was born in Bethlehem, but the "real" Jesus was born in Sandersville, Georgia. His reference was to the birth place of the late Elijah Muhammad (born Elijah Poole), whom he and other black Muslims, in times past, have claimed to be the Christ and the Savior! [45]

In another sermon he correlated the prophecy of the coming again of the prophet Elijah and the coming of Jesus. He very passionately told his audience that these two prophetic persons, Elijah and Jesus, were one and the same, which by the way is a gross error and the farthest thing from the truth). With great hand motion, he continued his fiery delivery. He merged his two index fingers into a parallel, indicating the "sameness" or "oneness," of the two; then he made the startling statement that HE was "the prophet Elijah which was to come, who is now COME!" The man was proclaiming himself to be Christ the Savior!!! His mostly Nation of Islam audience seemed spellbound. And given "the Nation's" strict code of allegiance to their self-proclaimed, "Messiah," none would ever dare question his remarks or his theology, less they too face the fate of Malcom X and others who have dared to defy their leaders.

It is obvious that the majority of Christians which have flocked to this man have no idea of his claims to divinity. For a Christian to have knowledge of such claims and still follow him would be apostasy of the worst kind. Mr. Farrakhan has carefully kept these type remarks "in-house," among Nation of Islam followers for the most part; apparently in an attempt not to startle those Christians, or offspring of Christian homes, who are leaning toward, or sympathetic to, his teachings. He knows that as long as he keeps his rhetoric based upon "us" against "them," or blacks against whites, he knows that he has a hot issue and some ready-to-hear audiences.

He is truly a master of disguise when it comes to keeping secret his true person and purpose. An article in the October 30, 1995, issue of Newsweek, states that "Louis Farrakhan has always been a man of many faces. Now the calypso singer turned separatist wants to move into the mainstream of American politics. Even blacks are divided about his appeal — but they're listening." [46] Furthermore, when we consider the success of his Million March Man March, in October and the recent $1 BILLION pledged to him from one of the chief sponsors of international terrorism, Col. Kadhaffi of Libya, we begin to see more clearly the danger and threat to national security, as well as what his ultimate agenda really is. Incidentally, Col. Khadaffi's gift was for the purpose of promoting "Islamic concerns" in the United States. In light of these things it would seem unwise to buy into Farrakhan's rhetoric that his ultimate goal is centered exclusively on the betterment of black people in America.

The Million Man March: It has been well established among black people that if you attach racial or cultural meaning and significance to an event and make it anti-white and limit it exclusively to blacks, it will go over well. All other events going on at the same time which can be labeled "for white folks," will be de-emphasized and abandoned by many blacks. Both Kwanzaa and the Million Man March were labeled as "black only" events. Judging by the enormous success of both, the vast number of black males who traveled from all over America to be in the Million Man March and the increasing number of African American's, in general, expressing a keen interest in Kwanzaa, while de-emphasizing Christmas, they are gaining territory and converts. However, on the Million Man March, even though it was attended by many very sincere and well-intentioned black males, Farrakhan was the greatest winner. As I have stated before, by charging $10 per person to participate in the gathering, from concession sales, and march related paraphernalia, any thinking person can see that Millions of dollars could have been collected!!! Once again, I ask, where did all that money go? Have you heard of any major contributions to our financially strapped and floundering, black colleges? Have you heard of any major contributions from this group to other black institutions and causes since this event? Enough said.

Any clear-headed evaluation of the entire tone and events of the Million Man March will surely reveal that this was more than a day of reconciliation for black men in America. I have talked about the economic brilliance of the man, and now for the spiritual implications. Any time a religious man from another religion is able to bring people to a meeting at the command of his god; and then have those people bow down to his god, and lead them into chants and a traditional prayer within his religion (the Islamic "Evening Prayer"), that religious man has successfully led the people into the worship of his god. It is so because the people have bowed down and acquiesced to his god's "call to worship." Farrakhan's "call to worship" was much like the one faced by the Hebrew boys who were called to bow down and worship the "god" of the Babylonians, unlike those "brothers" in Washington, DC, the Hebrew boys refused to bow down to another god. [47]

The Nation of Islam has long gone on record as denying that Jesus Christ was the Messiah, as the Bible claims. It denies that He is the Son of God; as well as deny His resurrection from the dead. In that these beliefs have been public knowledge for many years, it would seem that most Christians would know this by now. However, as incredible as it might seem, given the divergent and incompatible theologies of Christianity and the Nation of Islam, through his suave tactics, many of those who are now following him, claim to be Christian!

Today Farrakhan is considered "the most controversial black American leader" for his "dual message of self-help and hate. The message of hate predominate[s]." [48] He obviously has a dual purpose in his proselytizing. He is doing all he can to get all African Americans to abandon the Christian faith and to withdraw from the American way of life, as ways of fighting American racism.

To many black Christians, Louis Farrakhan might seem like a close friend when we consider the hate-filled acts of many white racists. Today we see a resurgence of racist Whites burning Black Christian churches; and only a few of our White Christian comrades ever open their mouths against it, to any degree of significance. Are we expecting too much of them? Maybe so, but many of these same individuals can be read in books, heard on radio, and seen of television espousing the teachings of James, the Lord's brother, which says that "faith without works is dead," while collecting large donations to show our concern for the oppressed in other lands. And there is nothing wrong with that; however, such inconsistencies only add credibility to those anti-Christian, who highlight the contradictory nature of the church's message of "love thy neighbor as thyself," when we fail to love right next door. This is why people like Louis Farrakhan have a field day in highlighting the contradictions and prejudices within Christianity, itself.

Let it be known clearly, that Louis Farrakhan is now waging a major battle for the souls of black people's allegiance, and to corner this part of the Western world for unfriendly Islamic concerns. However, he is not alone, for there are others like him, who are using more mild-mannered strategies in the battle for the souls of black folk. The celebration of Christmas and the reunion of African American families which have traditionally been associated with the Christmas holidays, is under serious attack. This is coming in a very subtle manner as more and more blacks are migrating to the celebration of Kwanzaa, the holiday created by Ron Karenga. The elaborate preparations outlined for the holiday begins a week before Christmas; then the holiday extends from December 26th through January 2nd. It doesn't take a genius to figure out that the Christmas holidays are being swallowed up in these cultural celebrations.

Those familiar with the Holy Bible will soon recognize the Biblical quote presented in the Introduction, as that of the Apostle Paul. Although Paul's answer to his own question declared that "nothing ... shall be able to separate us from the love of God, which is in Christ Jesus our Lord," there is now some separation going on among black people in America. There is a diabolical force of evil which has penetrated the very core of the African American Christian Community threatening to rip many from the Christian faith, so dear to our fathers and mothers, much like an aborted fetus is ripped from the lifeline connecting him/her to the life-giving mother. My hope is that well-intended and good hearted Christians, taken unawares; or caught up in the passion of finally seeing the brothers do something positive together, will also recognize the dangers inherent in actions which cross over into the spiritual realm. And although it does not have to be, the true fact of the matter is that this is a spiritual battle being fought in invisible realms, yet being played out in human characters on earth. [50]

136

CHAPTER TWELVE

THE HYPE SURROUNDING KWANZAA

One thing which I think I should say at the outset is this: Ron Karenga had a very great idea, but he polluted it by attempting to use it to overshadow Christmas in the life of African American Christians. Consequently, Kwanzaa can be grouped along with Mr. Farrakhan's attempts to sway black Americans toward his pseudo-Islamic faith. This challenge to Christmas came with the sudden appearance of Karenga's curious holiday, which he called "Kwanzaa." He claimed that it is a harvest festival; but who ever heard of having a "harvest festival" in the dead of winter? This is an insult to the intelligence of any objectively minded African-American, as well as, to that of our forefathers. While our African ancestors embraced the highest of moral and social principles, never was such a holiday celebrated in the motherland, in any way, shape, form or fashion. He should have been honest and courageous enough to call it what it really is, "The Anti-Christmas Festival."

Some persons who have an ax to grind concerning the Christian celebration of Christ's Birth, on Christmas, have argued that Christmas originated as a pagan festival. This, however, is simply a misstatement of the facts surrounding the choosing of December 25 as the day for observing the birth of Jesus Christ. The Evangelical Dictionary of Theology states that,

> The Scriptures do not reveal the exact date of Christ's birth, and the earliest Christians had no fixed time for observing it. . . December 25 eventually became the officially recognized date for Christmas because it coincided with the pagan festivals celebrating Saturnalia and the winter solstice. The church thereby offered the people a Christian alternative to the pagan festivities and eventually reinterpreted many of their symbols and actions in ways acceptable to Christian faith and

practice. For example, Jesus Christ was presented as the Sun of Righteousness (Mal. 4:2) replacing the sun god, Sol Invictus. As Christianity spread throughout Europe, it assimilated into its observances many customs of the pagan winter festivals such as holly, mistletoe, the Christmas tree, and log fires. At the same time new Christmas customs such as the nativity crib and the singing of carols were introduced by Christians. [51]

Therefore, the open-minded reader can see that Christmas was not started as a pagan festival, but as a day for commemorating the birth of Jesus Christ. The December 25th date was simply chosen in response to a great error which was drawing Christians into its satanic tentacles. Christianity has also responded in like manner to the pagan, satanic festival of Halloween, with All Saints Day. There are some Christians who see no harm in this festival, claiming it to be simply a fun-filled day for children; while others see the subtle work of Satan poisoning the minds of children with this witchcraft.

My point is that most informed Christians are well aware of the origins of their holidays; and I believe that most are intelligent enough to realize that all humans, including Christians, possess the tendency to pollute and/or add to many good ideas, in order to appease their fleshly whims. However, this untoward tendency does not, by any means, negate the original good intentions of the originators of the idea. Just as some self-serving, racists, attempting to protect the institution of American slavery and prevent blacks for voting, by polluted the US Constitution with ungodly amendments which declared each black man less than a full man, therefore, rendering him unable to cast a full vote. Does this mean that the entire Constitution should be dismantled because a few evil men polluted it? I should think not; and feel certain that the majority of the readers would agree with me. The correct and most logical procedure, is to implement those measures which fix that which is broken, and not "throw out the baby with the bath water," so to speak.

The critics and attackers of Christmas use ever imaginable trick in the book to win a place in the hearts of black Americans. Unfortunately, sometimes the deceivers do win. Our job as Christians is to make sure that we don't go to sleep on the job, or become so unduly deceived by their tactics, that we allow them to gain full advantage and gain an entrance into our own hearts, nor those around us. In spite of our best efforts, many are yet being deceived. Nothing better illustrates this than the story of the

Trojan Horse.

THE TROJAN HORSE COMES TO BLACK AMERICA:

The classical Greek legend, concerning the "The Trojan Horse," is one of my favorite stories of strategic warfare. It tells how the Greek army, when it could not penetrate the defenses of the city of Troy, devised an ingenious plan to get into the city. They built a huge, hollow wooden horse with wheels and filled it with Greek soldiers. It was left at the gates of Troy, like a giant gift. That night, after the people of Troy, brought it into their city, the soldiers came out and opened the gates to the Greek army, which destroyed the city and many of its inhabitants. It happened because of the gullibility and lack of perception by the people of Troy. They were easily deceived because the Greek army knew what touched their "hot button." Ron Karenga knew what touched the souls and "hot buttons" of African Americans, during those days.

In my opinion (don't get angry yet; please, hear me out), the Kwanzaa holiday, is just another Trojan Horse. It was conceived and constructed in the mind of Ron Karenga, during the turbulent years of the 1960's. When he rolled it out in front of a racially embattled black America, as a strictly black event, it was a source of pride. The people were reluctant to accept it at first, however, over the years more and more of them have brought it into their lives and made it a part of their existence. Now, greedy, white businesses in America, seeing another opportunity to exploit black people, are now promoting it as the holiday of black folks. I have already heard these distinctions being offered on one television talk show: "the Jews have their Hanukkah; the whites have their Christmas; and the blacks have their Kwanzaa!" It will not take too long before the idea is owned by more and more black people. The meaning and purpose of Christmas will be further neglected, as black people desperately seek to own something that's uniquely their own. But for the American business community, which subverts and perverts all, in pursuit of the almighty dollar, Kwanzaa simply means a new multimillion dollar, money-maker. The makers of this type paraphernalia have already begun flooding white-owned department stores, with Kwanzaa dolls, made in China! These items were quickly bought up by eager black shoppers, all too proud to own something "black." Oh, if we would only stop to consider the source before committing ourselves to things just because they are considered a black thing.

Now concerning the principles embodied in "Kwanzaa" holiday, Dr.

Karenga, incorporated seven of them which are highly desirable, being both morally and culturally focused, which is fine and dandy. Yet, I can find none which can supersede God's free gift of love offered to us in the sacrifice of His own Son's life, to reconcile for the sins of us all. Nor can his seven principles surpass Jesus' own mandated behavioral principles for His true disciples, found in John 15:12-13:

> "Love one another as I have love you.
> Greater love hath no man than this,
> than to lay down one's life for his
> friends."

Love is still the highest principle among humans, among every race and nation. Although the practice of love among some Christians can be called into question, none can question the intent in God's unadulterated message. The love which the Bible speaks of is that active love which comes from God the Father through our Lord and Savior Jesus Christ. God loved with such intensity that He was willing to, and did, give His only begotten Son to die for the sins of the world. And to know the true and living God, is the beginning of that wisdom which leads to everlasting life.

In all fairness to Mr. Karenga, we must understand that the holiday he fostered, was created in the bitter and frustrating years of the '60s. Many younger Black people, if they were not strongly rooted and grounded in the Christian faith, were easily drawn away to other, seemingly, more humane religious faiths. After all, the whole nation and the world, had not seen very much love displayed by many White Christian leaders and church bodies. The only impressionable things which they had seen were mostly hostilities and wide-spread hatred for fellow human beings, who happened to be black; from a white dominated nation.

Through television we witnessed the bombing of Black churches, one in which 5 little Black girls were killed in Birmingham, Alabama; the repeated denial of entry of a Black minister to a White "Christian" church in Georgia, and his unexplained and questionable death several months later; the assassinations of President Kennedy, Dr. Martin Luther King, Jr., Senator Bobby Kennedy, Malcolm X, and a host of Civil Rights workers; the open beatings and police dog attacks on marchers, and other atrocities. The White Christian churches rarely spoke out against these atrocities, with any notable degree of intensity. Most never took any actions to educate their memberships as to the wrongs of racism, White supremacy, and segregation.

Mr. Karenga, in creating his holiday, saw the evils of a white, oppressive nation, and the, almost, total neglect of white Christianity in preaching and teaching against racism. He appeared to be trying to reach out and find something morally and culturally uplifting, with special meaning for Black people. He, thus, designed Kwanzaa to emphasize the celebration of a black cultural experience, borrowed or created from the motherland of all black experience, Africa. However, irregardless of how noble his intentions, we must not fail to see that there was no example for him to borrow from in the context and lunar events celebrated among our African foreparents. There was no harvest celebration in this period of the lunar year; for there was no laudable harvest in the middle of winter, that we know of. Therefore, we would have to conclude that Ron. Karenga definitely had a counter motive in mind, when he juxtaposed Kwanzaa, above and beyond, Christmas.

THE BEST DEFENSE AGAINST DECEPTION IS THE PROMOTION AND PRESERVATION OF OUR CHRISTIAN TRADITIONS:

As we know, Christmas is one of the most important religious holidays in the Western World. It was intended to celebrate the birth of Jesus Christ, the rejected Messiah of the Jews and the cherished Savior to those who believed in Him. Traditionally, the Christmas Holiday Season, has always been a time of celebration and renewal among black families, Christian and non-Christian. It was not only a time of celebration of the birth of Jesus, but one of the few times during the year, or years, when most of the family got together; many coming thousands of miles, from across the nation, and even from foreign lands around the world, if they were in the military.

These family "get togethers" during the Christmas Season, also included extended family members, such as god-mothers and god-fathers; uncles and aunts, not seen for many seasons; cousins; old class mates; and our concerned and friendly neighbors: many, who helped raise the neighborhood children, and who kept us "walking the straight and narrow" paths, when parents weren't around. And, by the way, it did "take the whole village," to raise us, the right way (as stated by First Lady Hillary Rodham Clinton, wife of President Bill Clinton). Mrs. Clinton was right on the mark with her assessment!

At the church, old acquaintances and memories were renewed. The whole "village" would gather for the annual Christmas Play, attended by Believers and non-Believers. The older folk never missed a time of watching nervous, sometimes crying little children, stammering and stuttering while giving their speeches, and remembering the old days when they had to get up and give theirs. Many recalled how this one or the other one "went completely blank;" or "ran out of the church;" or "said the wrong speech," and so forth. These were exciting times. After church, almost everybody could be heard saying, "Ya'll stop by the house before ya' go back." When you stopped by the many houses, there were many culinary delights: Sweet Potato Pies, 'Tater (sweet potato) Bread; bread puddings; ginger bread men and cookies; cracklins, and cracklin bread; chitterlings; greens; plain and hot-water corn bread; coconut cakes (which was my brother Charles' favorite); caramel cake (my brother James' favorite) and chocolate, my favorite. Then, there were the best tasting turkeys and hams; and home-made and home-smoked sausages, that smelled so good that "it met you outside the door" and almost drug you inside, says a former brother-in-law, Willie Brown, of Lakeland, Florida.

"Christmas Time" was a time of going to church and worshipping; as we remembered the birth of Christ. But it was also a time for refreshing memories. At night, the young children would sit on the floor between the older folks, and listen to the stories of how life was "back in the olden days," when they worked anywhere from $0.25 to $1.00 per day (all day)! When they would turn to stories about the precious memories of loved ones, "gone on to get their reward in heaven," sometimes tears would be hard to hold back. They talked about precious mothers and fathers, favorite uncles, aunts, grandmothers and great-grandmothers. Mu'Dear (my dear mother) would talk about what Papa used to tell them about dealing with foolish folk in their times; of the great exploits and wisdom of my great-grand-mother, Hettie, whom I remember so well; and took care of when she was very old, while just a little lad (she died at home, at the ripe old age of 97). I was there in the house when she breathed her last breath. I never will forget it: Mu'Dear jumped up from her bed and rushed to "Grand's" bed, when she heard her taking her last three breaths of life. With that done, my dear, angel of a great-grandmother slipped off into that great land of no return, where Job said "the wicked cease from troubling; and there the weary be at rest" (Job 3:17).

After the Christmas Play was over, or on the following day or so, many who were brave enough, would visit the family plots at the cemetery. My family would never failed to visit Grand's grave site; standing there frozen in the present, while our minds raced back in time to see her loving face and hear her voice. Then, silently, and watery-eyed, they would walk from one grave stone to another. Occasionally, I would ask a question or two about those who, like tired soldiers, had quit the battle of life and had gone on to get their reward. We were told of the hard life and hard times many of them had to endure because of racism and the resultant poverty. Many of the old songs spoke of their mournful hope; such as this one entitled "Soon-a Will Be Done,"

> *"Soon-a will be done a-with the troubles of the world . . . Goin*
> *'home to live with God."*
> *"No more weep-ing and a-wail-ing, No more weep-ing and a-wailing . . . "*
> *"I want t'meet my mother, I want t'meet my mother, . . . "*
> *"I want t'meet my Jesus, I want t'meet my Jesus, . . . I'm goin'*
> *home to live with God."*

As they stood around the grave sites with their arms folded; often with tears trickling down the strong faces of the men, and the ruby red cheeks of the women, somebody could be heard humming softly, one of the old songs of Zion. I felt that, even among tears and sorrow, I was among men and women of great strength and character. They would break the silence by assuring us that they knew that they were at home with the Lord Jesus Christ, for these all had died in faith. But every now and then they would come across one whom they said "never came to know the Lord." They'd say, "You know, he sat on "the mourner's bench" with us, and came back year after year, but he never came through" (meaning he never accepted Christ as his personal Savior). "The Mourner's Bench" was a front row pew where unsaved sinners sat, while seeking the Lord during Revival Meetings.

I was often glad to leave the cemetery, because there was always talk of giant rattlesnakes lurking in some brush pile or in some sunken grave. I know that it's true because I had to kill one with a 32-caliber revolver, I filled with "shot shells," while cleaning the grave site of a former in-law in Madison, Florida. Where I grew up, our culture was very rich, filled with memories of family and exciting things which we learned to cherish.

I have related all of the above in order to state that Christmas was a time of Black Family reunions and remembering family and family values. It was also a time when parents and loved ones got the chance to reinforce the teachings they had been given during their younger days. They would remind us of how strong and proud our foreparents were, even while facing the harsh realities of racial oppression, they remained dignified. They lived, and taught us to live, by the Golden Rule: "Do unto others as you would have them do unto you." They taught us to respect our elders, no matter what color they were. Never a boy, no matter how big and burly, would rise up against, even his mother, no less his daddy. I have heard my mother and many other mothers say to near grow fellows, "Boy, don't you dare talk back to me. You're getting too big for your britches; I've got a mind to cut you down a button-hole lower." The one being disciplined would look all sheepish, and broken down, while the rest of us would hide our big grins and crack our sides laughing at the big shot being put to shame and being "dressed down" by a frail, little woman; or being jacked-up by an irate dad or uncle.

In just a few generations back, in the South where I came from, there was no such thing as disrespect for elders!!! I don't know where Ron Karenga or Louis Farrakhan grew up, but I know that where I came from, our elders commanded, and got respect. I suspect that what has happened is that many people who came from good homes and cultural environments, went to the big city, and while chasing the bright lights, women, wine, reefers, heroin, and the fast life, forgot the values which their foreparents had taught them. Now Mr. Karenga and Mr. Farrakhan are trying to sell as "something new," the "old teachings" which most of us had all along, but abandoned. While I love my African heritage, I don't need anybody to import any values from anywhere else, other than the ones I received, as a little lad, at my home down in Greenwood, Florida; and at the Buckhorn Missionary Baptist Church, where I first found Christ, heard the gospel preached by our pastor, Rev. Blackshear, and learned Christian and cultural values!!!

I can say to Mr. Karenga, and to all others, that I know that the "local" values, I received in my village while growing up, did, and still does, work. Where I grew up, about the only time that a young man went to jail was for public drunkedness or and occasional fist fight, and even those were rare. However, every now and then some drunk would "pull out a switchblade knife," but most of the time it was broken up by some respected person, who wasn't afraid, but considered it a duty, to get involved and stop the foolish behavior.

I can say to Mr. Karenga, Farrakhan, and others, that in my home, my folks followed Christ, who was the leader and the instigator of culture. It was from the teachings of Christ that I learned how to appreciate and apply both Christian and black cultural values. While we faced racism and many other difficult life conditions, we faced them with dignity; and we made it! From a little high school which typically graduated 40 to 60 people (in my class were 47 graduates), there have arisen nurses; doctors; a pharmacist; business owners; teachers; distinguished military men; public health officials; principals; coaches; preachers; professors and deans at major universities; Doctors of Philosophy in various subjects; and lawyers; just to name a few.

I refuse to allow Mr. Karenga or Mr. Farrakhan, and their followers to tell me that Christianity and our rich, local, cultural values and heritage have no meaning. This seems to be the idea projected by Ron Karenga's imported, but most likely, self-made holiday, called Kwanzaa; as well as Louis Farrakhan's false teachings concerning the religious heritage of our ancestors. I say, as those in the past have said so well, "the proof of the pudding is in the taste." The old Christian ladies and gentlemen, in my village, and similar villages all across America, raised many generations of well-behaved, un-jailed, un-doped, un-hating; un-welfared; hard-working, Bible-believing youngster, with nothing but their faith, their love, their hope, the Holy Bible, learned words of wisdom, leather straps and peach switches for discipline, and a determination that we would live orderly and decently among young and old in the village.

Our foreparents did not blame Christianity, nor "every" white person, for the perversions perpetrated by the ungodly living among us; and neither should we. Just as it is wrong for white, and other racists, which have included a recent Japanese Prime Minister, to place the blame for all of the ills and problems of our nation on the backs of black Americans, it is equally as wrong to accuse all white people of being racists. There are good and bad people among every group. Jesus indicated that this is a universal problem; for there are tares (weeds) among the good wheat (Matthew 13:26); and goats among the sheep (Matthew 25:32). The wise farmer, remembering the success he has had, certainly will not burn up the whole wheat field, nor kill off his whole herd in an irrational attempt to get rid of the few bad ones, living among the good ones. Life is an assortment of good and evil in every camp.

CHAPTER THIRTEEN

THE GATHERING OF VULTURES IN A FALLEN COMMUNITY

"For wheresoever the carcass is, there will the eagles be gathered together."

Matthew 24:28

The word "eagles" in the biblical text could be rendered "vultures," or "eagles." Both definitions would work, for in desperate times, even the noble eagle will feed on fallen prey, or "road kill." With this clarification, the implication is clear: In nature, whenever an animal is observed to be in a weakened condition, of if it falls to the ground, vultures and/or eagles soon gather to consume their carcass. In the spiritual realm, the spirit of anti-Christ feeds upon those who have fallen spiritually. The Apostle Paul warned the Thessalonians that "where there is spiritual corruption judgment will follow. The world will have become the domain of Satan's man, the Antichrist, the lawless one (2 Thes. 2:8), and many people will have been corrupted by false prophets (Matt. 24:24)." [52] In my estimation, one of the greatest false prophets to threaten the Black Christian church in recent times has been Louis Farrakhan. This man, asides from pointing out the ills of racism, fits perfectly the description of such an individual. He claims to be savior of the black Americans; and he boldly claims that he has come in the form of the prophet Elijah, as well as the Christ (see Chapter 5), in order to save us.

The Greek word "pseudoprophetes," describes those who claim to bring true messages from God, but they are corrupt inside and are simply deceiving the people. Jesus said these deceivers "come to you in sheep's clothing, but inwardly they are ravening wolves" (Matt. 7:15). One commentator has stated that "These false prophets are not merely wicked at heart and opposed to the truth, but they wish to injure you, and that for their own gain." [53] Mr. Farrakhan is a powerful man, who is seeking universal recognition as the key spokesman for Black Americans through religious and political means. His major contributions have been to antagonize those sincere folk who have been some of our chief political allies, including many sincere Jewish brothers; and to attack the Christian faith.

In almost every arena, false prophets and teachers are able to get a hearing and claim a following when the church is vacillating, uncommitted, or ineffective in fulfilling its role in the community. As we look at the accomplishments of the church in this post-Civil Rights era, after displaying such phenomenal courage, faith, growth and strength during the Civil Rights Struggle, we can only conclude that there now exists a great vacuum when it comes to strong leadership. The black Church in America seems to be without direction, strong leadership, and a vision for the future, therefore, the church has failed when it comes to reaching and leading the masses. Whenever a religion has failed an oppressed people, the oppressed is open to any who comes along offering what seems like relief and hope.

The African-American community, in general, is in a very bad condition. In so many ways it resembles the broken down condition of Jerusalem during the Babylonian Exile, in that Old Testament story, found in the Book of Nehemiah. Nehemiah was one of the living in Babylon, however, he had risen to the honored position of cup-bearer to the King of Babylon. This is how he describes what was relayed to him:

"The remnant that are left of the Captivity, there in the Province are in great affliction and reproach: the wall of Jerusalem also is broken down, and the gates thereof are burned with fire" (Nehemiah 1:4a).

Nehemiah went on to say:

"When I heard these words . . . I sat down and wept and mourned certain days, and fasted, and prayed before the God of heaven . . . and prayed, I pray thee thy servant this day, and grant him mercy in the sight of this, man. For I was the king's cupbearer" (Nehemiah 1:4b).

There are just too many similarities between the conditions in the time of Nehemiah, and in our conditions now, to be just coincidental. I believe that our histories overlap in the will of God; and therefore, in a limited, but significant way, we, like Israel of old, can find relief through the same plan outlined by Nehemiah.

As we look around the African American community, we find it broken down in many ways. Abandoned and dilapidated homes and many buildings which once housed churches are being used as "crack houses." Many are crying out for help. Seniors on social security and young mothers on welfare can't feel safe when they get their checks or food stamps. There is lawlessness; drug abuse, and the associated evils which it produces. It was bad enough with marijuana, alcohol abuse, and heroin; but then enters that monstrous phenomenon called "crack cocaine." Regular cocaine was too expensive, therefore, it seems that there was an organized effort to make a less expensive version, readily available to black people; which many claim that this was the primary reason it was developed. Since it's so cheap, almost anyone can afford it. And since it's so highly addictive, almost everyone who tries it is hopelessly trapped under its intoxicating spell.

Crack cocaine is known to take complete control of the users total person. As a matter of fact, evidence seems to indicate that the user of this "monster drug," becomes less of a person and more of an automaton. makes once sane and upstanding boys and girls rob, and, sometimes, even seriously injure or kill their moms, dads, sisters, brothers, aunts, and uncles; and anybody else they spy out with something with value to cop and hock. With all of this going on, and law enforcement often seeming to turn its head; or worse yet, profiting from the carnage in the "hood," it's no wonder that there is a sense of hopeless despair in many of our black communities.

The US Government sent well armed and technologically advanced troops to the Panama Canal Zone, in order to arrest General Noriega. We shot up and bombed the city until we found him and brought him back. We also sent some of the most sophisticated aircraft, weaponry and ground forces into the Middle East to take care of the problem with Saddam Hussein, precisely bombing marked out targets in Baghdad. It seems that we have a pattern of going around the globe to solve other peoples problems; yet there is more death and carnage in our own streets that threaten the safety of our own citizens, yet we are constantly being told that we are losing the war on drugs. It is not really a loss, but it seems more like a give-away. All the reports seem to indicate that there is simply too much money being made by people in key positions to ever allow the flow of these deadly chemicals to be stopped. The only way for black people to impact or stop it is through the strength of Jesus Christ in our lives and our own personal choices.

There are still many good people living in predominately black neighborhoods. Many find themselves trapped, unable, or unwilling to leave, for various reasons. These individuals want safety, peace and order in their neighborhoods like other people. Many have invested their entire lives in the old neighborhoods where they grew up; and where their families had their roots. They don't want to leave the street where they used to meet their fathers and mothers coming home from work; or where most of their childhood memories were formed. Yet, many of they live in fear; the "hood" is becoming run down; and young criminal elements often terrorize them and their neighbors. In spite of the different breed of inhabitants, who have long since abandoned the strong family and community values, which earlier residents shared, many still want to stay put, with the continuing hope that things will change for the better. Therefore, when anyone who promises to bring control and order to their doorsteps is often welcomed with open arms. Theological and religious arguments are thrown to the wind, especially since many feel that these are out of touch with reality, while at the same time they're being told that Christianity is more an enemy, rather that a friend; and that it has not helped solved the real problems they face anyway.

In some ways, this prevailing atmosphere of mis-trust and apprehension concerning the church's ability, or lack of ability, to be an effective theocratic administrator of the will and plan of God, has been created by the churches themselves, which include their leaders. Many have been in some neighborhoods for decades, yet have done nothing significantly constructive which the community can point at and give credit to. And to further complicate and deteriorate matters, is the negative publicity surrounding many television evangelists, as well as community-based, preachers, who have been caught in the spotlight because of various types of misconduct. Then there are those white individuals who claim to be Christian, yet behave more like hate-filled racists, rather than members of the family of God. These situations have taken their toll in the black community, and the Christian world, at large.

The spiritual and emotional carnage caused by racism in America, has claimed many fatalities; some physical, some social, and some spiritual. Vultures have little trouble finding the carnage left behind. There have been countless numbers of young boys, who have no heroes other that dope dealers, continued to fill our graveyards. The pain and suffering has been wide-spread, that it has literally devastated the life and hope of many black communities. The turmoil and squalor left behind, has left many African-American open to spiritual corruption brought by false prophets; an ever increasing number of cults; and lying psychic pretenders.

Since many relate all of the evils of our society to white racism, they become easy targets for false prophets, offering them a united effort which will soon deliver them from their oppressor. And in America it is all too easy to find African-American males who have been victimized by the evils of racism. It is sad, but it's true, that, on a global scale, the Christian church has done little to do significant battle with this situation. Consequently, it is now facing very strong competition from the growing popularity of Louis Farrakhan, and the Nation of Islam.

Farrakhan and his organization have displayed the wisdom to target for proselytizing and helping the very group which the Christian church, and society in general, have neglected. Those who are rescued, and find new meaning and a sense of significant personhood, love him supremely; simply because he was the only one who cared. They feel that he alone cared enough to risk his life and reputation in order to save them. He rescued them from what is perceived as a highly sophisticated and well-structured system of genocide, designed to annihilate African American from American soil. It is such a simple plan, that we have missed it. Some of the greatest loyalties come from those who can say, "When I was in trouble, you were there for me." Louis Farrakhan has a loyal following because he was there for so many of them.

Many see Farrakhan as the one who foiled the plans of the great destroyer of black males in America: American racism. They see the neglect, the imprisonment of black males, and the infiltration of drugs into our communities, as being no different in its ultimate intent, than that of Adolf Hitler's planned annihilation of the Jews, during the Holocaust. However, unlike the salvation of the Jews, the nations of the world have not come together to form an alliance to protect the rights of this endangered group. As a matter of fact, it seems that many nations around the world are becoming participants in expatriating black people from their lands, on an international scale. One only has to follow the headlines in places like Berlin, and other places in Germany; England; Japan; and France.

In America, those young black men who don't kill off each other, are found in disproportionate numbers, populating our jails and prisons. A recent poll indicated that among African American males between the ages of 20 and 24 years, 1 out 3 are either in jail, awaiting trial, in prison, or on parole!!! In the October 30, 1995, issue of Newsweek magazine, Rev. Henry Lyons, President of the National Baptist Convention USA, Inc., is quoted as saying, "We've got a million black men in prison, and they're quickly becoming Muslims... And we're standing by idly doing nothing."

However, that was back in 1995. Given the current headlines concerning Rev. Lyons, himself, we find him battling charges of misappropriating convention funds, and allegations of misconduct with a convention employee. Like others, he deserves due process. While many wish him well, we wonder what will happen concerning his statement: "We're standing by doing nothing," while so many of our young men are being converted to the Nation of Islam. Satan is out to destroy every good leader; and the greater the leader, the greater the weapon of the devil. Let us pray for our leaders and for the survival of endangered black males.

In those few situations where black males have decided to get involved, becoming mentors, Big Brothers, and the like, there have been phenomenal success stories. I recently read of one neighborhood where successful black males really got involved, it resulted in a greater than 90% high school completion rate, and at least 90% of that group went on to college. This testifies of the desperate need for fathers and father-figures in the rearing of children. So many of our young people are born into "families" where there is no father present. Most of these children in single-parent homes have to suffer because many absent fathers refuse to support their mothers in the care of their children. In many cases, the only father-figures are the drug pushers, gangs, and other negative figures, who hang around them waiting for a victim. And in other cases, there are those who have bragging fathers, who talk of how many children they fathered, sounding more like the "studs" used by slave owners during Slavery to provide fresh workers, but many of them do very little to support their offspring.

In the film documentary, "Crisis in Black America," journalist Bill Moyers, interviewed one young African-American male, who, like a roving "baby-maker," had fathered several children by one young woman, but felt no compunction to marry her nor make any meaningful economic provisions for his offspring. However, it seemed rather doubtful in his current economic state that he would provide her and their offspring with any meaningful support. For not only was he penniless and unemployed at the time; he had been unemployed for a very long time and had virtually given up on looking for a job. Their uncontrolled desire for carnal satisfaction and self-gratification prevented them from seeing the long-range negative impacts from their irresponsible actions.

Psychologically, by fathering many children, this was a demonstration of his virility, which he substituted for his low self-esteem; his poor education, or lack of it; his inability to find and keep a steady job; and his lack of ability to be a man, in the traditional way, by being able to provide for his family. And having failed educationally, economically, and socially, by siring all of these babies, he seemed to feel that he finally was successful at something. This type of destructive behavior seems to be some of the cruel "left-overs" from slavery, which is kept alive by a constant need for the psychological-self to create a world where the individual can feel good about himself. While it would be less than honest to shift the blame for the irresponsible actions of many black Americans to others, each of us must face up to our part in creating these sordid conditions which have created these ills. None of us can completely escape blame, and therefore, responsibility for these conditions.

While we do not advocate an atmosphere of wholesale guilt, which can only cripple, white America must join hands with the African-American Christian church, in looking for ways to formulate a positive reconstruction of Dr. Martin Luther King, Jr.'s "Dream." We must all join together in honestly seeking ways to bring about lasting peace among the races. After all, if we can do it in Bosnia; and since we have done it in Japan, Germany, Great Britain, France, and in other far-away places; spending billions of dollars in the process, surely we can do it at home. The major hurdle which America must first overcome, however, is the issue of the color of our black skin. She has been quick to rebuild everywhere except where the people have been black. Another stark example is the thousands of black Haitians whom America has allowed to drown at sea rather than land on her soil; while at the same time we welcome Europeans by the boatloads, and even escorted and imported hundreds of thousands of Vietnamese to America after the Vietnam War; and then gave hundreds of millions of dollars to support them. I have nothing against any of these nationalities; they were simply people who needed help. This is the proper response which we should, likewise, extend to "all people" who need help; not to just a select few. My sole purpose is to point out the gross disparities of how black people from "Anywhere, World," are treated, when compared to other groups.

CHAPTER FOURTEEN

THE GROWING CONFLICT: CHRIST OR CULTURE?

Whether we will allow it or not, there is a growing conflict between cultural and spiritual loyalties in the African American community. The fact is that we live in a culturally oriented world order. These cultural orientations are often allowed to supersede, even those theological principles which define our religions, when it comes to accepting other racial and ethnic groups as equals. There are very few white people who are willing to accept, carte blanche, the "oneness," indeed, the equality of us all, in a literal sense. Men who have been known to argue vehemently for the inerrancy of the Holy Bible, find difficulty as it relates to praxis, that is, when it comes to the literal and practical sense of living what our creeds and declarations define as Christ-like actions! The ultimate challenge is to take to its logical conclusion, the declaration which Paul made in his address to the men of Athens on Mars' hill:

> *"God that made the world and all things therein . . . hath made of*
> *one blood all nations of men for to dwell on all the face of the earth*
> *. . . For in him we live, and move, and have our being"(Acts 17:22-28).*

This statement is just too hard for most Whites to accept, in the literal sense of the declaration. It is equally, if not more so, difficult for most Black's to believe that such an acceptance will ever be realized, literally; given their global, negative experiences with the white race and racism, both past and present. If you will check a variety of commentaries, you will find that Verse 26 of Acts Chapter 17, is probably one of the most skipped or glossed over verse in the New Testament. Thus, we have both a theologically and culturally conflicting dilemma.

SOURCE OF THE CONFLICT: GOD, OR MAN?

God's Word, the Bible, says that all people on the face of the earth are equal, which is the literal meaning of "made of one blood;" however, most white commentators, reluctantly deal with the literal sense of these words, even though they are stated clear and simple in the Bible. Many choose rather to spiritualize the meaning, and forget the literal sense. But if we are ever going to make true progress in living out God's intent for humanity, we must face these things honestly. The beginning of our solution to the problem, is to first of all bring our true selves to the table of resolution; realizing that most of us will bring that which has been stained either by our prejudices or our suspicions; both of which foster mistrust and dishonesty. If we begin with the truth, and endeavor to stick with it until the end, we shall conclude with a much closer semblance of the mind of God.

We must first acknowledge that God is not the author of our conflicts. He has declared the brotherhood and sisterhood of all humanity. Many whites still believe in the superiority of the white race. While the Bible indicates that the Israelites (descendants of Israel, formerly known as Jacob, cf. Genesis 32:28), were the original "chosen people" of God (Deuteronomy 7:6); many Whites, thinking along the lines of Hitler, seem to feel that they are the only chosen ones. Adolph Hitler called the German people "the master race." Elaine Pascoe observes that:

> Hitler believed that the Aryan race—basically, white people of northern European stock — was by nature superior to all other races and was destined to conquer and rule them. In his book Mein Kampf, he argued: "Everything that today we admire on this earth — science and art, technique and inventions—is only the creative product of a few peoples and perhaps originally of one race. On them now depends also the existence of this entire culture. If they perish, then the beauty of this earth sinks into the grave with them." His theories led him to vehement racial hatred and ultimately to genocide—the attempt to destroy an entire people, in this case, the Jews, and other "inferior races" of Europe. [54]

This distorted and wicked thinking of Adolph Hitler did not die along with him and Eva Braun, in the bunker at Berlin on April 30, 1945. Many of his distorted beliefs concerning white supremacy are being promulgated by a variety of white elitist and racial supremacists, to this very day.

However, we must never forget that God places, in opposition to every evil, those good men an women who are willing to lay down their lives for right. One such person in Germany, even during Hitler's reign of terror, who felt that for him his commitment to Jesus Christ overruled the cultural thinking of the leader of his nation. That man was Dietrich Bonhoeffer, who gave up his life fighting against the evil rule of Adolf Hitler. Bonhoeffer, though a Christian theologian, joined other German revolutionaries in a drastic attempt to help end Hitler's monstrous rule in Germany. It is said that he participated with other Germans in a plot on Hitler's life; for this Bonhoeffer would pay the ultimate price: His own life. John W. De Gruchy notes in his book "Bonhoeffer and South Africa," that,

> Bonhoeffer was executed by the Gestapo at Flossenburg on 9 April 1945, a week before the prison camp was liberated by Allied Forces. Today there is a tablet at Flossenburg that commemorates his death. It reads "Dietrich Bonhoeffer: a Witness to Jesus Christ among his brothers." Such a statement clearly implies that Bonhoeffer died the death of a Christian martyr.

It is quite evident that Dietrich Bonhoeffer felt that it was not God who was confused in His choice of who the "chosen people" were, but Adolf Hitler, one of the most wicked human beings, who ever lived.

THE COMPLICATED CULTURAL AND RELIGIOUS MILIEU:

Over the years, from slavery to the present, American racism has often raped, victimized, and brutalized many in the African-American community of equal opportunities and justice. This has created an environment of polarization and wholesale mistrust among many blacks, against all who represent the white racist system. All of those fanatical, extreme fundamentalist, cold-hearted, far left-winged, ultra-conservative, white Christians running around promoting the heartless "system," and labeling most poor Blacks as lazy, dishonest, and welfare cheats, only compound the problem. Many of these black victims of white racism, in turn look for any "savior," whose face is not white. Louis Farrakhan has been most happy to fill this role.

He has walked upon a field of human oppression, ready to harvest. This is true because most African-Americans feel culturally isolated and economically deprived in the only place they can really call home. While it is true that somewhere in the past 400 years their ancestors were brought from Africa, the only home that most have known has been America; which, incidentally, was built on the backs, blood, sweat, and tears of their black forefathers and mothers. Yet European, Asian, and White immigrants from South America, and even South Africa, can show up in this country and become overnight successes through special favors, which are often denied, or unavailable to Black American citizens, whose ancestors have lived here for centuries. This unfortunate situation has relegated many poor blacks to the status of economic refugees in their own country. After being exploited and victimized as a form of cheap labor, they are then blamed for their hapless situation. Such conditions have contributed to high unemployment, low literacy rates, and lack of self-esteem.

In order to propose a "quick-fix" for the problem, the welfare system was created by Congress, which compounded, rather than, fixed the problem. The abuse of this system probably has contributed more to the destruction of the traditional idea of the family than any other factor. Under this wicked system, the government replaced the father as the head of the family, or bread winner, with free goods. Before the back of this demoralizing system was broken, the damage had already been done. In that many of the young mothers, who raised babies using welfare as their chief support, were forbidden to have an adult male living with them, many young boys grew up without fathers and therefore, without positive affiliations with adult males. This group constitutes a large portion of the robbers, muggers, and gang members. These young minds are in desperate need of attention from responsible black men. The black church and its many organizations can play an important role in reaching this group.

In the past, it has been unfortunate, that it has been pagan or cultic religions which have responded to the emotional and spiritual needs of the disenfranchised among Black Americans. Jim Jones; David Karesh and the Branch Davidians; the Reverend Sun Moon and the Moonies; and other false prophets and religions have profited from this unfortunate set of circumstances. Now Louis Farrakhan, sensing a weakness in the leadership in the African-American Christian community, is seizing a ripe opportunity to harvest many who are in desperate need for somebody to lead and guide them through this storm.

CHAPTER FIFTEEN

AMERICAN RACISM: FERTILE GROUND FOR BLACK RACISM

Louis Farrakhan was partially right when he stated that: "The real evil in America . . . is called white supremacy." **56** This, indeed, has been a sad American saga for centuries. For a brief period stretching from the very late 1960s through the mid-1980's, the past years which had been clouded by the evil of blatant racism; gave way to tremendous progress. However, since the rise to power of the Republican Party, which, incidentally, is the Party which broke the back of slavery under the greatest Republican and the greatest President, Abraham Lincoln, there has been subsequent return to a racist agenda throughout our nation. I must quickly note that this has not been a strictly Republican agenda, but a joint effort, comprised of conservative Democrats, as well as Republicans.

As is noted in chemistry and physics, "for every action, there is an opposing reaction." When applied to the racial climate in our nation, we might say that with the rising tide of white racism, there is a counter-increase in attitudes of black racism and hatred. As Dr. King noted years ago, "a doctrine of black supremacy is as evil as the doctrine of white supremacy." The destructive power of racism is all too evident on the written and unwritten pages of American history. Everywhere you turn, we find where it has raised its ugly head. It has been through the shameful legacy of American racism that anti-Christian, charismatic, radical leaders such as Louis Farrakhan have gained a window of opportunity for planting his racist views and commentaries among a growing number of African Americans, and even within some Christian churches. Mr. Farrakhan has been effectively using race and racial injustice as unifying forces among African Americans to forge a way into the hearts of Christians, and some Christian ministers are allowing him free use of Christ's church to do this.

Admittedly, many cases of racial injustice still exist in our country, however, I cannot subscribe to giving the Farrakhan the "favor" of speaking from the Christian pulpit in order to spread his messages of hatred.

The history of racism on American shores, had much of its beginning with the ugly event of slavery near the very outset of this nation, and continuing with the shameful treatment of Native Americans (white European Christians tricked the Native Americans into selling Manhattan Island, New York, for about $24.00, then, beginning from the East Coast, took most of the rest of the new frontier through violence and bloodshed). After slaughtering thousands of Native Americans, and taking their land, the US Government, then put them on reservations, in unnatural settings for these open-range hunters. These depressing situations seems to be a major contributing factor to the high rates of alcoholism found on many reservations. As with their wide-spread participation in the immoral and dehumanizing system of African slave trading, history records the worst case scenarios of European greed and racial supremacy attitudes firmly planted in the New World. The pervasive power of American racism continues to dominate almost every aspect of our society today.

Politicians keep it alive with little catch words like "welfare cheats," "reverse racism," and by attacking "affirmative action programs," and "the illegality of minority set asides." I have as little use for young and healthy individuals, who sit at home collecting free money from working tax-payers, just as every white person in America does; whether they are black or white. However, statistics do show that the majority of the recipients of different types of welfare benefits are white. You would never know this by looking at the national and local news programs; because they always find a black or other minority when negative reporting on these issues are being done. But, it is true that blacks do make up a disproportionately large percentage of this group, when we look at it based on population percentages. However, in spite of these things, this is no reason to dismantle Affirmative Action and other corrective programs, which were designed to right the long-standing evils of discrimination in the past.

It is well-known in American history, that blacks, certain other ethnic minorities, and women, were discriminated upon either by law or by traditions and practices, in areas ranging from education to employment. These practices went on for several hundred years; while white men benefited in almost every way from preferential treatments. The Affirmative Action legislation in the early 1970s was instituted in order to create a fair and level playing field for all citizens. As early as 1978, when a white medical student, challenged the quota system in the famous University of California Regents vs. Bakke Case. Mr. Bakke won his case in the Supreme Court, thus setting the tide for future attacks on Affirmative Action. However, no thinking person can believe that in the 8 years since Affirmative Action had been in place, that several hundred years of discrimination had been reversed, and that African American had the same opportunities as whites. Today, Affirmative Action is still being attacked.

In the often childish political shenanigans of 1996, House Speaker Newt Gingrich and Presidential candidate Pat Buchanan kept the race issue alive, through their sometimes subtle, sometimes overt references to "give-away programs" directed to minorities, etc.. It seems as though, whenever there are high stakes in the political arena, most white candidates know that they can add momentum to a lackadaisical campaign by injecting issues laden with racial overtones. Why is it that it is only during the campaign seasons that we hear men and women promising to fix the welfare systems, and rid our streets of violent crimes, drug dealers, and youth violence. The truth of the matter is that these are ever-present problems three hundred and sixty five days a year, not just during election time. Politicians know that these issues keep the race problem alive, and to insure that the white electorate gets the picture, they even add pictures. Remember "the revolving door" campaign ad used by George Bush; with the addition of a picture of the black man identified in the ad, who, among other crimes, had committed a crime against a white woman, the ad didn't leave you to wonder about who they portrayed as the main criminal elements are in our society: mostly black males.

The race problem in America is a like the land mines left in the fields and roads of Vietnam and Bosnia; maiming and killing innocent victims who are simply trying to get through this life. The tremendous carnage left behind by this monstrous and shameful American preoccupation with White supremacy and racism, and the seemingly "silent consent" of the White Christian church, make it all too easy for false prophets and dangerous personalities to lead off and even "deceive the very elect" of God. [57] Although there has been much notable progress in our nation, American racism still exists, in spite of marches, church rhetoric, legislation, bloodshed and death.

This affliction has destroyed, and continues to destroy, the lives of many African Americans people. I was tremendously shocked after discovering the depth of hurt and bitterness it inflicted upon one of our most respected and noted African American poets, Langston Hughes. Listen to Mr. Hughes' forgotten or shunned poem called "Good-bye, Christ:"

Listen, Christ,
You did alright in your day, I reckon—
But that day's gone now.
They ghosted you up a swell story, too,
Called it Bible—
But it's dead now.
The popes and the preachers've
Made too much money from it.
They've sold you to too many.

Kings, generals, robbers, and killers—
Even to the Tzar and the Cossacks,
Even to Rockefeller's Church,
Even to THE SATURDAY EVENING POST.
You ain't no good no more.
They've pawned you
Till you've done wore out.

Goodbye,
Christ Jesus Lord God Jehova, ...

One can feel the bitterness in this great man's writings. Mr. Hughes lays bare his heart's feeling of hopeless despair; along with the dreadful pain of, what seems to him, a failed religious experience. Although Mr. Hughes says "Goodbye" to Christ, one wonders if it is really Christ, who has failed him? A cursory reading might leave that impression; however, such a reading would be superficial; for behind the disappointment he expresses in Christ, we actually see a man disgruntled with many, so-called religious men and women. He decries those who, under the pretense of Christianity, were self-serving looters of the unsuspecting, often looking, for what he called, "the Consecrated Dime." This latter reference has to do with a religious gentleman called Elder Becton, "The Dancing Evangelist," of Harlem fame, during the 1930's. It is reported that the flamboyant preacher had a following of over 200,000, and one of the most elegantly dressed men in the world. Becton is reported to have said, "I told the Lord before I started that I didn't come cheap ...." [58] Too many persons, such as this flamboyant black preacher and white racists Christians, have given Christ a bad rap.

On the one hand, white supremacy and racism is a real evil in America, while on the other hand, black racism is another hate-filled evil, which is just as deadly at destroying both human character and personality. General Colin Powell has warned that America must avoid the "swamp of racism," for it is just as bad "whether it comes from Minister Farrakhan or a Mark Fuhrman, it's the same thing." [59] The African-American community is being duped with this same bitterness, as Louis Farrakhan offers it a highly emotional charged blend of black racist, anti-Jewish, and anti-Christian rhetoric, while calling for a new black militancy, cultural pride and separatism. This whole thing is nothing more than a massive effort by Mr. Farrakhan and other disciples of the Nation of Islam to win converts, and support from the African-American population.

While Mr. Farrakhan uses concrete proof and evidence of White racism in America, much of his arguments, as he attempts to proselytize black sympathizers involves the inverse, negative reasoning which highlights the evil actions of some White people, American racism and Christianity (which his group regards as a "slave" religion), as the root causes of the oppressive conditions under which they live. The antithesis of these conditions, which they are quick to point out, is to be found in the racial unity offered under the umbrella of the Nation of Islam and their liberator god, Allah, and Louis Farrakhan, their "savior."

Sometimes their efforts have been subtle; sometimes overt. However, the most recent efforts have been highly overt. An example of the subtle efforts is the introduction of the "new" holiday called "Kwanzaa," strategically placed the day after Christmas and extending past New Year's Day to January 2nd: a brilliant plan by one brilliant man, Dr. Ron Karenga. When one thinks seriously about it, one must admit to the brilliance of his tactic, which we shall discuss later in the book. The overt actions which we referred to above have been spearheaded by the highly controversial and charismatic, chief minister of the Nation of Islam, Louis Farrakhan. Though, often steeped in controversy, Mr. Farrakhan, has found great success in feeding on the racial unrest, caused by real, as well as, perceived injustices suffered by African-Americans. He also sites the obvious poverty, economic exclusion, community neglect by government, illiteracy, selective, negative reporting by the news media, and other evils experienced by the African-American community, at-large. He has found this to be a fertile ground for planting the seeds of reverse racism, strife, and anti-Christian sentiment.

Mr. Farrakhan has scrupulously veiled his anti-Christian comments, by carefully wording his speeches so that they even appear tolerant and friendly toward Christianity. Some of his sermons sound very much like the preaching found in many Christian churches because of his many quotes from the New Testament and the words of Jesus. Consequently, in heretofore, unprecedented actions which would make our Christian forefathers turn over in their graves, many Christian pastors have opened their church doors, and most astonishingly, their pulpits, from which Jesus Christ is proclaimed as the Son of God, and Savior and Lord, to those who deny all of the above!!! Muslim, or Nation of Islam, ministers would NEVER permit a Christian pastor to grace their pulpits and talk about the grace of God in Christ!

Are these pastors saying that their God is too small, too slow, or too powerless to be able to bring about needed changes under the time curves which they have established? These and other questions, they must answer for themselves. However, let all who will hear, be aware that the Nation of Islam troops, under the brilliant and highly effective leadership of Mr. Farrakhan, have mounted a mass offensive to separate African-American Christians from their Christ!

WE ARE LIVING IN SCARY TIMES:

These are scary times for African American people, socially, politically, morally, and spiritually. Socially, because of the breakdown of many family units; escalating unemployment and poverty; a growing underclass of impoverished people, and a lack of sympathy from an unconcerned government run by radical extremists. Then there are the growing numbers of violent militia groups all around the country who openly defy and flaunt their hatred and disgust for our government, black people, and Jews. It is scary politically, because of the assault on the disenfranchised by a right-wing Republican and conservative Democratic movement that is sweeping across America, threatening to take away many hard fought for and costly gains during the Civil Rights era.

These are scary times morally because of a breakdown of values which in times past clearly defined what was right and wrong. These values are either missing or seem hopelessly corrupt because of bad or no teaching taking place in our homes. Many out of control youths are roaming the streets, the hallways of our schools, and our streets robbing, killing and maiming at will, with no sense of remorse or conscience. The American Civil Liberties Union and other ultra-liberal factions, while posting some worthwhile victories in the past, have almost destroyed all the moral fiber which has made America and African American people great. With its constant attack on religion and overemphasis on personal freedoms, there is hardly any place for parents or teachers to stand in raising and educating their children. Their aim seems to create a hedonistic society where every man does what is pleasing or "right in his own eyes". [60] Such was case during the Period of the Judges in Israel's history, a period marked by gross corruption and immorality.

It is scary because of the disillusionment with the Christian church because at the forefront of the aforementioned political establishment we find an ultra-conservative, incompassionate "so-called" Christian movement, the Moral Majority, and others like it, leading the charge in a frontal attack on minorities, the elderly, and the poor, in what they describe as their attempt to "take back America." Again, we find Newt Gingrich, Speaker of the House of Representatives, one of the main spokesperson for many of these radical, extremist groups. Then it seems that those on the ultra-right are finding greatest support among Whites in America, those with ties and sympathizers in white supremacist groups, which is alleged of some high profile figures such as Pat Buchanan.

It is scary because we are being challenged by black Muslims (Nation of Islam) and other militant blacks to abandon Christianity, and join their black nationalist hate groups. However, any astute and careful reader of the biblical record of the ancestral lineage of Jesus Christ will eventually declare that Jesus was the Universal God-Man. His ancestry covered many tribes and races of people. It appeared that God intended it so. Further research of New Testament history as recorded in the Book of Acts reveals that the Gospel went to African via a very studious and inquiring Ethiopian eunuch long before it went to many parts of Europe. [61]

CHAPTER SIXTEEN

THE PROBLEM OF UNDEFINED BLACK POWER FOR CHRISTIANS

One of the rallying cries of the 1960s among Black Americans was that of "Black Power." The cry was heard long and often. There was a sincere groping for a chance to be heard; a chance to belong; a chance to be regarded as having meaning and significance in the world. Too long had black people been ignored; too long had they lived in fear; too often they had been the victims of fear and incomprehensible violence by organized white mob action when they spoke up as men. Now they were organized; and it felt good to finally be able to stand with clenched fist thrust forward and upward, while shouting "Black Power," and "Power to the People." Most of us liked the sound and many of us secretly admired those courageous brothers and sisters who were bold enough to stand and declare it. We wanted a piece of the American pie; and we wanted to be heard and recognized. So we cried (at least some of us) cried out "Black Power," yet we had no real power that we could claim as our own.

We heard the words, but most never knew the deep meaning behind the words. Many thought of finally being equal to be equally violent as our white counterparts. A few saw it as a time when we would soon be in power, politically, socially, and economically. Few of us seriously thought about how we would attain these high and noble goals. A people who has not been exposed to real power, or those who have been oppressed do not really understand the philosophy of power among the mighty. Therefore, since many did not fully understand Black Power, most could not define what it entailed, what it cost, or even how to get it. We knew that we wanted it, but getting it was so elusive. Dr. King attempted to define it more clearly in his book, "Where Do We Go from Here: Chaos or Community?"

Dr. King understood that one of the dangers encountered, and even created by the black masses who following after an undefined concept, was the real possibility that their confusion could easily turn into chaos. He knew that power required time in order to be attained, yet he was faced with the dilemma that we as black people could not afford to wait any longer. Black power needed to be understood in the proper context. He wrote that "in our society power sources can always finally be traced to ideological, economical and political forces." **62** The realization of these power sources in our lives, experientially, continues to elude the masses of Black people in America.

The philosophical, or ideological makeup of Whites in America, seems to be "we have the power and we're going to keep the power." There never has been an overall honest attempt to equalize opportunities for sharing power in this country. There have been many good gains through Affirmative Action policies in the past, however, the establishment has now determined that they've run their course. It's back to the "good ole boy" system. Most of these ideologies have a direct relationship to economics, which is really the way America measures power. It, therefore, behooves Blacks in America to stop talking distantly about becoming empowered, and really begin to develop power sources in the American economic system.

One of the greatest African Americans who dared to venture into the very depths of the American economic system, was Reginald F. Lewis. Mr. Lewis, who found great success at Harvard Law School, in the chaotic and exclusive networks of Wall Street, as well as in the international business community, took full advantage of every opportunity afforded him. His keen business acumen and thorough understanding of the economic systems, vaulted him to the top of corporate America. He became the CEO of TLC Beatrice International, a billion-dollar corporation, with world-wide connections and influence. Reginald Lewis never believed his detractors, who said such a venture could not be pulled off. He knew that true power in America, was founded in its economic system, and with hard work and determination, he became one of the most powerful men, black or white, in our nation.

Before Mr. Lewis died, at an early age in January 1993, he had become the wealthiest African American in the nation. His vast holdings eventually landed him in Forbes 400 list of the richest people in America. At the time of his death, Mr. Lewis was co-authoring his autobiography, along with Blair Walker, a former reporter with USA TODAY. The title of the book: *"Why Should White Guys Have All the Fun? How Reginald Lewis Created a Billion-Dollar Business Empire"*. His life story and his incredible business ventures and successes, would be well worth emulating. His story defines power in any culture.

The story of Reginald F. Lewis should encourage all African Americans to pursue their dreams and goals with greater determination. The legacy of the late Reginald F. Lewis will continue to live on in the hearts of those who believe and live in the pursuit of excellence. While Mr. Lewis' story is quite unique, there are countless other African Americans, who have found great success in mainstream America. However, in order to accomplish these things, the seeker must have at least these three things: (1) a very positive concept of self; (2) a strong belief in God and his grace; and (3) a goal worth pursuing with all of one's heart and soul.

BLACK POWER DEFINED IN TERMS OF AN EDUCATED MIND:

Another sad development in the area of education has been the ludicrous proposal to formalize black street slang as a second language and call it "Ebonics."

The rise of the idiotic idea about creating a so-called "Black English," came by way of a mostly black school board in Oakland, California. These supposedly educated, egg-heads, call it "Ebonics." Well, the only things that it is certain to create is a new name for black people, namely "Idiotics," for it will guarantee that none of our children will qualify to get in a decent college or university. It will also give the impression to young people, that if they don't want to "buckle down" and learn that which is difficult, just "rig up" something, so you can just get by. The ultimate message being: "Don't worry about striving for excellence, you are doomed to failure." Even the Reverend Jesse Jackson seems to lend his support to this nonsense. I say to black America, "we have followed Jesse many places, but this is one place which we should all refused to go!!!" We have had enough of our leaders, lead the people into ignorance. Jesse was even a speaker at the Million Man March. It seems that he goes everywhere and anywhere he can get press and recognition. Come on, Jesse, I know that Dr. King trained you better than that.

The folks in Oakland, and other so-called research findings, claim that the reason that some black children's language is so awful, is because of their African heritage. It seems very strange that all of the generations before them learned standard English, as well as the slang language used at home and in the "hood." Slang is all that "Ebonics" is. Even the children know this; it's these so-called "educated" buffoons that's causing the problem. Secondly, if the horrible language spoken by our youth is a result of their African heritage, why is it that the many African friends that I have had, from places like Ghana, Nigeria, and South Africa, have all spoken almost perfect English? Why is it that Vietnamese, Chinese, Ethiopians, and practically every other race, which comes to this country can excel in standard English in a year or two, while we try to make excuses for our kids, whose foreparents date back over 400 years on American soil!!! Will somebody please answer these question!

The fact of the matter is that we have a group of unchallenged and undisciplined children running the schools and the school boards. They are children, and children need guidance. Most children, left to their own devises and lack of wisdom, simply take the pathway of least resistance. Many parents, some teachers, some educational leaders, and congressional leaders, do not want to meet the challenge of requiring and demanding that our school children put away all the foolishness and begin to dig deep and learn the language of the land. My mother's high school class had to learn Latin as well as English, way back in the 1940's. She also studied, REQUIRED, Latin and English, when she attended Florida A&M College in the 1940's. She did it, and did it well, making A's and B's. My mother's teachers did it before her.

My generation studied and excelled in English; and so did many generations before and after me. We still had our "special" language we spoke to each other, that we called hip, cool; and then there was the slang, which we called "pig Latin;" but we had sense enough to know the difference between that and standard English. Now, it seems that they have even drawn our national leaders into this downward spiral of ignorance, who are trying to offer explanations for this awful silliness. I believe that our children can learn the same things that others learn if they are challenged, and held strictly accountable, for doing so. The major problem with black children not learning is that we have some irresponsible parents who are not willing, nor do they care enough to demand a disciplined life-style from their children. Teachers are finding every day that an undisciplined child and unsupporting parents are the greatest detriments to learning that this country has ever had. And the reason that teachers can not do their jobs more effectively is because the courts, Congress, and the Civil Liberties Union have taken the authority away from our teachers and given it to the students, parents, and others, not qualified to run the affairs of a classroom, or a school. Real change will come in our nation's schools, when the Congress and the President pass and enact laws which restore power to those in charge of educating our nation's children. If there are parents who don't want their children to be held accountable in our nation's schools, let them establish their own privately supported schools.

One of the reasons that other cultures come to America and excel, is that their parents demand discipline and devotion to study. They realize that only through an empowered and educated mind, that their offspring can empower their lives, in order to make the best of life. It is all a matter of pride.

Instead of blaming white folks and other groups for the sorry plight of those black Americans, too slothful to empower their lives, we need to spend our energies on those who are willing to discipline and demand excellence from their children. I believe that we still have some of the brightest and the best; they simply need the refining touches of a quality education. We should be demanding that the legislatures, state and national, re-empower parents, teachers, and educational bodies in order to return full control of the learning institutions and learning environments, to conditions conducive to learning. I believe that parents who fail to properly discipline and control their children, should be subject to fines, up to and including jail time. Why so harsh? I believe that a child left to rear himself or herself, without discipline and respect for societal standards, is the worst and most destructive kind of child abuse. I do not, by any means intend to belittle those real, horrible, yet rare cases of child abuse, for there are some; however, I feel that undisciplined children, thrust upon society, is the ultimate disrespect for society and children. The courts and the liberal agencies, such as the Civil Liberties Union, and extremists in some so-called "child protection" agencies, have taken the ideas of personal freedoms to the most detrimental ends. All of the good that they have clearly done, have been overshadowed by the ills heaped on society by their pet projects. We must get rid of some of these detrimental forces, if we ever hope to have a real democracy again. Only when we take actions in this direction, will we be able to rid our society of those who over-burden us with their irresponsible actions and reckless living.

DEFINING BLACK POWER IN TERMS OF MUTUALLY BENEFICIAL COALITIONS:

There was a time when we had a comfort zone, for consistent, if not for rapid change. That was when we had stable leadership in organizations such as the local and national chapters of the NAACP, and highly respected leadership in the black community; which knew of the importance of multifaceted coalitions, with interests outside of the black community. After the retirement of Benjamin Hooks, much of that comfort, trust, and integrity in the NAACP seems to have flown away. The national office has been clouded with scandals; as well as having leaders who have failed to understand and respect the deep cultural, religious, and social differences between Jews and Palestinians. Then there are leaders in many local chapters, who are reverting back to pre-1970 tactics of open and hostile confrontations with every segment of the population.

Recently, in Dallas, Texas, the School Board elected a female, Hispanic educator, who came equipped with a Doctoral Degree in Education. The black members of the Board walked out of the election and did not vote. The local leader of the oldest, predominately black Civil Rights organization, spearheaded several highly visible and vocal protests against her. Although race was not mentioned, however, race appeared to be at the center of the controversy. Granted, the new Superintendent resigned after charges of personal improprieties with another District employee and misuse of public funds had surfaced; still minorities must somehow get beyond this "our race-only" mentality, when it comes to supporting other minorities for positions of leadership. When we had a black male serving as Superintendent, in this same district, there was an organized effort among Hispanics attempting to oust him. It appears that America has conditioned minorities to always be at war with each other, where territory and influence are involved. Many years ago, Dr. King spoke of a day when "Our loyalties must transcend our race, our tribe, our class, and our nation; and this means we must develop a world perspective." [63]

We must also come to realize that we indeed need each other, blacks, whites, Hispanics, Jews, the elderly, females, and other minorities and classes. For those who have taken time to analyze it, there is clearly an anti-poor, anti-elderly, anti-ill patient agenda at work in America. The number of health programs to help stem the growing mortality among black babies born to poor mothers and the terminally ill, are slowly disappearing. As a matter of fact, the elderly and those with debilitating illnesses, are being encouraged to seek "doctor-assisted suicide," as a way out. In that way, there is less of a burden on the precious health-care dollars. We are in a hostile crisis, while at the same time we are being prompted to continue the in-fighting among the poor and the minorities. God help us all to come to our senses.

In his famous "I Have A Dream" speech, Dr. King said, "The marvelous new militancy which has engulfed the Negro community must not lead us to a distrust of all white people [nor, I feel, Hispanic or other people] . . . This offense we have mounted to storm the battlements of injustice must be carried forth by a biracial army. We cannot walk alone . . . I have a dream my four little children will one day live in a nation where they will not be judged by the color of their skin but by content of their character . . ." **64** The brilliance and humanitarian character of Dr. King does not seem to be shared by many of our leaders today.

DEFINING BLACK POWER FOR PROSPERITY AND PROGRESS:

It is no secret that American, or Americanized power-brokers are willing to share, even if to a very limited point, some of the power with those who are able to generate capital. This, in part, accounts for the incredible success of Reginald F. Lewis, discussed above. Reginald Lewis understood the financial markets and he knew how to make money! People listen to people who know how to make them money!!! Reginald Lewis knew how to make money. However, you don't have to be a Reginald Lewis in order to be able to make money for yourself and others. If you can, many power-brokers will stand back and take notice. When they see that you have marketable skills or goods, they will join your team. These are the kind of coalitions we should seek. It has been by these methods that so many young athletes, musicians, actors, etc., have been to cash in on the American money market.

No one can deny the incredible success, wealth, and prosperity obtained in mainstream America, by individuals such as the late, great business tycoon, Reginald L. Lewis; Oprah Winfrey; Bill Cosby; Will Smith; John H. Johnson, Chairman and CEO of Johnson Publishing Company; Diana Ross; Michael Jordan; Maya Angelou; Michael Jackson; Whitney Houston, the great singer and actress; Shaquel O'Neal; Hakeem Olajuwan; Bryant Gumbel; L.L. Kool Jay, the rapper turned actor; Evander Hollyfield; Alice Walker; Toni Morrison; Tiger Woods; unsung heroes such as Remer C.

Prince, former high-ranking NASA official, mathematical genius and one of my former house mates while in college, etc.. Why is this so? How have many of them been able to go from just young kids on the block, to super-rich persons, making mega-bucks. It is simply because they have worked incredibly hard in order to have undeniable, and highly marketable skills!!! They have prepared themselves to make a valuable contribution to society. Others of them have the ability to help others make a whole lot of money; therefore, the power-brokers allow them to share the wealth.

It is obvious that most of us will never possess the remarkable skills of these ladies and gentlemen; however, each one of us can do something. Look at the number of immigrants who come to this country and start up businesses and do exceptionally well. While it is true that blacks are often denied the same privileges as immigrants, that is no excuse for us not to get in the race. Most of these foreigners open mom and pop stores, or Dollar Stores, $1.25 Dry Cleaners, and the like; and before you know it they are well established in the economic and financial arena. Why? Again it's because they make themselves and their product marketable. They work hard; they work together as families; and sometimes with friends in their culture; and more importantly, they smile at you and charge a reasonable price for their goods and services. Now, I know that they are not smiling because they like you so much; not after all those pictures I've seen of some of them shooting down brothers and sisters, just because they disagreed with them. But that aside, we find that most of these foreigners catch on quickly about successful American marketing schemes. They quickly learn the marketing concepts of super stores such as, Wal-Mart, K-Mart, Target; and other successful discount operations: sell a reasonable good product, be kind to customers, and charge a comfortable price. It's an almost unbeatable combination.

There are numbers of black businesses which have done well in this area. These include the Williams Chicken Chain and Proline Hair Products of Dallas; Johnson Publishing Company; Carson Inc., led by Dr. Leroy Keith, former president of Morehouse College, and Soft Sheen Products. However, these are the exceptions rather than the rule. Most often we find financially-strapped black businesses, with few sources for raising needed capital, charging higher prices in hopes of raising quick cash. This, along with poor customer relations, often destroy their customer-base, dooming many to failure. Many of these businesses fold very early; or they never make enough profits to get beyond the break-even point. Then when these businesses fold, they blame other blacks for not supporting us. The simple fact is that black shoppers want the same kind of quality products and services from other blacks as they get from every other retailer. If black entrepreneurs are ever going to make a major impact in the American marketplace, we must change the way we do business. You must remember that at the beginning of this work, I asked permission to be as critical of African Americans as I was of Whites, or any other groups. Jesus said that "the truth shall make you free," when we know it and accept it. [65] I am not writing to simply offer folk pleasing words which help keep them enslaved to tactics which continue to fail, but to wake up a sleeping and dying culture, my culture.

Black power, then, must be defined in several terms. One term in which it must be defined is in that of economic clout, not in military or armed resistance. Any fool who wants to wage war against an enemy in which he is outnumbered 88 to 12; who is outclassed in sophisticated weapons, much like a fellow armed with a stick going up against 7 men with automatic shotguns; and whose monetary resources are housed in a piggy bank; while the other group has world-wide monetary banking systems. It is ludicrous, at best. While I realize that ridicule is counter productive, African Americans must simply face the facts that mass armed confrontation is not our greatest strength. Our strength has, and always will be, centered in God through the Lord Jesus Christ. And the Holy Ghost says "If God be for us, who shall be against us?" [66] This leads me to the second way in which black power must be defined; which is faith in God.

This may sound corny to some, and to others it might seem like an excuse for not taking personal responsibility for our lives, but it is my unshakable belief that if it had not been for God on our sides, we would not have made it. I would dare say that our greatest strength has been our close walk with and dependence on God in Christ. Those who have walked in our shoes clearly understand this. Others simply look at our situation and either marvel or scoff. Karl Marx, the German philosopher, who, along with Friedrich Engels, founded modern socialism and communism, once stated that,

"Religion is the opiate of the masses."

However, I would contend that Karl Marx had no idea what he was talking about!!! He was certainly a well-learned scholar and is still highly respected by many today; however, in reading excerpts from his background, it seems that he, like so many rich kids, took up this cause for the working class as a pet project. Karl Marx really knew nothing about suffering, poverty, or conditions which foster melancholy, or, simply put, "the blues." He was born to an affluent family; the son of a lawyer. He grew up in a well-to-do home; had the best of schooling; and went on to study law and philosophy. It is often found in such environments, that religion is most often de-emphasized. Many of these individuals have the best that life offers, therefore, they often see no need for God, for they become gods unto themselves. What would he know about the religion of the masses?

It is said that Karl Marx rejected the idealism of G. W. F. Hegel, instead becoming a disciple of Ludwig Feuerbach and Moses Hess. It is obvious that this man knew nothing about real suffering, poverty, or living as a member of the underclass. He like so many social revolutionists took up the project of socialism as one of his "pet peeves," or a cause to toy with.

In the lives of so many of the masses, which include the poor, the struggling mothers and fathers, single mothers, the elderly, and so forth, a connection with God or a spiritual, higher power, is the only hope they have. Religion, and especially the Christian faith, has been exceedingly more than just an opiate for the oppressed. To them, it invigorates and lifts them above their circumstances. An opiate on the other hand, is not uplifting. It is a downer. As a Registered Pharmacist, I know that an opiate is an opium-containing narcotic, having sedative and pain relieving properties. The opiate induces sleep, sedation; or causes dullness or apathy. It deadens ones senses; it does not cure the condition. The opiate simply increases ones threshold to pain: you still have the pain, but you can't feel it as much, because of the false sense of relief of the condition. This dismal description is a far cry from the religion of the masses which I grew up with. It is certainly not a description of the Christian faith; nor of the heart and soul of a Christian; especially among African Americans.

As an African American, and especially being male, I know, first hand the pitfalls of living in an oppressive society. I have seen many examples of "the masses," who have been in the depths of suffering; and were down with "the blues." Much of this suffering was caused by poverty, a lack of education; feelings of hopelessness and helplessness; and the breakdown of their families and their personal relationships, in which most could be traced back to white racism. I know full well that it was not some sort of religious opiate that they turned to for relief, while they were in their condition. Oh, yes, there were many who succumbed to the trappings of opiates and other powerful narcotics by the dope dealers, and alcohol; again run by white, drug lords. But, there were those who found another hope in order to make it through the storms and vicissitudes of life. It was the Christian faith and its hope-filled messages, and powerful worship and praise services which "brought us out of the wilderness."

African American Christians, who have suffered some of the worst conditions on American soil, found ways around the oppressive conditions in which they lived. They sang songs of hope and coming victory, in spite of their "low valley experiences." One such song says:

"I went into the valley, but I didn't go to stay,
My soul got happy, and I stayed all day."

Then, another related one goes like this:

"Tell me how did you feel, when you, come out the wilderness,
come out the wilderness, come out the wilderness,
Well, I felt like shouting, when I come out the wilderness,
come out the wilderness, A-leaning on the Lord."

Also, consider this one:

"How I got o - ver, (How I got) o - ver my Lord, And my
soul looked back and wondered, (wondered, wondered), How I got
over my Lord.

Lord, I've been 'buked (and) I've been scorned, And I've been
talked ('bout as) sure as you're born } And my soul looked back and
won-dered (won-dered, won-dered) How I got o - ver, my Lord." [67]

These songs tell of being raised from spiritual melancholy, making the soul glad, while implying the instilling of a spirit of hope. It raised the worshipper's expectation and hope of deliverance; instilling in him and her a fighting, faith-filled spirit. With the help of Almighty God, this was the basic driving force behind the world-changing, Civil Rights Movement. The success of this movement is still changing people's perceptions of their conditions in today's world. It is what eventually caused the downfall of the oppressive forces of Communism, which was started by Karl Marx, himself. Even in Karl Marx's ancestral origin of Germany, this spiritual of liberation, started by black Americans, brought down that great icon of oppression in Berlin, the Berlin Wall, where the people kept fighting the oppressor until that wall, too, came tumbling down.

Marx knew nothing about the depths of sufferings and feelings of oppression by the masses, nor how far they were willing to go until they cast off their oppressors. He certainly knew nothing of the fighting spirit of African American people. Our only opiate was faith in Jesus Christ, which supplied the motivation and courage to keep going till the victory was won. Marx's attempts to describe religious experiences for all people, represents yet another white person, expressing a typical, self-imposed, superior, know-it-all, and "we know what's best for you all" attitude. The great sin of us all is that we allow such "mental giants" to describe life and faith for those whose shoes do not fit him, and in whose shoes he (nor those today) can never walk in. For understanding such experiences, the white person must come to the oppressed, be silent, and listen!

OUR GOD HELPS US DEFINE TRUE BLACK POWER:

The Holy Bible gives clear evidence that not only does God want to empower us spiritually, He also wants to empower us economically. In the Third Epistle of John, we find these words: "Beloved, I wish above all things that thou mayest prosper and be in health, even as thy soul prospereth." [68] Prosperity and power for the Christian, are products of lives lived in obedience to the Word of God, the Holy Bible. It is in the Bible that we find the words, "Seek ye first the kingdom of God, and his righteousness; and all these things will be added unto you" (Matthew 6:33).

CHAPTER SEVENTEEN

CONCLUSION AND SUGGESTED SOLUTIONS TO THE PROBLEMS

In these writings we have tried to address a very fundamental problem which has surfaced with the resurgence of Louis Farrakhan into national prominence. Mr. Farrakhan, being no friend to Christianity, has pressed the issue that there is a great conflict between Christianity and the true interests of persons within the African American culture. He contends that Christianity is, in fact, an enemy of the black man in America. This should come as no surprise, in that history records that similar views have been expressed by previous leaders of the Nation of Islam, or Black Muslims, as it was most popularly known in the past. These were held by its founder, Walleye D. Fad; its second leader, Elijah Muhammad; and by Malcolm X, before his demise. The one big difference in these latter days is that, while in the past some Christians and non-Christian blacks, listened politely to their peculiar claims, but for the most part ignored them. The majority eventually returned to their usual way of life and religious practices after the hype of the moment was over. However, I sense a different atmosphere and a very different kind of receptivity toward the fiery and racially charged perorations of Minister Louis Farrakhan. Farrakhan has developed a message and a method of presenting his message into a finely tuned and highly acceptable package, which thousands upon thousands of black people are now flocking to him in order hear what he has to say. His success in organizing the Million Man March, along with the support of Rev. Benjamin Chavis, the ousted, former President of the NAACP, proves that he is a man to be contended with; and that his influence and power are growing.

As a Christian minister and believer, Mr. Farrakhan's growing influence disturbs me most because of his false teachings concerning Christianity, in several areas. First, he has proven to be a vehement opponent of the doctrine of Jesus Christ, the risen Son of God, and Savior of the world;

literally, rendering him anti-Christian in his world view. Secondly, it disturbs me to see Christian pastors open their pulpits to a man who denigrates the Person of our Lord and Savior Jesus Christ. Such a thing would never happen in a Muslim mosque!!! A third area which disturbs me is the false teachings of Farrakhan concerning his own claims of being savior; for not only has Mr. Farrakhan denied the reality of Christ as Messiah and the Son of God, he has on occasion claimed that he, Louis Farrakhan, is the literal fulfillment of the prophetic Jesus! Such heresy can only be contended with through sound and accurate teaching of the Word of God. Each believer, whether layman or minister, has been called by Jesus Christ to contend for the faith. Additionally, they are to go into the world and spread the hopeful message of salvation, which is found only in the Cross of Christ and His Resurrection. The most effective way to sway the tide of Farrakhanism among black Americans is to become more zealous and committed to our duties as Christians; and to be more effective in serving the needs of our communities, as concerned citizens. If we continue to fail in doing these things, persons such as Louis Farrakhan will always be able to get a hearing. A person can only be deceived if that person does not know the truth; and/or if the person is unable to recognize and discern the difference between the truth and a lie. Every deceiver realizes this and therefore, lays carefully masked plans of deception before springing the trap on the intended victims. Thus, we find the ultimate and essential value of wearing the proper "mask" to fit the deception.

The diabolical masks of Louis Farrakhan by which he continually deceives so many black Christians are many-fold. He is a highly intelligent man, and is using this to keep his opponents off guard. He keeps abreast of many of the fine details of history and current events, which, most often, concern themselves with some of the most vile acts of racism and injustices perpetuated by Jews and whites, against black people. Too often, I have seen and heard so many white journalists, who came unprepared to match his wit and acumen, get "blown out of the water" in interviews with him. This further elevates him in the minds of his growing following, that he is beyond reproach. He is a great orator; having the ability to combine his great oratorical skills, with his eloquence of speech, and charisma, into a show of flamboyant arrogance, which has earned him the title "the angry charmer." His commanding presence, affords him the ability to hold many audiences spell bound, as he rattles off detailed acts of injustice perpetuated by whites and Jews, against blacks. He presents himself as the ultimate leader and friend of all African Americans in this country. However, I believe that, above all else, his commanding knowledge of the Bible, and his ability to sound so convincingly friendly toward Christianity and Jesus Christ, while at the same time telling his intended African American victims that the culture of Christ is an enemy of black culture, without alarming them of his diabolical plot, is what delivers the fatal *coup de grace*. Far too many black Christians are falling for this race-baited hook; being lured into thinking that the culture of Christ and the black culture are mutually exclusive. The strong implication is that one has to choose either the culture of Christ (which is presented as being the same as choosing white oppression); or to choose the culture of black nationalism (which is presented as choosing liberation and being on the side of their black brothers and sisters). The latter choice is further fortified by citing many examples of continued acts of white racism in this country. Many on both sides are confused, being blinded by the age-old issue of race.

With that having been said, I now turn my attention back to Louis Farrakhan and the Nation of Islam Muslims. My unanswered question to them is this:

WHERE WERE THE MUSLIMS DURING THE MULTIRACIAL BATTLE AGAINST BLACK OPPRESSION?

The walls of segregation and southern Jim Crow public policies came tumbling down, not because of our military might, which is often advocated by militant hate groups. The walls of segregation came down because God was for us; God embraced our cause; and God got us the victories. God's love and providence looks after spiritual and physical matters. BUT GOD DIDN'T DO IT ALONE: HE ENLISTED THOSE WHO HAD COURAGE ENOUGH TO FOLLOW HIS CHOSEN LEADERS! Many of us marched, sang hymns and songs of faith, many were whipped, and unfortunately, many of us died for the freedoms we now enjoy. But where were the Muslims, or Nation of Islam disciples when we needed them? You see, while many African Americans marched and put our lives on the line for freedom's cause during the 50's and 60,' Mr. Farrakhan and other Muslims stayed home. They couldn't march, Sit-in, or Swim-in with Dr. M.L. King, Jr. and the rest of us Black soldiers who laid our lives on the line for equality, justice and freedom; and a piece of the American pie. Now this Johnny-come-lately and his followers are parading themselves as saviors of Black people, when many were too afraid to stand up for our rights when it really counted. And anyone falling for Farrakhan's bull does not know, nor do they wish to know our history. The fact of the matter is that the members of the Nation of Islam did not participate in the many public demonstrations for freedom for African Americans. Again, I repeat: THERE WERE MORE WHITE AND JEWISH AMERICANS WHO PARTICIPATED IN THE MARCHES AND OTHER DEMONSTRATIONS FOR THE FREEDOM OF AFRICAN AMERICANS, AND MANY EVEN DIED, THAN THE WHOLE NATION OF ISLAM, COMBINED!!!

What every Christian must come to realize is that the battle being waged is not about race and cultures. The ultimate battle being waged against the influence and false teachings of Louis Farrakhan, is a very serious one, indeed. We are contending for the souls of persons on the earth. We can only compete by following the instructions given by the Apostle Paul in Ephesians 6:11-12, which says:

> *"Put on the whole armour of God, that ye may be able to stand against the wiles of the devil. For we wrestle not against flesh and blood, but against principalities, against powers, against the rulers of the darkness of this world, against spiritual wickedness in high places" (KJV).*

In this battle for freedom from oppression in America, we all must recognize, both blacks and whites, that the oppressed are greatly outnumbered. Such a condition calls for great courage, unity, and concerted efforts from all of the true soldiers of the Cross which can be mustered. Our white, Hispanic, Native American, Asian, and other true brothers and sisters are needed in our struggle. Therefore, I must make yet another declaration in this endeavor if I am to be truthful: I refuse to view all white and Jewish people as enemies and devils, as Farrakhan and the Ku Klux Klan have declared. It seems that racist birds-of-a-feather tend to flock together. Such an attitude is not only self-defeating and hateful, it denies us our true humanity as defined by Christ Jesus our Lord. In St. John 13:34-35, He said,

> *"A new commandment I give unto you, That ye love one another; as I have loved you, that ye also love one another. By this shall all men know that ye are my disciples, if ye have love one to another."*

His words are self-explanatory.

1 Woodson, Carter G., "The Mis-Education of the Negro," (African World Press, Trenton, N.J., 1990), p. xiii.

2 Washington, James M, A Testament of Hope: The Essential Writings of M.L. King, Jr. (San Francisco: Harper & Row, 1986) 258.

3 The National Baptist Hymnal, "The Lord Will Make a Way Somehow," (National Baptist Publishing Board, (Nashville, 1980), Song #286.

4 Romans 8:38.

5 James Patterson and Peter Kim, "The Day America Told the Truth," (Prentice Hall Press, New York, 1991), p. 182, 183.

6 Panati, Charles. "Extraordinary Origins of Everyday Things," (Harper & Row, New York, 1987), p. 272.

7 Marable, Manning., "Beyond Black and White," (Verso, New York, N.Y., 1995), p. 137.

8 Second Timothy 1:12 (Kings James Version of the Bible).

9 National Baptist Hymnal, "Amazing Grace," (National Baptist Publishing Board - Nashville, 1977), Song# 135.

10 The Epistle of James 1:17.

11 Richardson, Harry V., Dark Salvation, (Anchor Press/ Doubleday), p. ix.

12 Patterson, Orlando. "Freedom," (Basic Books - HarperCollins Publishers, 1991) p. 357.

13 Ibid., pp. 9, 10.

14 Morey, Robert, "The Islamic Invasion," (Harvest House Publishers, Eugene, OR, 1992), p. 170.

15 Ibid., p. 168.

16 Spence, H. D. M., and Exell, Joseph S., The Pulpit Commentary, vol. 18, (Eerdmans - Grand Rapids, 1977), p. 253.

17 Morey, Robert, "The Islamic Invasion," (Harvest House Publishers, Eugene, Or, 1992), p.182.

18 Ibid., pp. 182, 183.

19 Ibid., p. 183.

20 Everett, Susanne, "History of Slavery," (Magna Books, London, 1988), p. 6.

21 Everett, Susanne, "History of Slavery," (Magna Books, London, 1988), cover flier.

22 Ibid., p. 6.

23 Everett, Susanne, "History of Slavery, (Magna Books, London, 1988), pp. 22, 23.

24 Ibid., p. 24.

25 King, Martin Luther Jr.. "Strength to Love," (Harper & Row, New York, 1963), p. 39.

26 Morey, Robert. "The Islamic Invasion," (Harvest House, Eugene, Or., 1992), p. 161.

27 Ibid., p. 171.

28 Ibid., p. 163.

29 Perkins, Useni E., "Harvesting New Generations," (Third World Books: Chicago, 1985), p. 5.

30 Ibid., p. 8.

31 Everett, Susanne, "History of Slavery," (Magna Books: Leicester, 1988), Chapter 4.

32 Frazier, E. Franklin, "The Negro in the United States," (MacMillian: New York, 1957), pp. 307-309.

33 Willie, Charles V., "A New Look at Black Families,: (General Hall: Bayside, 1982), p. 5.

34 Frazier, E. Franklin, "The Negro in the United States," pp. 310-311.

35 Perkins, "Harvesting New Generations," p. 9.

36 Frazier, E. Franklin, "The Negro Church in America," (Schocken Books: New York, 1963), p. 4.

37 Frazier, "The Negro in the United States," p. 313.

38 James, Clarence, "A Message to Youth," is a sermon preached at Concord Baptist Church, Dallas, TX., August 1991.

39 Frazier, "The Negro Church in America," p. 45.

40 Morrey, Robert, The Islamic Invasion (Harvest House Publishers, Eugene, Or. - 1992), P. 163.

41 Newsweek, October 30, 1995, "An Angry 'Charmer,'" p. 38.

42 Ibid., p. 38.

43 Morey, Robert, The Islamic Invasion, (Harvest House, Eugene, Or, 1992), p. 169.

44 Morey, Robert, The Islamic Invasion, (Harvest House Publishers, 1992), p. 168.

45 Ibid., p. 172.

46 Newsweek, October 30, 1995, "An Angry 'Charmer,'" p. 32.

47 The Book of Daniel: Chapter 3.

48 Lang, Susan S.. "Extremist Groups in America," (Franklin Watts, New York, 1990), p. 129.

49 Romans 8:38.

50 Ephesians 6:12.

51 Elwell, Walter A., Editor; Evangelical Dictionary of Theology, (Baker, Grand Rapids, 1985), p. 220.

52 "The Bible Knowledge Commentary," Walvoord and Zuck, pp. 77-78; Victor Books, 1983.

53 Spence, H. D. M. and Exell, Joseph S., The Pulpit Commentary (Erdmans, Grand Rapids - 1977), p.284.

54 Pascoe, Elaine, Issues in American History, (Franklin Watts-New York, 1985), pp. 38-39.

55 De Gruchy, John W., Bonhoeffer and South Africa, (Erdsman, Grand Rapids, 1984), p. 16.

56 Newsweek, October 30, 1995, "Perspectives," p. 27.

57 Matthew 24:24.

58 NEGRO, "Harlem Reviewed", p. 51.

59 Newsweek, October 30, 1995, "Perspectives," p. 27.

60 Judges 17:6; 21:25.

61 Acts 9:26-39.

62 Washington, James M., A TESTAMENT OF HOPE: The Essential Writings of M.L. King, Jr., San Francisco (Harper & Rowe, 1986), p.303.

63 Washington, James M., "A Testament of Hope - The Essential Writings of Martin Luther King, Jr.," (San Francisco, Harper & Rowe, 1986), p. 253.

64 Ibid., p. 219.

65 St. John 8:32 (KJV).

66 Romans 8:31b (KJV).

67 The National Baptist Hymnal, "How I Got Over," by Rev. C. H. Cobbs, (National Baptist Publishing Board, Nashville, 1980), hymn # 266.

68 3 John 2 (KJV).

MAIM- disable or disfigure usually by injury or removal of a persons limb or member,

IGMA -a mark burned into the skin of a criminal or slave; brand. 2 a mark or token of infamy, reproach or disgrace.

RF- a slave esp. of the lowest class in medievil urope bound to the land and owned by a lord. a person in servitude.

CRID - harsh to taste or smell 2 caustic (able to burn, sharp and bitter wit.) in language or tone.

-PIATION- to make atonement for.

MPUNITY- exemption from punishment, penalty, or harm.

REVARICATION- stray from or evade the truth.

NCIPIENT- beginning to exist or appear.

ESIST- to cease doing something. 2 forbear (to refrain from, resist)

ENIGMA- an obscure (not clear, deficient in light) speech or writing. puzzling. ambiguous. OK speak in riddles.

BIGOT- a person who is rigidly devoted to his own group, religion, race, or politics and is intolerant of those who differ.

ACUTE - having a sharp point or tip. 2 keenly perceptive or discerning: shrewd. sensitive.

BLATANT- unpleasant, and often vulgar loud & noisy. conspicuous, obvious.

REPRISAL- forcible seizure of an enemies goods or or subjects in retaliation for injuries inflicted retaliation as injury for injury. also using political or military force without actually resorting to war.

VARMINT- a bird or animal that is considered undesirable or troublesome.

DISDAIN- to regard or treat with haughty (proud arrogant) contempt (being dispised or dishonered, dis grace). 2 consider or reject as unworthy of oneself.

DESPISE- look down on with contempt or scorn. 2 regard with extreme dislike and hostility.

UNTENABLE- incapable of being defended or maintain

VICISSITUDES- a change or variation. sudden or unexpecte changes or shifts in ones life.

ANOMALY- deviation or departure from the norm. out of form or rule. abnormal.

PERNICIOUS- tending to cause death or serious injury.

MISCEGENATION- interbreeding of what are presumed to be distinct human races.